OF

ALASKA

A Stirring Saga of The Great Alaskan Gold Rush

Enjoy!

Charles af Forselles

A

Biography

by

Charles af Forselles

Published by
Alaskakrafts, Incorporated
Anchorage, Alaska

First Printing

Library of Congress Catalog Card Number.....93-73089

ISBN 0-9623192-3-6

Printed in Korea

General Editor---Frank G. Pratt

Technical Editor---Charles af Forselles

Photographs are from af Forselles family files unless otherwise credited to:
Anchorage Historical & Fine Arts Museum, 121 W. 7th Ave., Anchorage, AK
Carrie McLain Museum, McLain Archive of Photographic Materials, Nome, AK
Consortium Library, Univ. of Alaska, Anchorage and Alaska Pacific Univ. Anchorage
Oakland Public Library, 125 14th St., Oakland, CA 94612
Wolfsong of Alaska, Box 110309, Anchorage, AK 99511-0309

FRONT COVER PHOTO:
Georg af Forselles, "Count of Alaska", demonstrates how to use a spade.
"The man who can handle a spade properly does not find it very hard or laborious work.
He first lets the spade fall of its own weight, down to the spot where the spadeful is to be
taken up, taking care that the breadth on the surface ground is not more than four inches.
Then he draws back the spade a little, which takes off much of the friction of the descending
blade. One good thrust of the spade with the foot then sends the blade down its full depth.
A backward pressure makes a lever of the handle and heel of the spade, and a dexterous
turn of the wrist sends the spadeful upside down just where it is wanted. There is no raking
or 'sputtering' needed to make the ground level. A slight tap with the corner of the spade
makes the work as regular and plane as if laid off with an instrument."

TABLE OF CONTENTS

ACKNOWLEDGMENT

A letter from Mr. James A. Michener gave me the incentive to write this book. The following is Mr. Michener's letter, dated November 23, 1987:

"Dear Mr. af Forselles:

How interesting that you should write to me about your Swedish manuscript about the gold rush days in Nome and elsewhere during the last years of the nineteenth century.

Two years ago I finished a long chapter in my forthcoming book about the Swedes in Nome in those hectic times, but I used imaginary characters made up from a variety of sources, none of them based on real persons. My book, of which Nome material is but one relatively short chapter in a long entity, will appear some time next year, perhaps in October, I should think, and it will, I hope, awaken real interest in that fascinating historic period.

I would think that my account, even though it is fictional, would rouse much interest in the period your book covers and thus increase the possibility of finding an American or even an English publisher.

Legal considerations prevent me from reading other people's manu-scripts, but from your table of contents I can see that you have covered excellent material, much of which has appeared in one casual book or another, but which has not been gathered together as you have done.

In the meantime, I am returning your manuscript and I wish you the very best luck in finding a publisher. It's always a search but worth the effort.

Sincerely,

James A. Michener"

ACKNOWLEDGMENTS

I would like to express my thanks to my many friends who have, over the years, encouraged me to persevere with the writing of this volume.

Special thanks to:

Inga-Lisa Evers who so graciously and indulgently translated my father's letters, diaries, transcripts, contracts, and Swedish books. (Without her I could not have written this manuscript.)

Jane C. Fredeman, Editorial Consultant, Vancouver, Canada;

Amy Laverne Greeson, Freelance Writer and Proofreader, Anchorage, Alaska;

Bruce Merrell, Bibliographer, Z. J. Loussac Public Library, Anchorage, Alaska;

Betty Wright, Publisher of Rainbow Books, Inc., Highland City, Florida.

And last, but certainly not least, Frank and Verna Pratt, owners of Alaskakrafts, Inc., Anchorage, Alaska, who produced and published this work.

DEDICATION

This book is dedicated to my father, Georg Jakob af Forselles, who gave his many long memorable early golddigging years to Alaska, a frontier that he loved, until his death at Lindingö, Sweden in 1952

and

to my brother, Thomas F. af Forselles, who with great endeavor, devoted his time to our father's Swedish books until his death in 1983.

Georg Jakob af Forselles--"Count of Alaska"

PROLOGUE

More than fifty years have passed since the "Swedish Count" Georg af Forselles left Alaska for the last time, and only a few survive who met him when he was engaged in the adventures recounted in this book. Georg was one of thousands of men in far-flung places around the globe who heard the news of the discovery of gold in the Klondike by George Carmack and Skookum Jim, and set off to join the rush.

Georg made it from Hawaii to San Francisco, Seattle, and Alaska in record time. But he was too broke to get to Dawson in the winter of 1898; and so, he was still in St. Michael, drinking in Tex Rickard's saloon on the night that Jafet Lindeberg showed off the gold that launched the rush to Nome. In later years, the Count was sure to find other Nome pioneers everywhere he went in Alaska, and his reputation as the discoverer of Candle Creek gave him an easy entrè into local society.

Probably Georg would never have written about his adventures during the next decades, if he had stayed in the United States or if he had held on to any of the gold that he had washed out of creeks from Nome to the wild Koyukuk country. But he dissipated it, as most of the others fortunate enough to find any did, and he went home broke to Sweden when his marriage to his much younger wife ended in divorce in 1931.

By 1947, Georg had published six books and many magazine articles about some of the extraordinary characters he met during the Nome rush and in the following years. They went by names like Bronco Bill and the Scurvy Kid, and they were a hard, coarse lot. But they were also generally honest with strict rules of frontier justice which they quickly applied. Georg tells first hand how the news of real discoveries, as well as rumors, made the rounds, and from his own experiences at Nome, Candle and Fairbanks, he reveals what a rush to a new field was like on the inside.

Making the Count's stories available in English has been a dream pursued by his younger son, Charles, for many years. When Georg af Forselles left California, his three young children remained behind with their mother and her brutal second husband. In those unhappy years, the romantic life their dynamic father had lived intrigued Charles and his brother and sister, although their childhood memories of him had dimmed. Charles escaped from the household by joining the United States Navy and was on Battleship Row aboard the U.S.S. Maryland BB-46 when Pearl Harbor was bombed. Charles continued to serve in the Pacific, and it was not until two years after the war was over, in 1947, that he was finally able to seek out his father. He spent six months with him in Sweden, and in the 1950s, he went to Alaska himself to begin a long odyssey as he followed Georg's footsteps on the Seward Peninsula and elsewhere in the state while collecting adventures of his own.

Charles managed to get taped and written translations of parts of his father's books, but they remained unpublished. Finally, he came in contact with a Swedish journalist, Tord Wallström, who was fascinated with the extraordinary Swedes who made their way to that last frontier, and Wallström wanted to use the Count's books as the basis of a new work about them. Their collaboration resulted in the publication of *Guldgrävarna* (Gold Prospectors) in 1986. It was immediately successful and was even produced as a talking book for the blind. Then began work on a polished English translation and a search for an English-language publisher.

In the end, this book combines the best of *Guldgrävarna* with material from the Count's own books, particularly the first two, *Svenske greven av Alaska (The Swedish Count of Alaska)* and *Guld och gröna skogar (Gold and Green Forests)*. Some of the people he knew, men like the legendary Wyatt Earp, had reputations before they came to Alaska, and others he knew, like fight promoter Tex Rickard, novelists Rex Beach and Jack London, were more famous later, but the details of the hard lives of ordinary miners and their simple pleasures--mostly drinking and fighting-- that make the Count's recollections lively reading.

Georg af Forselles, on right, with friends aboard ship bound for Alaska.

Nome, Alaska, 1900   (Photo-Carrie McLain Museum)

Illegitimus non carborundum

The Nome Nugget

Old newspaper headline from *The Nome Nugget*. Loosely translated from the (Pseudo) latin, it means "Don't let the bastards grind you down!"

Chapter One

To the Gold Fields

Gold!

Most men would have waited in the dark cellar. The walls of the cellar were damp and the floor was slippery. Rats slithered under the refugees' feet. With no candles, the group of deserters had only a few matches to light their way through the labyrinth of walkways. It was not the life 19-year-old Georg had imagined when he left Sweden.

Georg Hjalmar af Forselles was the third son of a distinguished but no longer wealthy family. His great-grandfather, an innkeeper in Weckelax, Finland, had been elevated to the nobility in 1867 by King Adolph Frederick for his service in Sweden's wars against Russia, and his descendants had developed a large iron works.

But after Georg's father died in 1886, his fortune soon disappeared, and its remnants went to the eldest son. Georg was tired of big cities and had his own plans for making his fortune. For him, a 35-year adventure began when he decided to see the world and signed on to work on the cargo ship Nordstjärnan in the port of Härnösand, Sweden.

The trip wasn't what he had expected. The ship lurched and rolled through rough weather, the captain was grumpy, and the ill-tempered cook served them salty, half-raw bacon. Still, when they sailed into the Bay of Biscay to unload their lumber, he thought he had reached paradise, sunshine, clear blue skies, and warm gentle breezes.

The ship docked at Marseilles where it was to pick up a cargo of salt for the south Brazilian port of Santos. The sailors on the ship were fearful, since Santos had a bad reputation as a place of sickness and fever. After meeting Scarface Harry, a man who ran a hotel for sailors, several members of the crew, including Georg, saw a way out.

Georg as a young sailor

Scarface Harry was no beauty. A quarrel over a girl in his youth had left him with an ugly knife scar down his cheek and through his lip. But Georg thought he had an honest look all the same. Harry told the crew members he would smuggle them away from Marseilles, for a price, from their commitment to go to plague-ridden Santos.

Georg thought about how he had come to this horrible cellar, hidden from the police, while Scarface Harry worked out an escape for himself and his shipmates. After a full night and another day of the dark pit, Georg had had enough of the waiting and decided to make an escape.

"We had a meeting and decided that I should try to get out," Georg said in his memoirs. "I disguised myself with some of the others' clothes and rubbed dirt on my face. Then I went back through the labyrinth. I was not frightened of the rats anymore, nor of the dark.

"I struck a match when I got back to the door and saw a lock. It was old and rusty, and it gave way under pressure. I went up a stone staircase, until I was stopped again by an iron plate. Its hinges were easy to force. I was hit by a shower of dirt and gravel, and then a blast of sunlight hit me."

Georg came out cautiously into a trash-filled backyard. He slipped into a grocery store he spotted around a nearby street corner. A fat Frenchman behind the counter eyed him suspiciously. He raised his eyebrows, but they went down again when he saw the coin Georg held out. Georg bought food and candles, and hurried back to his friends. They greeted him enthusiastically, and they partied by candlelight. Full of meat and wine, the group fell asleep.

Scarface Harry returned to the cellar the next morning. He didn't waste any time asking where the food came from. He told the men that a reward of 500 francs had been offered for their capture. But he was as good as his word, and that night he smuggled them aboard a German vessel, the Marco Polo, bound for San Francisco.

"We sailed around Cape Horn, and the trip took four months. The rations were meager, and there wasn't much to do except make plans. I was all ready. I was going to the Wild West. The cowboy life was tempting, a fiery mustang and two revolvers were all that I would need."

But fate had something else in store for Georg af Forselles.

After the Marco Polo arrived in San Francisco, Georg decided to go into a tough-looking bar called Three-Finger Jack's, which was on Stewart Street. Three-Finger Jack waited on Georg himself. His eyes were cold as ice, but he seemed friendly enough as he welcomed the young Swede to San Francisco and sat down at his table.

"I noticed that the bar was empty for the middle of the day, but I thought little of it as we chatted and I started on my second drink. Suddenly everything started to get fuzzy and distant, and then the world turned black. When I woke up, I felt a familiar movement. I jumped out of the bunk, and shouted at a sleepy, dirty face lying near me, 'Can you tell me where in the world I am?'"

"On the J.B. Brown, of course, bound for Australia!"

Georg had been shanghaied. Apparently Three-Finger Jack had drugged him and brought Georg to the ship. He had even stolen Georg's pay in advance by explaining that the involuntary crew member owed him for room and board.

When the ship arrived in Sydney after three months, the crew members went to the consulate to be paid. Only 10 shillings was owed to Georg. He told the consul what had happened, and the official questioned the captain. The captain replied that he had no way of telling whether people were drunk or drugged when they signed on.

Hard words were exchanged, and the captain cursed. But he wanted his sailing papers, and in the end he had to give Georg a pound. The consul was sympathetic, and he matched Georg's wages to help him get on his feet again.

Georg hurried back to the ship for his belongings, avoiding the captain who had promised to kill him if he saw him again. Then he went to a boarding house where he met a young German named Fritz. He asked if Georg had heard about the gold in Coolgardie. This was Georg's first experience with gold fever.

The young men didn't have much money, but they decided to go to Newcastle on the way to Coolgardie anyway. Newcastle is a seaport on the Pacific in east New South Wales, Australia. The men struck out on foot for the town, which was 94 miles away. Farmers fed them on the way when they showed their seamen's books. They heard that the farmers were repaid by the government for their trouble.

The reality of their situation struck the boys when they arrived in Newcastle. After the long trek, they realized they would need money for provisions to go farther. Pack mules for the trip cost hundreds of pounds. So Georg said good-bye to Fritz and hired on an American clipper, the Colusa, which was bound for Honolulu, Hawaii. The clipper ships were called the "greyhounds of the sea", and Colusa flew over the waves.

The crew was mostly Irish as was the captain, a tough old bird who liked to drill his sailors. Georg fell ill with a fever after a couple of weeks and lay sick for a month. Soon after he recovered, and the Colusa arrived in Honolulu. Georg was astonished to see more than a hundred ships in the harbor waiting to load sugar for far-away ports.

"We soon knew the reason there were so many ships," Georg wrote. "The plague had broken out in the islands, and they were quarantined. People were dying all over. Someone thought that it had started in Chinatown and had started a fire there that killed dozens of people."

A guard was put aboard to make sure nobody went ashore. But Georg became restless, and one night he sneaked ashore with one of the Irishmen. The young men were not afraid of the plague and only intended to have a quick look at the city. The guard was asleep, and they rowed ashore silently.

The sailors stumbled around in the dark, until they found the Anchor Bar, an American saloon. They had a glass of whiskey, and then another. They sat there all night drinking. When they went out at dawn for a look around, they were overwhelmed by the smell of rotting flesh. The pair hurried down to the beach to return to the boat and escape the horror.

As they pushed the boat out, three men from the Coast Guard appeared.

"Where are you going, boys?" one of them inquired.

"Out to the Colusa; we're crew members."

"Come ashore," he said coldly.

Since the Coast Guard officer was armed, the sailors had no choice. They found themselves quarantined in lovely Honolulu.

Georg managed to build himself a shack and acquired a rowboat. When the quarantine was lifted, he ferried passengers to and from the shore. Then he discovered he could get American and Australian newspapers free off the ships and peddle them in town.

Georg acquired a uniform with a fancy hat from an American ship, and soon he became a well-known figure in the harbor.

Life seemed good in the mild, sunny climate. Georg swam at Waikiki and basked in the white sand. He read the newspapers he sold, and one day he saw a story that was to bring an end to this idyllic life.

On the front page of the *San Francisco Examiner* was a large picture of a gold digger asleep under a spruce tree, with a bag of gold dust as his pillow.

"The Klondike was discovered! Here it was warm and heavenly; up there, only snow and ice. But, gold fever had struck me and I had to get there."

Georg had $800 saved, and the Mariposa was sailing for San Francisco that night. He packed his things, pulled his boat up on the beach, and closed his cottage.

Soon Georg was in Seattle along with thousands of others from all over the world. Craftsmen had left their workshops, farmers had sold their land, office workers had quit their jobs, workers had left their factories.

The gathered would-be golddiggers were almost insane; they talked only of gold and cursed the boats that were already full. To realize the mining dream, one had to get a seat to Skagway, and then there were two ways to the Klondike. You could take a boat to St. Michael and then travel 1800 miles up the Yukon River to Dawson, or you could go by land through the Chilkoot Pass over the glaciers and mountains.

The boats went north loaded to the smokestacks. The cabins and the cargo holds were full of passengers, and there were tents on deck. The fare was $500. While the gold-seekers waited impatiently for a boat, they bought supplies, tried out different equipment, even took lessons in gold panning from sourdoughs on the Seattle beach.

There were also plenty of bars and places to gamble. Georg didn't have enough for the fare, so he tried his hand at poker. In short order, he had only a couple of nickels in his pocket.

Georg's fortune turned with the arrival of a ship called the Roanoke. It had come around Cape Horn loaded with provisions and destined for St. Michael. The helmsman was so sick he had been taken off to the hospital, and Georg got his job.

The 10-day journey to St. Michael was rough, and most of the passengers were seasick. All of the ship's drinking water was gone, and Georg went ashore with four others to replenish the supply. After he had put the other men to work, he looked around the tent city. He hadn't wandered far when he came to a big circus tent that housed Tex Rickard's Northern Saloon.

Georg stepped inside and met real gold diggers from the Klondike for the first time. Weatherbeaten men with high boots, guns in their belts, and Stetsons on their heads, they hung around the roulette table or stood at the counter drinking whiskey. There were four scales for weighing gold on the long bar. There the sacks of gold were weighed in and put in a safe behind the bar. The owner of the gold got a receipt or bills for the deposit. Thus, the saloon also functioned as a primitive bank.

"Tex" Rickard (Photo-Oakland Museum of Fine Arts)

Men carried smaller pouches in their back pockets and used either gold or bills in the roulette games. One oldtimer with a wrinkled face saw Georg watching the game and asked if he was Swedish. When Georg replied that he was, the old man said, ''Then you are a lucky bird! I've seen Swedes look for gold in Dawson. Here's a hundred dollars. Play it now!''

The old man threw a 100-dollar-bill into the young Swede's hand. Georg put the bill on red. Red won. He let the $200 stay on red. Red came again. Georg turned around and looked bemusedly at the old man. He then put $200 on the black. Black came up. $300 stayed. Black won again. Then Georg moved $200 to red. Black won. He put more money on red, and won again. It seemed like Georg couldn't lose. The stack of bills grew in front of him. When he finally remembered the boys down on the beach, he handed the old man the stack of bills.

"Well," he grinned. "what did I say about Swedes? Here's your share."

Georg stuffed the bills in his pocket, nodded, and left. As soon as he was out of sight, he sat down and started to count. Incredible! Georg, who made wages on the boat of $30 a month, had made over $1000 in 10 minutes. He now had the fare to go to the gold fields. He went down to the beach and waved his bundle of money. "Tell the captain I'm off to the Klondike."

The next boat for Dawson didn't leave for three days, so Georg went back to the Northern Saloon and watched the others play. The air was full of the smell of tobacco and frying pork. Georg soon discovered the outrageous prices of meals and accommodation. Pork and beans with bread and butter, $12.00; coffee, $4.00; a hammock in a tent with whiskey or coffee in the morning, $20.00. What money the young man had wouldn't last long.

Georg began to gamble again to increase his nest egg, but soon he was as broke as he had been when he arrived.

For a week, Georg worked for Tex, the bar owner, keeping order and cleaning up in the saloon, and then he met Frank McWellen. McWellen was slightly older than Georg, and said he had been involved with Soapy Smith's gang. He had been shot, however, and now was a law-abiding citizen.

Frank invited Georg to his cabin and explained that he made money by cutting wood for the Alaska Commercial Company. Soon Georg agreed to become Frank's partner and moved into his cabin. Since everyone was off to the Klondike, they could make $75 a cord cutting up driftwood for the riverboats.

Frank and Georg liked the time outdoors, sawing and sweating, saving and making plans for their trip to the Klondike. But sometimes they had to have an evening at the Northern Saloon. It was fun to meet the gold diggers who came down the river and hear how they had made out. They drank with the prospectors and sometimes tried a little roulette.

When the last boat for Dawson lifted its anchor, the men were not aboard. They wanted to buy a dog team and drive up there themselves, and so they worked even harder at their driftwood business.

One day at the end of November, they got a visitor from a firm in Eureka who was looking for someone to saw wood along the Yukon during the winter. Being out in the wilderness during the winter didn't appeal to them; they were happy enough where theywere. The man offered the team $150 a cord for the wood, however, so they agreed to the conditions. To finalize the deal, they went to Tex's Northern Saloon to set up a contract.

A slim, dark boy, maybe 22-years-old, had come into the saloon. He went up to the bar and threw down a bag of gold dust. It weighed up at hundreds of dollars.

"I come from Nome," the young man said, "and there is more of this there."

That was Jafet Lindeberg. Nome was discovered!

Pandemonium broke out all over St. Michael. The wide-eyed miners asked Lindeberg where Nome was. He told them it was named Cape Nome, an insignificant little headland on the treeless south coast of Seward Peninsula. It was 115 miles above St. Michael, on the Bering Sea across from Siberia. It was nothing but a flat stretch of gray beach, with frozen hills. It may have derived its name from a mistake made by a cartographer with the British Admiralty. On the sketch map, someone had written "? Name" to indicate that the headland was nameless. But perhaps the cartographer read the question mark as a "C" and the "a" in Name as an "o", and so, it became known as Cape Nome.

Another story claims the name comes from an Indian expression "No-me", meaning "I don't know", when some-one asked the name of the headland.

There are many versions of the story of the discovery of gold at Nome. As early as January 1, 1900, the *Nome Nugget* published, in its *Special New Year's Edition,* a long article about "Who Discovered Nome?":

"Who discovered the Nome dig-gings? Was it Lindeberg (sometimes spelled Linderberg), Lindblom, Brynteson, Blake, Hultberg or the Laplanders?

Or was it some unknown whose modesty prevents him from putting in a claim for the honor?"

Jafet Lindeberg (Photo-Consortium Library, UAA/APU)

The *Nome Nugget* also records a part of Lindeberg's account of his first expedition to Anvil Creek with Brynteson and Lindblom:

"It was on the 6th of September, 1898, that we panned out our first gold dust at Anvil Creek. The first pan produced $5. Sizing up the situation at a glance, we saw that we had made a strike indeed. After a ratherhurried consultation, we decided to return to Golovin Bay with all haste, stock ourselves out with provisions, get two other men, and form a (mining) district in the new region."

The *Nome Nugget* noted that Lindeberg did not reveal which of the three washed out the first rich pan of gold. Nor did he reveal that fact in his later accounts.

Erik Lindblom was credited by Ivan Boström, an early gold seeker in Nome, with being the first man to find gold in the Nome district. According to that version, Lindblom discovered gold in the Sinuk River on his journey from Port Clarence to Golovin Bay. He found a little bit of gold there and also panned a little more during a short stay by the Snake River. He told Hultberg about his discoveries. While Lindblom was panning by the Fish River, Hultberg began to organize an expedition to the Snake River. On his return, Hultberg stated that he had not found any gold and that Lindblom's information was incorrect. However, Lindblom did not give up and eventually went to the Snake River with Brynteson and Lindeberg.

On June 5, 1900, a report by Harry L. Blake titled, "The History of the Discovery of Gold at Cape Nome", was presented to the U. S. Senate in Washington, D. C., and was also published as an official act of Congress:

"The following account of the discovery of gold at Cape Nome is the correct and only truthful account ever written. This account is vouched for by over 300 miners and claim owners, both in the Cape Nome, Eldorado, Discovery and Blake mining districts."

Blake then vividly described Hultberg as a gold-mining missionary who always made a point of exhibiting his piety:

"The Rev. Hultberg, like the good, true, God-fearing missionary that he was, wanted to get some more gold mines for the poor natives, and asked me if I had any objections to his going with me." Blake wrote that Hultberg didn't fare well in the wilderness and always seemed to be sick. At Snake River, Blake stated that Hultberg burst into tears and, when asked what the matter was, said: "My poor wife and children...I must go home and see to my mission duties."

There may be good reason to believe that perhaps Hultberg really was seeking the gold, not for himself but for the mission, and that he saw the quest as a kind of service to God.

Sworn testimonies, designed to support Blake's account, end the document. One such testimony by John Waterson, a shipmate of Lindblom's, dismissed the idea that Lindblom panned gold on his way to Golovin Bay:

"John Waterson, being first duly sworn, deposes and says: That during the month of July, 1989, he was one of the crew of the bark *Alaska* bound on a whaling voyage in the Arctic Ocean; and that one Captain Cogan was the master, and one Erik O. Lindblom was one of the crew on said bark and shipped with affiant as a member of said crew from San Francisco, California. That owing to severe treatment by said Captain Cogan and other hardships of said voyage said Erik O. Lindblom and affiant decided to desert said bark at Port Clarence, Alaska, and in the month of July, 1898, did desert said bark and started along the coast in a skin boat, made by natives, for Golofnin (Golovin) Bay. That having no provisions other than what fish we could get at the mouth of Sinook (Sinuk) River the natives supplied us with fish and we continued on our voyage. We had no pan, pick, shovel or implement of any kind and did not prospect for gold or discover any place of prospecting, and did not meet any white men on our trip.

"At the head of Golofnin Bay, we were given shelter at the Swedish Mission by N. O. Hultberg, who employed us to go up Ophir Creek in Eldorado mining district to work on a claim owned by Hultberg. At Ophir Creek, we were much about the cabin of H. L. Blake, D. B. Libby, A. P. Mordaunt and L. F. Melsing, and we heard said Blake telling his partners about gold discoveries he had made at a point 15 to 20 miles west of Cape Nome. Said Blake said a creek came in by a mountain on the top of which was a rock anvil, which landmark was very conspicuous from the coast. That thereafter said Erik O. Lindblom left said Ophir Creek to see Hultberg and tell him what Blake had reported to his partners. Said Hultberg sent Lindblom as one of a party for the place designated by Blake to stake claims, but I, affiant, was not included, as Hultberg, Lindblom, and others spoke the Swedish language, which I did not understand, and I was left to my own resources from and after that time. Later, I met said Lindblom and he told me that he and others had gone to the place said Blake had described; that they had named the river Snake River, owing to its winding course, and that they named the tributary Anvil Creek, owing to the rock anvil which said Blake had described. He said they found plenty of gold on Anvil Creek and staked plenty of claims.

"Further affiant saith not, except that this affiant was made in the interest of truth and correct information as to the original finding of gold in said locality and by whom found and first reported."

This testimony was, in due course, certified and stamped on October 14, 1899, by the public notary of the District of Alaska.

On the golden sands to the headland of Cape Nome, by midsummer 1899, the beaches of Alaska proved to be true; gold had been discovered!

The Cape Nome sands occupied in a short time hundreds of men who were able to take $2 million in beach gold over a single season. After the 1899 season, the beach sands of Nome were worked out, but more conventional placer discoveries continued to be made in the Nome region.

Jafet Lindeberg with bank personnel in the Bank of Nome. These bricks are solid gold worth millions of dollars. (Photo- Archives, Alaska and Polar Regions Dept.,Rasmuson Library, University of Alaska, Fairbanks)

Chapter Two

Georg Heads for Nome

"We shall all be rich, rich as kings."

There are different versions of the discovery of gold at Nome, but three men later known as the "Three Lucky Swedes" got the lion's share of the new claims in the area. The three men were Jafet Lindeberg, a Lapp reindeer herder, Erik Lindblom, a Swedish tailor from San Francisco, and John Brynteson, another Swedish man. Jafet Lindeberg, whom Georg af Forselles met in the Northern Saloon that November night, had signed up to herd reindeer in 1897 when an American delegation arrived in Norway to buy reindeer for naturalizing in Alaska. Lindeberg did not know very much about the reindeer, but he had been brought up at Varanger in the north of Norway, and in the summer the reindeer came down there to the coast from Kautokeino. Lindeberg saw the job as a way of getting to Alaska. He intended to press on to the Klondike gold fields as soon as he could. When the reindeer project collapsed, he resigned his position.

"The Three Lucky Swedes"
Erik Lindblom, age 43; John Brynteson, age 30; Jafet Lindeberg, age 27 ---Nome, Alaska, 1901

As a result of a meeting with Dr. A. N. Kittilsen in St. Michael, he headed for Council City instead of Dawson. There in August he fell in with Erik Lindblom, from San Francisco, and John Brynteson, who had earlier mined coal in Michigan. Both of them were Swedish-born, naturalized American citizens. These three prospectors have gone down in Alaskan lore as the "Three Lucky Swedes" who discovered the gold at Nome, but from the beginning angry words flew about who had actually found the first diggings.

Lindeberg, Lindblom, and Brynteson certainly staked the "Discovery Claim," but they did not stumble on it accidentally as gold miners George Carmack and Skookum Jim had done at Bonanza Creek in the Klondike region on August 17, 1896. More than 30 years before, in 1866, an engineer named Daniel B. Libby had been shown gold by natives. He found traces himself, while he was working on the Western Union telegraph line. When the news of the Klondike strikes hit San Francisco in 1897, Libby set out for the Northland with three companions, Louis F. Melsing, H.L. Blake, and A.P. Mordaunt.

In April of the following year, 1898, Libby's party staked their first claims at Melsing and Ophir Creeks. Months earlier, however, they had encountered other men who were prospecting on the Seward Peninsula, among them the Swedish missionary at Cheenik in Golovin Bay, Nels O. Hultberg, the teacher, P.H. Anderson, Dr. Kittilsen, and a Lapp reindeer herder, Johan S. Tornesis. They also staked claims on the creeks, and the two groups established the Discovery and Eldorado Mining Districts at Council City.

Hultberg and Blake had traveled together, using reindeer as draught animals, to Cape Nome in January. They went with an Eskimo named Too rig Luck, who had shown Blake ore that contained gold. While they found excellent prospects, Blake argued that they should wait until spring to stake their claims. Hultberg made further forays in February and March, but it was not until July that he and Blake made their return trip to Nome. Thereafter the story is confused.

Hultberg provided two Eskimo kayaks, and Blake contributed a whaling boat. Hultberg wanted to take along two Swedes who had recently arrived in Golovin Bay, Brynteson and John L. Hagelin. Blake didn't want the party to be dominated by the Swedes, so he invited two friends to join him, Chris Kimber and Henry L. Porter. In later accounts Hultberg was

N. O. Hultberg
(Photo-Consortium Library, UAA/APU)

to claim he invited all five men, while Brynteson said he and Hagelin organized the trip and invited Hultberg, who then included the remaining three. Henry Blake gave a third version. He recorded that Hultberg did not want Kimber and Porter to join the party. "This made the little missionary white with rage, and he acted ugly and spiteful all the way," Blake wrote of Hultberg's mood on the trip.

Nonetheless, they all set out together on July 31. A heavy storm assaulted them on August 4, and as they headed for the mouth of the Snake River, five of them were swept overboard by the strong winds and towering waves. They escaped with their lives, but they lost most of their food and equipment. They spent that night drying out by a big fire, then set out across the barren tundra.

When they arrived at an unnamed stream, later called Anvil Creek after nearby Anvil Mountain (four miles north of Nome), Porter, Blake, and Kimber panned a little gold. Hultberg went upstream with his pan and shovel. Two hours later, when he saw Blake approaching him, Hultberg picked up his tools and hurried downstream. He told Blake in his heavily accented English, "Dey is not any gold up dare."

There was, of course. Hultberg evidently wanted to lead the others astray and head back to Cheenik where he would prepare another expedition. At this point, the two groups set out on different return routes, but they met again at Sinuk Mary's place, some 20 miles to the west. There they found some other white prospectors.

A story told by Jed Jordan, the first bar owner in Nome, credits Mary Antisarlook, a Russian-Eskimo woman married to a reindeer herder, with the first discovery of gold at Anvil Creek. He said that she saw stones glittering in the creek when she stopped there for a drink of water and that she showed these stones to Lindeberg, Lindblom, and Brynteson.

Jordan went on to say that Mary did wind up rich. She was far more the lady than many sourdoughs were gentlemen. At the time she was probably the wealthiest Eskimo in the world. She lived about 50 miles from Nome, and her wealth derived from reindeer, not gold. Her husband died leaving her several hundred reindeer, and she enlarged the herd. Lindeberg took a million dollars out of Anvil Creek; Sinuk Mary at her richest was worth a few thousand dollars.

At any rate, by this time Hultberg's health had taken a turn for the worse. Then Blake was sure the illness was genuine, but later he wrote: "I had not been gone more than one day when this sly, crafty, avaricious, God-fearing, Eskimo-loving missionary fooled me. He got a boat from some white man at the mouth of the Snake River, slipped off in the night, left Porter alone in the tent, and went directly to Golovin Bay, got two more Swedes,

Lindblom and Lindeberg, and a small sailboat, and drew a map of the place, told them exactly where we had been and exactly where to go, gave them his power of attorney, and off they started, taking the power of attorney of every Swede missionary in the vicinity and located the whole country."

Hultberg was certainly completely exhausted when he reached Cheenik, to which Brynteson and Hagelin also returned at the end of August. A few weeks later he went home to Sweden. But before he left, he made sure that Brynteson would return as quickly as possible to Anvil Mountain.

Brynteson would have not have needed the map Blake refers to since he was one of the original party. Whatever actually happened, Brynteson did leave Cheenik on September 11, 1898, taking Lindeberg and Lindblom with him. Lindblom later claimed that he had told Hultberg in July about gold he had found in the Snake River on his journey from Port Clarence, where he had jumped ship, to Golovin Bay with an Eskimo family. Probably the three men had met in Council City, where Lindblom and Lindeberg were both looking for gold. However, they became a party, and now the "three lucky Swedes" were working together.

In 1934 Georg told his version of the story in *The Swedish Count of Alaska*.

"Many favorable circumstances contributed to the Scandinavians getting the honor of having discovered the biggest Alaska gold field. The first step in that direction was taken on a cold autumn day in 1897. One of the Coast Guard boats was returning from its usual round of provisioning all the missions that worked with the Indians and Eskimos, when it stopped at the Swedish mission at Golovin Bay so the crew could visit and have a drink. There were Sheldon Jackson, leader of the mission, Captain Tuttle, commander of the boat, and the missionaries Hultberg, Karlson, and Kallman. They discussed the Klondike discoveries and their regret that they had not been there for the big rush.

"Kallman had a different opinion. 'Why should we have to dig for gold to be rich?' he said. 'I know a much better way.'

"Everyone wanted to know what he could mean. Kallman explained his plan.

"'Why not rent a boat, go to Norway, and ship a full cargo of reindeer along with families of Laplanders over here? Reindeer are tough, and they make good draught animals. Their meat is delicious, you can drink the milk, and the skin is excellent.'"

After Jackson thought it over, he decided the idea was brilliant. That fall he and Kallman went to Washington to present the idea, and during the winter a cargo ship sailed for Vardo. Five hundred reindeer were purchased, and twenty Laplander families were hired. Among them was Jafet Lindeberg.

He was half Laplander, and being of mixed race had often made it difficult for him. Dark-eyed and handsome, he was popular with the girls, but on Saturday nights he was thrown out of dances along with the other Laplanders.

"When he left Vardo that winter, he promised he would come back and take his revenge on the Hammerfest boys. It was a promise he was to keep. But Jafet Lindeberg would never have made any gold findings had it not been for an old whaler who looked him up at the last moment. The whaler dreamed about the Klondike like many others, and he wanted a piece of it.

"'I cornered Lindeberg,' he said, 'and pressed some money on him. Buy me a gold mine if you find one over there.'

"Lindeberg took the money and promised to look for gold. By the time the Lapps and the reindeer reached Seattle, it was clear that the supply of reindeer moss would not last to Golovin Bay. Half of the animals and some of the Laplander families were put ashore at (the) Haines mission, where they could travel on by land to the Swedish mission. It took a whole year to make that trip, and many of the animals died. Lindeberg was among those who continued on by barge. He was a smart young man who already realized he could not buy a gold mine with the $2,000 he had. The money would buy provisions, however, and that is what he spent it on.

"Now that he had got to Golovin Bay for free, Lindeberg, who was a good carpenter, got work at the mission, where a new church was being built. There he met a tall, religious Swede named John Brynteson and two English brothers, Frank and Gabriel Price. They worked for the mission and prospected for gold in the surrounding area. Their findings were small and probably would have continued to be had it not been for the arrival of another Swede.

"Short and skinny with red hair and beard, Erik Oskar Lindblom was a tailor who had emigrated to San Francisco. No doubt he would have stayed there tailoring, if he had not caught Klondike fever. He became possessed with the idea of going North; he talked of nothing else during the day and dreamed at night that he was digging gold. Finally his mother decided that she would have no peace unless she promised to look after the business while he went to Alaska after those gold nuggets.

"Lindblom was short of cash, but he thought he could fix that. Down in the harbor he strolled around watching for boats that were heading north. Finally he found a whaling boat whose captain agreed to take him on as a seaman. Lindblom knew little English, and he was well on his way before he learned that the contract he had signed meant that he was to serve as a whaler in the Arctic Ocean for two years.

"Two years! The little tailor nearly had a stroke. He broke out in cold perspiration, but he clenched his teeth and didn't utter a word."

At Port Clarence there was a mineral well where the whalers use to take on water before they went   any further. When the boat stopped, Lindblom ran, and after a couple of miles, when he was sure no one was following him, he sat down for a rest. He was shaking, and sweat was pouring off him, but his eyes glowed with triumph. They had not managed to cheat him out of the Klondike, those villains.

There he sat in his coat, pants, and shoes in the middle of the most deserted Arctic country the Lord had created. He shivered when he looked around. A terrible silence lay over the tundra and the faraway snow-covered mountains. There was nothing living to be seen. Trudging over the tundra was like traveling on an immense wet sponge.

"But he had no time to be depressed; he was in a hurry to get to the Klondike. During the long, cold, black night he walked on, and then he slept for a while when the sun came up. When the cold woke him again, he continued south, avoiding the mountains.

"Soon he had run out of the crackers he had in his pocket, and he found no water as he walked on. On the third day, he met an Eskimo. He was frightened, but he was too weak to run away.

"Kahnooeepitch (How are you?),' the Eskimo said.

"Lindblom didn't understand, but he opened his mouth and put his finger in it as a sign that he was hungry. The Eskimo gave him some walrus meat, which he gobbled down. Then the Eskimo pointed eastward, said something else, and put two fingers in the air.

"Lindblom thought hard, and after many signs and gestures, he finally understood that eastward, by a river, there were two white men. The Eskimo showed him the direction to take, and Lindblom set off.

"Charlie Garden could scarcely believe his eyes when Lindblom walked up to his cabin. Where in the world had this white man come from, bare-headed and without any equipment?

"Garden was married to an Eskimo woman named Sinuk Mary. He made a living fishing and panning for a little gold in the Sinuk River. He exchanged the gold for food when he made his yearly trip to the trading station. When Lindblom came to Garden's cabin, another Englishman, John Blake, was visiting. He had panned for gold at Ophir Creek, which was now Council City.

"Lindblom had big news with him. Nobody there had heard anything about the Klondike. The little tailor told them about the discoveries and his own adventures, and then he asked if it was far to the Klondike. They looked at him with a smile and said it was very, very far.

"That evening as they sat around the fire talking about gold, Garden suddenly said, 'I found a river bed 30 miles to the east where I took up fifty cents worth of gold in a single shovelful.'

"'I'll look at it on my way back,' Blake said. 'You should make a hundred dollars a day there.'

"Lindblom sharpened his ears but remained silent. He was so tired, but this was about gold. It gave him energy just to think about it.

"Two days later they broke up. Lindblom was going to accompany Blake until he went off to Ophir Creek; then he would head for the Swedish mission at Golovin Bay.

"In the evening they rested by the winding Snake River. Blake had observed the rock formations and thought there might be gold there. Probably this was where Garden had made his findings.

"Early the next morning, they broke camp and left the beach they had been following to travel over the tundra in the direction of the mountains. As they came closer, they found a valley that cut through the mountains. A stream flowed through it, and Blake took out his gold pan, filled it with sand, and started panning. The pan was half washed when the bottom started to glitter. Blake jumped for a second but then restrained himself and emptied the pan in the water, pretending there was nothing.

"'But that was gold!' Lindblom shouted. 'The bottom of the pan was full!'

"'No, it was nothing,' Blake said. 'That was nothing. I'm going to show you places where there is more of it.'

"Blake had quickly valued the gold in the pan at about $15. But he didn't want to share the claim with this naive Swede. According to the law, the one who found a gold field had the right to make two claims. And as the two of them had found the valley, they would have to share it. That was not what Blake wanted to do.

"Lindblom didn't have the faintest idea about how to stake a claim, but when Blake was out of sight for a moment, he quickly peeled the bark of a branch and carved on it, Lindblom's mine.

"They continued walking for another two days, until they reached Topkok. Blake was now going to head for the Interior, while Lindblom struck out for the coast.

"'Follow the beach,' Blake told him. 'When you have walked for a couple of days you will come to a reef sticking right out of the ocean. There is a path towards the rocks, and when you climb over them, you'll see the mission on the other side. . .After you've been there, you can come to me at Ophir Creek, and I'll show you where the gold is.'

"Lindblom thanked him and said goodbye. But as soon as Blake had disappeared, he started running along the beach as fast as his short legs would carry him. That Blake thought he could cheat him!

"And that is how the sweating, skinny tailor arrived at Golovin Bay. Only Missionary Hultberg was in when he came. Lindblom was so excited that he could hardly speak.

"'I've found some gold,' he said, 'lots of gold.'

"Hultberg tried to calm him down.

"'Do you have some with you?' he asked.

"'No, but there is so much of it.'

Erik O. Lindblom
(Photo: Consortium Library, UAA/APU)

"Hultberg listened as Lindblom went on incoherently. He seemed to be delirious or crazy. How could anyone believe that a dirty bearded whaler without a shovel or gold pan had really found gold. It must have been mica. The mountains were full of it. And he knew about Blake from earlier episodes. He must have had fun with this whaler.

"Lindblom gradually calmed down and had a square meal, even if no one believed his story.

"When Brynteson and the Price brothers returned from their prospecting that evening, Hultberg took them aside.

"'Don't say anything,' he whispered. 'We have a crazy whaler here talking wildly about gold. He's been with Blake about 65 miles west and says he has found a mine full of gold.'

"They nodded and looked at the little tailor, who was still sitting at the table over his food. 'Well, if he was with Blake, it had to be mica.'

"The religious Brynteson found it difficult to see evil in anyone, There must have been something in what happened between the tailor and Blake. He talked with Lindblom and then came out again to the others.

"'There has to be gold,' he said. 'If you'll come along, we'll go right away.'

"The Price brothers laughed at him. 'Should we follow every crazy man who thinks he has found gold?' they said. 'No, Brynteson... and provisions, where are we going to get them? Winter will be here soon, and we'll starve.'

"Brynteson nodded. They were right. Without provisions, it was useless to think of a long trip like that. Lindblom would have to wait for spring.

"Then Jafet Lindeberg suddenly stepped in, and Brynteson remembered the provisions he had had when he landed.

"'Do you have any of your provisions left?' he asked eagerly.

"'Yes, I have a couple of tons,' Lindeberg replied. They were the provisions he had bought with the whaler's money.

John Brynteson
(Photo-Consortium Library, UAA/APU)

"'Come in,' Brynteson said. 'We have something to discuss.'

"That night Brynteson, Lindblom, and Lindeberg worked out an agreement on how they would share their claims and on other matters that were bound to come up. That night Nome's laws were written.

"I was told all this by those who participated. On the town hall in Nome you can read the words: Nome's laws were written before Nome was discovered.

"Now they had to find the best way along the coast in the fall weather. Lindblom was still weak, and the way over the mountains was hard at that time of year.

"Brynteson knew how they would do it. He went to Hultberg and asked to borrow the mission's barge. They loaded it full with Lindeberg's provisions and left early the next morning. As they sailed along the coast, Lindblom watched for the mountains where he and Blake had found the valley. He was alert and well now, and he could hardly sit still in the boat.

"After a couple of days, he thought he saw the right mountain, and they turned the barge toward the shore. They tied up at the mouth of the Snake River and took only the most essential items with them as they set off into the tundra.

"They reached Anvil Creek and found the bush Lindblom had marked with his name. Now they would find out the truth. Brynteson took out his pan, filled it with sand, and started to shake it as the others watched. The whole bottom shone and glittered.

"Brynteson looked at the others and nodded seriously. 'Boys,' he said calmly, 'we are millionaires.'

"During the day a big storm blew up, and they had to make camp.

"When they returned to the barge in the morning, they found only pieces of it left. Their provisions were gone, and they had nothing for the coming winter.

"They had to think fast. Soon it was decided that Brynteson would go back to the mission by land to get as many provisions as he could. The others were to build a cabin, make some claims, and wash for gold. Then Lindeberg would go to St. Michael to buy winter provisions.

"Brynteson was 6-foot-6, a physical giant of a man, with fists the size of crayfish nets and as calloused as elephant hide from all the devastatingly heavy labor he had performed in his life. He disappeared into the east with giant steps. He walked like a crazy man, but when he came to the mission he was able to throw a sack of gold dust on the table.

"'Here, old men,' he said, 'you can see the glitter.'

"The effect was amazing. When Lindeberg passed by two weeks later on his way to St. Michael, the mission was deserted.

"Gone were the Price brothers. The Laplanders who were going to watch the reindeer had disappeared. Yes, for the moment, even the missionaries had given up their hunt for souls and hurried west to make claims.

"The word spread like wildfire in St. Michael. New findings, richer than Klondike, a Laplander had come down with thousands in gold. From every direction men poured into the Northern Saloon and asked endless questions. Where was the Laplander? They wanted to hear it from him with their own ears. Was it really true? How far was it?

"'Fourteen days over the ice,' Lindeberg answered.

"There wouldn't be any sawing firewood along the Yukon for Frank and me that winter. We decided we were going to Nome too."

When John Brynteson returned home from America in 1906, he was one of Europe's richest men, and his fortunes nearly doubled by the time he died in 1959. In Sweden, he went by the name "the gold digger of Svanskog," because of his vast wealth, which was in the form of large estates in the United States, industries in Svanskog, Värmland and Gothenburg, Sweden and large forests scattered about Sweden. But, just as well, he deserves the name, "The Saint of Nome," and being unique, he deserves with all right another name, "The gold diggers' gold digger."

Chapter Three

Georg Stakes a Claim

"In the Northland they have discovered that prayer is only efficacious when backed with muscle, and they are accustomed to doing things for themselves."

Georg af Forselles and Frank McWellen were among thousands who headed for Nome that winter, but the news had leaked out to a few, even before Lindeberg went to St. Michael in November. The three lucky Swedes had returned to Nome in October in the Cheenik mission's schooner, accompanied by Dr. Kittilsen, Gabriel Price, who had been prospecting in the Kotzebue Sound area, Johan Tornensis, and an Eskimo named Constantine.

To get the schooner, they had paid a price. Lindeberg recounted the details in an interview in 1960:

"Hultberg would not charter us this schooner unless we built him a church. This was quite a job, but then there were five of us, because we had informed Dr. Kittilsen and Gabriel Price of what we had found.

"It took us five days to build that church because none of us were carpenters. As a matter of fact, not one of our group was able to handle a hammer or saw straight. When we were through with building the house, he insisted upon our building a steeple. It took us another half a day. Finally, we got the schooner, and we filled it with provisions.

"Five tons, that was the sum of my supplies. We loaded the schooner to its capacity, took some lumber, took a lot of my provisions and bought some from a trader by the name of Dexter. We went back to Nome in two days on the schooner. We had trouble getting it into the river; it took us all day. After we got the schooner into the river, the river froze solid

Dr. A. N. Kittilsen
(Photo-Consortium Library, UAA/APU

by next morning. We were just in time. Once we had anchored the schooner in one of the small creeks that run into the Snake River at the lower end, we started packing in the supplies up to the mines, tents, some lumber and some firewood. Nome had practically no firewood.''

There on October 15, 1898, with Dr. Kittilsen as chairman and Price as secretary, the party created the Cape Nome Mining District, which was to become the richest in all Alaska, adopting resolutions on the size and recording of claims. They proceeded to restake the claims made in September and located a number of others both on the Snake River and in neighboring streams. At the beginning of November, they returned to Cheenik by sled, leaving the ice-bound schooner behind.

Soon their news was out. Price wrote to some of his friends in Council City, telling them "not to make this known too much." Within 24 hours the place was deserted. About a hundred men went out into a severe snowstorm. It took them four days to cover the 80 miles to Anvil Creek, where Carroll M. Bennett and others took some of the best claims.

Meanwhile, Kittilesen and Lindeberg both revealed the strikes when they arrived in St. Michael on November 30. The stampede then began in earnest, and within a month more than 300 claims had been staked.

Georg's recollections give a picture of the chaotic conditions that prevailed during the rush and of the life the gold diggers led that first winter at Nome:

Everyone rushed from the Northern Saloon to the trading companies to get dogs, provisions, and equipment. The Northern Commercial Company and the Alaska Commercial Company had their own saloons where you could have a drink after you finished your business, but that night the drinks were all free. Whiskey, beer, cigars, what would you like?

Frank and Georg could not afford a dog team. They bought a six-foot pull sled, which they loaded full with 200 pounds of provisions. They also got knee-length sealskin parkas and mukluks that had walrus skin on the bottom. They were completely waterproof. They didn't wear socks on the long walks because they sucked up sweat, which turned to ice and froze travelers' feet. Instead, they filled their shoes with reeds from the trading companies and put them on over their bare feet. At night they took the reeds out and hung them up to dry.

Drift ice had come down the Bering Strait and went down Norton Sound and stayed. Snow fell on top of it, and the road was clear.

It was like a storm had passed over St. Michael that night. The tents went down like popped balloons, turned into white dots, and disappeared on the sleds. Tex Rickard's proud saloon was torn down and packed up to go to Nome too.

The trading companies' big dogsled teams, which had been ready from the moment the news came, left first over the ice. After them the other teams followed like a long snake. The whips and the commands for the dogs could be heard long after they disappeared.

Frank and Georg followed after the dog teams with their sled. The trail was much better since the larger sleds had paved the way. Frank went in front with a rope around his chest, and Georg went behind and pushed. There were some risks involved, for the men had no tents, only reindeer-hide sleeping bags, and a snowstorm would have been fatal.

Their luck held, however, as the weather was clear and cold; the ice glittered and the sled creaked. But the days were very short, and they camped as soon as the dark came in order not to get lost. The team made about 12 miles a day.

The shortest way would have been straight over Norton Sound, but the drift ice wasn't so

G. W. Price
(Photo-Consortium Library, UAA/APU)

secure farther out, and the danger of a snowstorm was more likely. The trail went north over to Isaac Point, which the men reached in three days. They rested there and dried their footgear over a fire, and the next day they continued over to Norton Bay. From there they went over the neck of land and came out on Golovin Bay.

That was good timing for the pair. The sky was gray and getting dark in the west. They knew a storm was coming and hurried to reach land. The sweat was pouring as the men ran, tripped, and cursed.

When they got to land, they looked around for shelter. While they were gathering driftwood for a cabin, the men met an Eskimo. He was very kind and let the two know by sign language that they could stay in his nearby igloo when the storm came in from the sea.

When the storm was over, they came out of the igloo. Everywhere there was evidence that people had passed in a hurry. Food lay about in the snow. They thought for a moment. They knew their provisions wouldn't be enough for the winter, and it would be hard to make any claims now while everything was frozen and snowed in. If they were a couple of days late, theirr chances would be the same, they reasoned. So they delayed and started to collect the provisions.

While they were doing that, other men began to move around them again. In the Yukon the *Courier Post* had reported the findings, and the news reached Kotlik; then it went farther up and came to Andreafsky. There were big gatherings of gold diggers there who were supposed to go up to Dawson. They changed their course in a hurry, while dog teams were brought along the Yukon.

Then the rush came over Golovin Bay. Big teams with nine to 17 dogs passed on their way to Nome. Three or four men ran after the sleds; they had put the teams together to get there faster. In their hurry they went in over land; they passed Frank and Georg as they were heading towards the mountains. Their whips whistled through the air as they screamed at the dogs. The dogs scratched in the snow, cried, slid backwards, and the sleds went down again.

More shouts, curses, noises from the whips. The dogs would never make it. "What in the hell do we need these sacks of flour for?" one man shouted as he dried his forehead. "They're too heavy. Throw them off!"

Out in the snow went the sacks.

"Throw out this bacon," another one shouted, and the snow blew as the bacon came off the sled.

The teams worked harder and harder to get up, and more and more provisions were thrown off. The sleds got lighter, and the dogs could go on.

Enterprising as always, Frank and Georg loaded their sled with sacks of sugar and flour and boxes of bacon. They pulled with all their might to get the sled up the mountain; it must have been 3000 feet high. Up in the pass between the mountains, they buried their provisions in the snow.

As they went on they could hear new shouts and swearing.

"You are a fool, you ass," one man shouted.

"Pull yourself, you son of a bitch," his partner replied.

Farther up it was quiet, they were fighting. Finally they stopped, and one of them said, "We had better continue if we want to get anywhere." Then Frank and Georg heard an axe.

"Now, take your share of the sled and go to hell," one shouted.

"These madmen have each taken a piece of the sled," Georg said to Frank.

"Yes," he answered, "they've lost their nerve."

And so it went on. More dog teams drove by; more provisions wound up in the snow. They would rather have gold than food. Altogether Frank and Georg collected four loads of provisions and buried them. They left a stick with their names on it over the supply, and then they went on. It was easier as they went downhill. Snow started to fall as they came to the other side of the mountain, but the trail was well-packed and easy to follow.

They went east along the coast and came to Nome after a six-day trip. A small tent city had already sprung up, and everywhere people were collecting driftwood to build cabins to get out of the long winter's icy grip.

Frank and Georg started on a cabin too. They measured an area 14 feet on all sides and started to collect logs. They had an axe and a saw, but they couldn't get nails anywhere, so they had to make do without. They wanted to make an A-frame cabin, but they had few resources and wound up with a flat roof like most of the others. They put moss and sand on top of it.

The men couldn't get any hinges for the door either, but Georg used his ingenuity. He found an old shoe and cut it into wide strips, which they attached to the door and walls with thread nails. Now they were only missing something to put in front of the window to keep the cold out.

They took an old flour sack and washed it thoroughly. Then they melted some old candles in a pan, dipped the material in it, and stretched it over the hole. The cloth let the daylight in like a glass window, and it was always free from frost.

They didn't have a basement or a floor, except for well-packed clay. In one corner they put their Yukon stove, which they had brought with them from St. Michael. It was a yard long, made of metal, but with no rings or holes to put the pots down in. However, it had an oven for bread making, and a long metal pipe went up through the roof.

Next the pair needed beds. They put some sticks in the clay, made some slats, and tied them up with steel wire from the bacon crates. Over the slats they put some more sticks and shoveled moss up from under the snow to put on top. The men had not had a more comfortable mattress for a long time.

After they made the beds, they decided they should make a couple of bunks above them. This proved to be an excellent idea, for they had hardly finished the cabin when Red Sullivan, and Frank and Jack Cooper stepped inside to ask if they could stay.

The guests agreed to make the extra bunks themselves. In return for the hospitality, they let Georg and Frank borrow their dog team. Jack Cooper and Frank used it to get the food buried up in the mountain pass, while Georg went out to make some claims for himself and McWellen.

It snowed almost every day as Georg started making trips into the surrounding valleys, and he plodded around in knee-high new snow. Anvil Creek was already claimed, but he succeeded in finding a bench claim on the slope on the way down to the valley that was still free.

Claims were allowed to be 1320 feet long and 660 feet wide. Georg walked around in the valleys and measured up the claims. He had already learned enough about finding gold so he knew where to look. In the valleys crossing the mountains were the greatest chances of finding gold.

In Otter Creek Georg made three claims for himself, at Glacier Creek half of one, and one each at Balto Creek, Specimen Creek, Bourbon Creek, Dexter Creek, and Nekula Gulch. It took him two weeks to do the job, and when everything was ready, he went up to Nekula Gulch one day. He dragged some bushes together and made a little fire. When the fire had melted the snow and thawed the ground a little, he took out his gold pan and filled it with sand. Then he put melted snow on it and started panning.

He came to the bottom of the pan and saw at least fifty cents worth of gold shining and glittering there.

"That was a proud moment," Georg said later. "For months I had heard about gold, seen gold, thought about gold, and dreamed about gold. And here I was, on January 18, 1899, with a gold pan in my hand and gold from my own claim. How much there was in my claims only the future would show. But one thing was sure; at the age of 21, I was the owner of eight and a half claims in the richest of the Alaska gold districts."

Chapter Four

Waiting for Spring

"The great hazards by trail and river were spoken of in the light of common places."

During the long, dark winter months, Georg and his companions dreamed of the gold they would take out of their claims in the spring. Meanwhile frontier life returned to normal.

Tex Rickard had left the roulette table in St. Michael since it was too heavy and too expensive to bring by dog sled. Instead the men played cards, poker, pangini, and solo. As far as Georg was concerned the camp was badly equipped, there was little food, no beer, and the whiskey was always running short. Rickard made an agreement with Charlie Hocks, who had opened another saloon nearby. He would manage both of them while Charlie brought the whiskey by dog team from St. Michael.

There was no paper money in the camp; everything was paid for in gold. Those like Georg, who had no gold yet, were allowed credit until spring. Dollar bills gradually rolled in with cheechakos who kept arriving.

Among these newcomers were some who took up lodging with Frank and the Georg. The first two were Oskar Olson from Stockholm, who was called the Lone Swede, and Frank Landström from Gothenburg. They had stayed up on the Yukon River, chopping wood for the Alaska Commercial Company's boats. But when the rumor about the gold findings had reached them, they put flour sacks on the sled, loaded up with fire-water, and left for the mouth of the Yukon. They traded the whiskey to the Indians for furs, and then they sold the furs for provisions, and that is how they were able to get to Nome.

As soon as they got their bunks in the cabin ready, they left to make some claims. They followed the Snake for a few miles and then turned into a valley that was later named Sunrise Creek. They found that there was still room for claims there, and they got so busy marking them that they took no notice of the weather.

The sky filled with clouds, then darkened, and suddenly a heavy snowstorm came through the valley and enveloped them. They looked for shelter, but there were no trees in the naked valley. They fought their way back to the Snake River, trying desperately to get to Nome.

Suddenly Frank shouted as the ice broke under him. Oskar had gotten over the river, but Frank, who was bigger and heavier, had been pushing the sled from behind. Now he was in the water up to his knees and his mukluks were full. He tried to crawl up, but his leg was starting to go numb.

"Oskar," he shouted, "I can't walk any more. My leg is frozen."

"Hurry up," Oskar insisted, "it's a matter of life and death."

So Frank clenched his teeth and grabbed the sled again. He fell heavily; his leg was dead. Oskar went over to his friend and felt the stiff leg. What were they going to do now?

"Goddamn it," he shouted. "I can't drag you into Nome. That would mean death for both of us. You'll have to stay here until I can get back with some help."

"All right," Frank nodded grimly.

Oskar spread a sealskin from the sled on the snow and put Frank on top of it. Then he covered Frank with the canvas, shoveled more snow over everything, and left the sled and a shovel as markers.

The storm was still blowing from the southwest, and Oskar knew that was where the beach had to be. He took the shortest way over the tundra, walking right into the storm. He could hardly see through the snow whipping into his face, but he forced himself on, staggering and falling, stubbornly fighting the storm. Eventually he tripped over something hard. He put his hand on his face, closed his eyes, and tried to orient himself. He had hit some logs; he was on the beach.

He knew the cabins couldn't be far away. He followed the driftwood into Nome. Panting, red-eyed, water from melting snow pouring off him, he fell into Tex Rickard's saloon.

"Boys," he said, "I need some help. My partner is lying up in a creek with a frozen leg."

"Impossible!" shouted a weatherbeaten old gold digger. "It would be madness in this snowstorm; we wouldn't find him."

"He'll freeze to death!" said Oskar.

"Can't be helped," came the reply. "We'd all die if we went out on the tundra; we'd get lost."

Oskar looked grim. He knew none of them would go with him, and he would have to let Frank lie out there until the storm was over. Finally, on the third day, they could leave. Jack Cooper hitched up his team of four dogs and followed Oskar up to Sunrise Creek over the well-packed snow. The sled still stood in the middle of the creek covered with snow.

As they began to dig, Oskar whispered, "I'll bet he's dead," and Jack agreed. They lifted the makeshift tent and looked in. Frank lay there smoking his pipe. The three men stared at each other until Oskar finally stuttered, "How are you, Frank?"

"O.K.," growled Frank, sucking on his pipe, "but why the hell have you been gone so long?"

"He's in a good mood," Jack whispered as they lifted Frank onto the sled and tucked in the furs.

As Frank warmed up on the way back, his leg began to thaw and the real pain set in. He was a tough old-timer, but finally, with beads of sweat on his forehead, he began to curse.

Oskar and Jack tried to calm him down, but the pain drove Frank out of his mind.

"Shut up, you damn idiots," he shouted. "If I had a gun, I'd shoot both of you and then myself."

"He must be in terrible pain," Jack said.

"He's hallucinating," Oskar replied.

They drove to the Northern Saloon, which Tex Rickard had kept open and tried to decide what to do as Frank lay there still sweating and moaning. Red Sullivan said he thought kerosene would help, and Tex gave them the last he had. When Frank's mukluk was cut off, the leg looked a bluish-white, as if it were dead. There was only enough kerosene to cover the foot up to the ankle, and they all knew it wasn't enough.

Frank McWellen said that he and Georg would take Landström home, but gradually he got worse and lay in his bunk screaming day and night. The leg got gray and then black, and finally it began to smell.

Sometimes Frank would shout, "Lend me a gun. Isn't there anyone with a gun so I can end all this? Won't any of you shoot me? I'm lying here rotting away."

He looked terrible when he tried to get up in his bunk. The hair on his head looked like a lion's mane round his square, twisted face. His eyes were on fire, and he continued to curse.

"Well, how about today?" he demanded.

"Frank, that would be murder."

"Hell, you can draw lots. Haven't you ever shot a moose before. This won't be any worse. I'll take full responsibility."

No one was willing to shoot Frank even though he was in such a bad way. But it was obvious something had to be done, and finally Red Sullivan started the ball rolling.

One night he went to Tex's saloon while Tex and the barkeeper were asleep behind the counter by the stove. Neither of them heard Sullivan as he cut a hole in the tent where the barrel of whiskey was standing and rolled it out. He went back with it to the cabin and dug a hole for it in a corner. Frank must have heard him, but he was only semi-conscious in his pain, and everyone else was sleeping like a log.

Despite Charlie's trips to St. Michael, the whiskey was always running low, and this was Tex's last barrel. When it was discovered missing in the morning, there was a terrible commotion. This was worse than horse theft!

There was cursing and threatening, and all the cabins were searched, but the barrel didn't turn up.

A couple of days later, Red Sullivan finally spoke up. "Something has to be done about Frank," he said. "I've got five quarts of whiskey from St. Michael. I'll open it up tonight and we'll settle it."

Crazy Louis must have had a fine sense of smell, for he showed up just as Red was filling the mugs. He licked his mouth, and Sullivan gave him a shot too.

"We're all tough men," said Sullivan, when everyone had had a drink. "We're not afraid of the devil himself, but we can't shoot Frank in cold blood."

"That's my opinion, too," said Oskar. "I think we should try to cut the leg off. If Frank makes it through to spring, we can take up a collection and send him south."

Everyone agreed, and Oskar got out a piece of paper and wrote down that the first $500 that came out of our claims would be spent on getting Frank to a hospital if he lived. All the people in the cabin signed.

The men didn't intend for Crazy Louis to be in on the collection since he wasn't a member of the household. But Louis got hold of the paper, wrote down his name, and put down a sum of ten thousand dollars.

Oskar went into a rage when he got the paper back. He had had problems with Crazy Louis when he was chopping wood on the Yukon, and Louis was the captain of one of the boats.

"What in the hell do you mean by doing that?" Oskar roared. "You're no damned good; you don't have a cent."

Crazy Louis didn't say a word. He slowly emptied his mug and walked towards the door. Suddenly he turned around with a gun shining in each hand.

"Hands up, all of you!" he shouted. "And you," he said, "Swede, get out in the middle of the floor and die."

Three shots rang out, but Oskar was nimble and rolled to the side.

One shot went through his ear, but the others hit the wall. Louis fired again just as Frank McWellen, who had been sitting near the door, landed a lightning punch on his jaw. The bullet went wild into the ceiling, and everyone jumped on Louis.

He lay there quietly as Jack Cooper said, ''What shall we do with him?''

''Hang him!'' said Oskar angrily.

Everyone was so angry and agitated that this seemed to be the lightest penalty Louis should suffer.

They all helped drag Louis outside and over to the Alaska Commercial Company's warehouse where there was a flagpole that could serve as a gallows. The flagpole had a good strong rope, and Oskar made a hangman's noose. Then the men all pulled until Louis was at the top.

From the cabin came a low booming voice. ''Pull the rope,'' Frank Landström said.

Louis was now dangling from the flagpole, but Oskar had forgotten to tie his hands. He had them under the knot and the noose and squealed like a pig.

People came running from all directions, but the first to get there was the little red-headed Lindblom.

''What is all this noise about?'' he shouted. ''Are you murdering people in the middle of the night?''

''He was shooting at us; he will be hanged,'' said Oskar bitterly.

A few more people came. ''Get him down!'' they shouted. ''He'll be judged when the law arrives.''

Oskar took out his sheath knife and cut the rope. Louis came down with a thump. He whimpered and couldn't get up.

''I've broken my leg,'' he said, and it proved to be true.

Suddenly Lindblom started to sniff the air, and so did some of the others. They could smell the whiskey. This time the barrel in Georg's cabin was discovered. Red Sullivan swore that he had taken it to give it to Frank as medicine. But his story didn't wear well with the others.

''We were all accused,'' the Count recorded. ''We had been drinking whiskey while the others were dry.''

''Never a law of God or man runs north of fifty-three,'' Kipling once wrote . There was no judge in Nome, but they called a miners' meeting in Dr. Kittilsen's cabin. The accused had to wait outside while the verdict was reached. It took a long time to come to a decision about both Crazy Louis's behavior with his firearm and the even less excusable stealing of the whiskey.

The votes were collected in a cigar box, and Dr. Kittilsen pronounced the judgment.

"Louis Renoir, otherwise known as Crazy Louis," he intoned, "is condemned to imprisonment until next spring and will then be sent south by the first boat, and he is forbidden on pain of death to show himself in this region again."

Then Dr. Kittilsen paused. When he looked up again he had a strange light in his eyes.

"All of those living in cabin 23," he said, "must build the prison where Louis Renoir can be put. Then they will provide him with food, pork and beans and bread, three times a day."

Georg and his pals looked around at the others' stern faces. It was lucky they had so many provisions.

While they were collecting the wood to build the jail, H.L. Blake arrived in Nome to claim Anvil Creek. After he had been to the valley, he came driving into the camp, hot and angry.

"What is the meaning of all the stakes that have been put down in my valley?" he demanded.

Everyone just shrugged. It wasn't written down anywhere that the valley was his. The claims had all been made and registered legally, and if he wanted to take the law into his own hands, he would find out how tough the men of Nome were.

Before they finished the jail, the men knew that they still had to operate on Frank's leg. There was no doctor or proper medical equipment, so they had to work the procedure out themselves. First they built a special stand, calling it ironically the butcher's bench. They spread a blanket over it and went around the camp collecting all the bandages and cotton they could get.

"Charlie Hocks had just returned from St. Michael with a new supply of whiskey, and he also had a small saw we could borrow. Tex gave us some ropes."

Now the only decision was who was going to handle the saw. They used matches to draw lots, but when Jack Cooper came up with the longest one, he said, "I can't do it; I'd faint."

They drew lots again, and this time it was Frank McWellen. He turned to Georg and said, "We'll do it together."

They built up the fire to make the cabin as hot as possible. Then they lifted Frank up on to the bench and tied a rope in two places above his knee and pulled it tight. A third rope went just below his knee, about an inch above the spot where they had decided to amputate.

Georg picked up the saw and McWellen went sneaking round the back and hit Frank on the head with a sand-filled gold pouch. This anesthetic knocked Frank backwards, and Georg set to work. He was nearly finished, when Frank opened his eyes. Georg saw them rolling back in Frank's head and shouted, "Hit him again!"

McWellen gave him another blow, and the operation continued. When the leg was off, he dipped his sheath knife in boiling water and then cut off more flesh, leaving some skin behind. Then he washed the whole wound with boiling water, pulled the skin over it, and stitched it together primitively with the only available tools, shoemakers' thread and a large sailmaker's needle.

They waited patiently for Frank to wake up. Eventually his eyelids moved, he blinked, then he looked around confused.

"Are you okay, Frank?" someone asked.

"My God, I guess I must be in heaven," he sighed, smiling through his cracked lips.

In a trembling voice, Georg told him his leg was gone, but Frank was so relieved to be free of the pain, he only said, "To hell with the leg."

He lay still for a few minutes, and then he sat up on his elbow. "Give me my pipe," he said, "I haven't had a good smoke in a long time."

After a couple of weeks, Frank's leg began to fester again, and he wanted them to cut it off higher up. But they were afraid they wouldn't be so successful a second time, and the drift ice was beginning to break up.

The first boat arrived about two weeks later, and the mining expert Sidney Lane was aboard with his two sons, Thomas and Louis. Louis became interested in Frank's story and took him back with him to San Francisco on the same boat. Frank had a second operation, and then he got a laminated cork leg.

The next spring Frank Landström returned to Nome. He couldn't mine any more, but he opened the Pioneers Cigar Store, where he was very successful. Everyone knew his story and would pay for their tobacco and cigars with five-, ten-, or even twenty-dollar bills, telling Frank to keep the change. Stinginess was one thing the mining men of Nome couldn't be accused of.

While Frank was away, the others worked their claims. Georg and Frank McWellen panned out almost $300 a day that summer. Oskar Olson and Red Sullivan didn't do so well; the claims they had staked were not very productive.

Tex Rickard, who was always an energetic man, was always looking around for something new to do. He knew that there were lots of valuable furs to be got in Siberia on the other side of the Bering Strait. So he decided to sail over there and exchange a shipment of goods for fur. He bought a small schooner with two masts, and Oskar and Red were ready to sign on. As a third crew member they got Curly Cooke; he was supposed to have been a prize boxer.

Tex's new undertaking was the talk of the town, something to dream about for the men standing at the bar. The boat was filled with a rich supply of food and lots of whiskey that was going to be traded for furs. Nome had a big party and cheered the crew aboard. They raised the sails and went out to sea.

After half a day, the tipsy Cooke found to his astonishment that they had forgotten to fill the water tanks. They didn't have a drop aboard. They couldn't very well return after the big party so the others somewhat doubtfully agreed with Oskar that the whiskey was drinkable.

The state of their sailing may be imagined. But the summer weather was beautiful, and it was calm. They were in no danger of shipwreck, and they sailed on continuing their party until they saw snakes crawling over the deck. They took some potshots at them, and the noise roused them to consciousness. They realized then that they could be in danger.

By this time, they had reached East Cape in Siberia, and they went into the bay. They expected to find Indians to trade with and Curly rowed ashore to investigate. He was ashore for a long time, and some Siberian natives came down to the beach and put out their kayaks. Suddenly Sullivan and Olson heard screams from the beach, and so they speedily pulled up the anchor and hoisted the sails, leaving poor Curly behind in the midst of his trading.

Curly was later found by a Coast Guard boat and taken back to the States dressed in luxurious Russian furs. The hapless sailors, however, knew by now that the expedition was a fiasco. They were sick at the sight of whiskey, but they didn't dare return to Nome with empty whiskey barrels and nothing to show for them.

They reached the coast of Alaska and decided to beach the schooner on a sand bank as soon as they could. When they did so, they found a whaler near by and were able to hitch a ride to San Francisco.

A few years later Georg met a bearded, grumpy man washing a claim in Candle. He looked familiar.

"Isn't that you, Oskar?" Georg asked.

"Hell," he said, letting go of the shovel, "it's you."

"Where in the world have you been?"

"To the Philippines to help Uncle Sam fight a war. I joined in Frisco; never thought I'd be back up north."

Together they went off to the nearest saloon, and Oskar recounted the whole story of how Tex's proud schooner had been stopped by cannibal Siberian natives! After that day, Olson, the Lone Swede, was just one of many who were never heard of again, swallowed up by the Alaska wilderness.

Chapter Five

Georg gets his Title

"The great spring murmur of awakening life came from things that lived and moved again."

Spring finally came to Nome. The snow began to melt, birds sang in the watercourses, the air got milder and the days longer. It was time to see what was in the claims.

People had come from all over Alaska during the winter. By June 1899, there were almost a thousand men in Nome but more than half of them didn't have any claims. Soon a townsite was laid off at the mouth of Snake River, and on the 4th of July, 1900, a post-office was established. The town which had sprung so suddenly into existence was called Nome, by the Post Office Department, but at a miners' meeting held February 28th, it was decided to call it, "Anvil City". Then, later, at a meeting held in September, the name was again changed back to Nome. There was widespread discontent and tension was in the air, especially between native-born Americans and the Scandinavian miners. Since claims were in such short supply, men who didn't have anyplace to mine began to blame the Scandinavians. They said the Swedes had no right to stake claims before American citizens, although many of the immigrants had indeed become U.S. citizens. It was mainly thanks to one man that an outbreak of violence was avoided.

Lieutenant Spaulding had been ordered to Nome, in the vicinity of Snake River, to avoid bloodshed among the miners. He left with a sergeant and ten men from the army's Third Artillery at St. Michael. On several occasions he intervened firmly and courageously.

On July 10th, the aggrieved men called a miners' meeting. Their plan was that all the existing claims would be declared null and void. As soon as the resolution was passed, they would light a fire as a signal to another group who were stationed on Anvil Mountain, eight miles away. These men would immediately stake fresh claims.

But the conspirators reckoned without Lieutenant Spaulding. He had anticipated trouble and went to the meeting in person. As soon as the motion to invalidate the claims had been put, he asked for an adjournment. He made sure that it took place by ordering his sergeant and men to fix their bayonets and clear the hall.

In August the discovery of gold on the beach dissipated the tension. Now there was gold for everybody. Jafet Lindeberg told how it was discovered.

"A soldier found it. I found the soldier myself, panning some sand on the beach with a mining pan. I don't know how he managed to obtain it, but he did. I looked in the pan and found considerable yellow dust on top of the dirt, and the pan wasn't empty, so I helped the soldier pan it out. The gold we obtained amounted to $26.05. When that became known all our men left."

This gold was so fine-grained that it was called "flour" gold, and rockers lined with felt were needed to trap the gold as the sand and water washed through them. But wood would be needed to build the rockers. Where would the material come from?

Soon a solution was found. Empty potato crates would do very well, and their price shot up; as much as $100 was paid for a single crate. But washing on the beach paid off. A man could take out two to three hundred dollars a day.

In June the first ship, the Katherine Sudden, showed up with a load of lumber, saloon equipment, and a few passengers from St. Michael where it had spent the winter. The captain was an enterprising Yankee, and he soon took note of the shortage of lumber in Nome. He could see that his boat was worth more on land than on sea, and he put her up for auction.

Lindblom and Lindeberg, who had already made their fortunes and founded the Pioneer Mining Company, were the highest bidders. The boat was dragged on to the beach, and in short order the hull was turned into a pile of wood.

All sorts of rockers were invented, and some people tried to construct dredges to scoop up as much sand as possible. Jed Jordan told of Mac Gulliver and his "Patented Gold Pan," a gadget he had bought in San Francisco and brought with him on the boat.

He took it with him to the beach and set it up with its pan, crank, wheel, sieve, pump, and belt. It even had a bell on top. Men gathered around this weird looking contraption, and Mac went into his spiel, mentioning that J. P. Morgan owned one and that President McKinley had unreservedly guaranteed it would produce $200 a day in gold. When he finished, he asked, "What am I offered?"

"Six hundred dollars," screamed one miner. And before Mac could catch his breath, the bidding mounted until finally one lucky sourdough carried it off for $975.

People were eager to work the beach, but it was more difficult to get men willing to carry lumber up to Anvil Creek. However, Georg put his tent up at his bench claim there and began to wash for gold at a claim called Nekula Gulch Three. Frank McWellen had the neighboring Nekula Four, and they were both getting out about $300 a day.

One day, while Georg was sitting in his tent eating pancakes, a stranger named Carpenter who had come in with the Valencia, the first boat from Seattle, approached him. Georg thought the behavior of the tall, bespectacled man was strange, for he had thin, well-cared-for hands that clearly hadn't done any gold-digging, and he wanted to know if there were any Laplanders nearby with good claims.

Carpenter finished his coffee quickly and left when he learned that the next claim down was owned by a Lapp named Isaac Hatt. A little later Georg went down to see what Carpenter had been up to. To his surprise, Hatt's name was gone from the stake marking his claim and a new paper with Carpenter's name on it was in its place.

Wondering how Carpenter thought he could get away with this blatant claim jumping, Georg went into Nome in the evening. There he learned that Carpenter had been all over the area finding out where the Laplanders' claims were and putting his own paper on all of them. Even worse, he had been to Dr. Kittilsen and registered them in his own name.

How could this have happened? Surely, they were all registered already. Then the truth came out. Carpenter was on a secret mission from Washington. It turned out that the Laplanders who had come with the reindeer had abandoned their herds to make claims instead. As far as the government was concerned, they were nomads without papers and could not be considered citizens. And so, Carpenter had been sent out to jump their claims. He had shown Dr. Kittilsen some papers from Washington, and his registrations couldn't be refused.

However, when Carpenter went south, everything went back to normal. The Laplanders cursed for a while, but then they destroyed his papers, put their own back, and continued to wash for gold.

All over the area men were working at full speed; the summer was short, and they wanted to get as much gold out as they could before it froze again. Down at the beach there was gold dust, but up in the creek there were nuggets to be found.

When they had taken out a few thousand dollars, Frank and Georg took a trip down to Nome like all the others. The town had gotten bigger; there were tents everywhere. The population was now about 7,000 people, and people were still pouring in. There were six bakeries, five laundries, 12 general stores, a book shop, four hotels, six restaurants, six boarding houses, four public baths, and four barber shops.

And there were seven saloons. Whiskey was available in bottles now; workmen and foremen alike, they all had their own bottles. The whole area smelled of whiskey. In the saloons, whiskey or beer, which was finally available, still cost a pinch of gold. And, of course, it was the owner's fingers that went into the pouch to get that pinch, not the customer's.

Jed Jordan, who owned the Ophir, had observed as soon as he landed in the place that there weren't many drunks about, which proved that there must be a shortage of whiskey. The "bar" in his tent consisted of a 20-foot plank laid on barrels. His whiskey was well-diluted, but only the best clean drinking water was used.

"The brew was seasoned with tobacco juice and tabasco sauce," Jordan recalled. "Sometimes, when I felt creative, I would add some boiled brown sugar or coffee to give it a little color, or red pepper to improve the body. I didn't get many complaints. Sourdoughs seldom moaned about the quality of a drink. They didn't seem to care much what they put down. What they complained about was the size of the drink."

There were still no banks. In the saloons men handed over their pouches to be weighed, and then the pouches were stacked like wood behind the counter. The first women came to Nome that summer too. They called themselves revue stars and claimed they had come from dancing halls down in the States. Among them were Diamond Hattie, who had all her front teeth replaced with diamonds, Carrie Plough, Holdup Fanny, the Oregon Mare, and Woodpile Annie.

Bar owner Jed Jordan recorded his impressions of these women years later. "I used to laugh so hard when I saw movies depicting the glamorous belles of the gold rush era. None of them was a Marlene Dietrich. Most of these women had one eye, or one tooth, or, worse, when it came to performing their duties, one leg. One of the best-looking trollops I knew in Alaska was called Nellie the Pig, and you will have to take my word for it. Lewd Nellie, who had a slightly imbecilic bell-like laughter, was given this nickname for a good reason."

They dressed exquisitely and behaved smartly, but they were not generous with their favors. They stayed in the saloons. When miners came in, the women would buzz round them at once, perch themselves by the bar, and start flirting. One glass of whiskey went down, then another. The ladies got a 50 percent commission on everything that was sold to their companions, so they made sure no glass was ever empty.

If a rich man came in, they would soon get their claws into him. "I need a new outfit," one would say, when the friendship was better established. "I hate it here," another would sigh. "I need a trip south. But who has the money?"

Many a gentleman paid for dresses that were never bought and trips that were never taken in order to spend an evening in their company. It was easy to catch an old weather-beaten gold digger who hadn't seen a woman in years. A hurried marriage would take place, and then a divorce with compensation for the pain and anguish the bride had suffered!

There were other women in the North at that time, however. On a sand spit at the opening of the Snake River, there was a small insignificant log cabin that was often visited by the newly-made gold kings from Nome. There they came all dressed up with their collars starched, new Stetson hats and their best suits on. But even with all that dressing up, they were sneaking carefully around other cabins and making sure that nobody saw them when they knocked on the door.

After a while, one could see the results from these mysterious visits. The gold kings ended some of their bad habits and started with a few new habits that really amazed their friends. Bull Frog Johnson, for instance, stopped blowing his nose in his napkin when he was eating at the Paris Cafe in Nome. Esak Hatle started to use hair cream with a violet smell. George Murphy started to say, "Otassat, mon ami," when one took a drink with him.

In the little log cabin lived Mrs. Staple, a widow from the States, and her daughter Elsie. Mrs. Staple gave lessons in English and manners. Even though it was considered embarrassing to need her services, she had many customers and made good money, with her bills paid in gold.

One dark evening, Jafet Lindeberg knocked on her door. He had returned to Nome from a trip he made to San Francisco, where he had fallen in love with a society lady. As a preparation for the fine marriage, he wanted to learn about etiquette. He had a good reason for this, as they had made a lot of fun of him in San Francisco. His fiance, Miss Matson, belonged to one of the richest families, and the *San Francisco Examiner* had published a drawing showing what happened when Jafet was a guest in the bride-to-be's home.

Jafet was eating turkey in the drawing. He had put two forks to the turkey, one at each end, and he was holding the big bird cross-wise in front of his enormous mouth. Jafet was gobbling it up so that pieces of bone and fat were dangling crudely from his mouth. At his side stood Miss Matson, shaking her finger at him. Below the drawing was an article about the rough-mannered and unkempt Lapp who was going to marry into the fine Matson family. The excusing circumstance was said to be his many millions. "They have so many things they're doing that I don't understand," complained Jafet to Mrs. Staple, "and whatever I do they laugh at me."

Mrs. Staple comforted the young millionaire. "My complete course in etiquette is exactly what you need," she said. "It contains everything that a gentleman needs to know."

She took out her diploma from an institute in New York. With old-fashioned letters, it assured that Mrs. Eleanor Staple had taken the highest examination at the New York Institute. The beautiful parchment paper, the five illegible signatures, and a shining golden stamp on the right upper corner had won Mrs. Staple many pupils in Nome.

Jafet smiled so widely at this that Mrs. Staple asked twice as much as usual for her fee.

Night after night, Jafet sneaked down to the sand spit in Nome. Mrs. Staple plucked away some of the worst curses from his speech, and put his little finger back if it stood out when he was holding his coffee cup.

One day Mrs. Staple asked Jafet to get a job for her daughter, and so he hired Elsie for the office. He also took her with him to parties sometimes, and Elsie had many good days with Lindeberg. She was only 19, round, happy, and full of budding love. Her highest wish was to catch one of the rich gold diggers. She probably would have caught Jafet Lindeberg, but he was already affianced, and let the pretty young lady go.

Mrs. Staple continued to hunt for a rich suitor for her daughter. One day she read an advertisement in the golddigger newspaper that interested her. It was about a picnic at the soldier barracks at Nome River, which was about three miles from Nome. The ladies of Nome were invited to the picnic. It was leap year, and Elsie looked around for an escort. Of course, that escort had to be a millionaire. She had heard that Caribou Bill was in Nome, and decided to invite him. They had never met before, but with the description of his picturesque face, she went out to look for him.

Bronco Bill was at the same time going from saloon to saloon, hoping to find some over-refreshed golddigger with a good drinking habit, as he as usual was looking for free drinks. They finally met on the street. Elsie could spot from far away Bronco Bill's shining red nose. She knew that Caribou Bill was very red-nosed, as he had once frozen his nose some time ago in Dawson. She stopped Bronco Bill and smiled her cutest smile.

"Hello, Caribou Bill," she said. "I have been looking all around for you to invite you to a picnic to be held near the Nome River."

"What are you saying?" stammered Bronco Bill. "There must be a mistake! My name is really Bill, but..."

"Ah, no excuses, now," chirped Elsie. "It's leap year, you know, you don't want to make me unhappy, do you? We'll have a real good time."

Of course, Bronco Bill couldn't resist her beautiful eyes. He looked deeply into them and found a happy invitation that he had been long missing from the other sex. They decided when to meet on the excursion day. Elsie was dreaming about marriage, then divorce, and a million-dollar alimony.

The picnic day finally came on a beautiful spring day, with a clear blue sky and glittering snow in the background. Outside a white house, the participants gathered around five day carts that were half-filled with hay and pulled by bell-covered horses. Bronco Bill came up in Scurvy Kid's wolf-fur coat, Harry Hunter's brown boots and Hilmer Lee's heavy shirt. Elsie and Mrs. Staple welcomed him whole-heartedly as Elsie's heart throbbed. They took their places on the hay cart, and the coachman cracked the whip. With jingle bells and accordion music, the leap year train started toward Nome river.

Captain Stapleton, the commander for the military camp, had offered one of the soldiers' barracks for the ladies' use, and there they had long tables set up for the food. In a corner of the room was a barrel of beer, and then a barrel of whiskey on wooden trestles. Under the tables were three cases of champagne. The alcohol had been donated by the three lucky Swedes.

Bronco Bill took his place at the table between Mrs. Staple and Elsie. George Murphy was there, and a couple of other gold diggers who knew Bronco Bill, but Bill's excited blinking kept the others quiet. Elsie Staple was known for her desire to get money from gold diggers, and if Bronco Bill wanted to entertain himself a little at Elsie's expense, then they did not mind.

A few soldiers were taking care of serving the food, and soon the party was going at its fullest. There were quiet coughs for the first few minutes, then serious faces, and then the usual everyday talk was exchanged for happy burps, laughs and noise.

The evening was full of happy surprises for Bronco Bill. How ever many times he emptied his whisky glass, it was filled in the next moment by some helpful soldiers. Bronco Bill ate a real square meal. His chin was shining from the young pig's fat that he was eating, and his eyes were shining in ecstasy. The golddiggers' rough hands were fumbling more and more often under the tables for more champagne. Finally tables and benches were moved away, and they started to dance.

Sailor Joe was in charge of the music, and his thin arms were moving in and out on the accordion. When he felt like it, he sang with his hoarse voice in the refrains. Sometimes he skipped a few notes, and then the dancers stopped for a few moments, but soon they again found the right rhythm and jumped ahead with the dance music. Nobody complained over little things like that. Sailor Joe had a very difficult drinker's hiccup, and who the hell could keep time? The heel irons made noise against the sandy floor. The dust was swirled in veils around the sweaty couples, and the barracks trembled. On stroll arms, the ladies were swung in spirals, and stretched their toes fearfully toward the floor, while their skirts flew high with the draft in every direction.

The gold diggers' knees were bobbing like drawn bows, and they stamped so that the floor was singing. Bronco Bill jumped around with the red-cheeked Elsie in his arms. He was bouncing around like a rubber ball between his friends. Elsie got her toes stepped on badly by his boots, but she kept a smile on her face. "Bronco Bill is so enormously rich," she thought, "the stupid dunce."

Bronco Bill experienced some unforgettable hours. A young, beautiful woman was smiling at him all the time. From a barrel in the corner, the whiskey was running, as soon as you touched the faucet. The following morning, the big dance broke up. Bronco Bill had been sleeping under a table. He refreshed himself with the last bit of whiskey, and sat down in the hay cart between Elsie and Mrs. Staple.

The horses took off at a good speed toward Nome. The road was bumpy, and on one turn, Bronco Bill lost his balance, fell against Elsie, and put a loud kiss on her red lips. The big kiss made everyone happy, but Mrs. Staple straightened up and looked hard into Bronco Bill's drunken face.

"Don't you have any sense?" she asked.

"I'm sorry, it was an accident," stammered Bronco Bill.

"Accident, it's not the way I saw it! Bah!" said Mrs. Staple loudly. "You have scandalized my dear daughter!"

Bronco Bill looked at her hard face and tried desperately to find an excuse. "I demand that you marry my daughter!" said Mrs. Staple, and Bill sighed with relief.

"If she wants me, sure," he stammered, with a shy look at Elsie. The gold diggers laughed so hard they almost lost their breath.

Elsie put her round arms around Bill's neck, and the rest of the journey they kissed while Mrs. Staple kept an eye on them.

They stopped outside a priest's house, and the ceremony was taken care of in just a few minutes. Mrs. Staple invited the newly-married couple to her house for dinner. Elsie packed the most necessary things in a couple of bags, and in the evening she went with Bill to his log cabin a short distance from Nome.

The truth was that Bronco Bill had not built the house they went to. He had found it abandoned, as it was situated in a valley at the coast, in which snow fell very heavily during the winter. The log cabin was completely covered with meter-high drifts of snow. Around Nome there were several such huts that had been built by unknown gold diggers, and the only thing one could see during the winter was a thin sheet-metal chimney.

"Do you live in an igloo?" asked Elsie in surprise. Then Bronco Bill pointed out the chimney. Elsie climbed daringly down the ladder to the door and went in. The old sourdoughs didn't care too much about glamorous cabins. Elsie told Bill he should buy a much finer house than the one she was in as soon as he could, as the one she was in was completely run down.

In the morning, Elsie and Bill were awakened by someone knocking at the door. It was Scurvy Kid who needed his wolf-fur coat, and he scolded Bill because he had not returned it when he had promised . After breakfast, Elsie thought it was time to talk business. "How are your gold mines going now, Bill?" she asked. "You can't be secretive with me now, Bill, I'm your own little honey baby."

"I don't have any gold mines," said Bronco Bill, "but today I'll get a job working, so we will have some money. I have a promise about a job in town."

Elsie looked at him with fear in her eyes, and her face grew pale. She started to ask him some more questions, and half an hour later she was back home again with her mother. The Nome papers had a couple of articles about the sorry marriage, and pointed out the danger of marrying the wrong person.

Elsie had a difficult time. Everyone was laughing at her, and thought that she got what she deserved. The marriage happened very fast, but the divorce took a longer time. Finally, Elsie was free again, and when they saw her the last time, she was happily married to a lawyer named Orton. He was of course rich.

In the fall of that year, wild rumors began to circulate that the Swedes couldn't hold property and that their claims would be withdrawn. Many associated Swedes with the gold findings and thought that Swedes and Laplanders were the same. Eventually lawyers came up from St. Michael and confirmed that the rumors were true.

The Swedes had doubts. As far as they could see, their papers were in order, but Washington was a long way off. Maybe the laws were written without knowledge of the situation in the North.

No one really knew, but Americans were sure the Swedes would have to give up their property and started to confiscate their claims, ripping claim tags off the stakes and putting up their own. The Laplanders began to sell their claims as fast as they could. They were already rich and were ready to go home with pouches full of gold.

Charles Lane was buying everything he could get his hands on, and so one day when Georg found strange claim papers on his stakes, he went off to see him. Georg offered to sell for fifty thousand dollars, and Lane countered with forty-five. Georg tried to improve the deal, but in the end he accepted it.

Frank McWellen sold out to Lane too, but he could hold out for a higher price since he was an American and no one dared disturb his claims. He got $175,000. The original discoverers, Lindblom and Lindeberg, kept their claims. They were so prosperous that Lane couldn't buy them out.

By this time it was fall and the Roanoke was in waiting for passengers for the last boat south. Georg af Forselles, McWellen, and Lindeberg were among those who went aboard before the ship went up to St. Michael to pick up more passengers laden with Klondike gold.

There were no vaults or safety deposit boxes. The gold sacks lay in the cabins while the men visited in the main rooms. The whiskey was kept under lock and key, and rationed out by the bartender; no chance of anyone getting too much. The guns were confiscated too and not returned until they landed in Seattle.

There the men rented rooms in the New Northern Hotel, the best in town, and went out to buy new clothes, getting ready to board the boat they had hired to take them to San Francisco. The townsfolk in Seattle had stared at them in their brand new Stetsons and black corduroy suits. But it was nothing compared to the reception that awaited them in San Francisco. The harbor was full of people who wanted to see the gold kings from the north.

Gold rings emblazoned with Klondike and Nome were already ordered, but they weren't enough. Soon diamonds were added, and a ring appeared on every man's hand. The newspapers arrived at the hotel as soon as the miners did.

A reporter from the *San Francisco Examiner* questioned Frank and Georg.

"Excuse me," he said politely. "Can I have your name?"

"Georg Hjalmar Jakob af Forselles."

The "af" caused some problems.

"What does that mean?" the reporter asked.

"Well, it means I'm a nobleman," Georg replied, stretching himself out.

"Ah, then you are a Count," the reporter said with surprise.

"You can call it what you want."

This was all news to the listening Frank, but he was not going to be outdone.

"And you, sir?" the reporter asked Frank.

Frank got up and made an impressive bow.

"I'm the Duke of Lumberland," he said.

The boy's eyes opened wide, and his pencil flew. Photographs were taken, and the next day the *Examiner*'s front page was filled with portraits of the northern millionaires. There, along with Klondike discoverers Skookum Jim, George Carmack, and Bob Henderson and Lindblom, Lindeberg, and Brynteson from Nome, were the Duke of Lumberland and the Swedish Count.

That night the hotel threw a fancy dinner for its guests. There were drinks and wine, fancy meat dishes, oysters and crab. Afterwards shiny bowls filled with a clear liquid were placed on the table. What was this?

As everyone looked around, Skookum Jim picked his up and put it to his mouth. The taste was familiar, but he'd already had so many different mixea that he wasn't sure.

Everyone copied him and then looked around whispering..."Yes, of course, it's water...only water...they're finger bowls. Damn hotel!"

The days began to disappear fast. Skookum Jim couldn't read or write, and checks and other papers were new to him. Carmack tried to make sure he wouldn't get cheated by the banks or other establishments. For that purpose he bought a box and filled it with twenty thousand dollars in gold coins. It was kept in Skookum's room to pay for running expenses.

One day while he was out seeing the sights, his wife was watching the crowds on Market Street below. She

Georg Jakob Hjalmar af Forselles "Count of Alaska" (Here Georg was a millionaire. He was going to San Francisco from the Nome and Candle gold fields in Alaska.)

knew that white men liked gold, so she opened the window and threw a handful of coins into the street. Soon a host of people was fighting and screaming, crawling over one another to get the coins. She had never had so much fun, and she would probably have emptied the whole box, except for the police who ran into the hotel and put a stop to it.

Frank McWellen decided to go home to his family in Chicago. On the train he ended up in the company of a contingent of soldiers from the Philippines. They were all thirsty on the long trip, and soon Frank was sending wires along the railroad to make sure whiskey barrels were waiting for them when they arrived. Never had thirsty soldiers been so well received after battle, and Frank was a hero. Eventually, the train personnel had to intervene, and there were no more telegrams.

Lindeberg went home too. He hired a freighter in New York to take him directly to Hammerfest. It was Christmas, and he arranged to rent the city's hotel for an enormous ball. He invited all the youths from Vardo, the girls and the Laplanders, not the boys. They had to stay outside and look in as he had had to do when they threw him out such a short time before.

The Count soon moved from the Palace Hotel to a simpler, quieter place. It had become a strain trying to live like a millionaire from Alaska. He had a good pile of gold; but still he was one of the poorer gold boys.

He thought of Hawaii where he had promised to return, and soon he was off to Honolulu on a relaxing boat trip to recuperate from the hectic days in San Francisco. He found the city much changed. There were far more ships in the harbor, and construction was going on all over now that the Islands were under American control, so he soon cut his holiday short.

Back in San Francisco, the Count met a German boat-builder named Vogel. Since he had often thought owning a boat would give him a chance to explore along the Alaska coast, he quickly contracted for a 50-foot barge to be built for twenty thousand dollars.

Vogel and the Count went along to the sawmill at Port Gamble where a sawmill was located. There they put up tents and soon erected a small cabin. Vogel hired four men, and in short order the keel was laid. The Count's job was to buy the materials and equipment while the construction went on. The fresh smelling lumber, the singing saws, and ringing hammers brought him pleasure as he saw his own boat taking shape.

But time was pressing on fast, and he was afraid the boat would not be finished in time for him to get it up north that season. Vogel calculated that it would be ready in July, but that would be too late.

So the Count opened an account for coming expenses, told Vogel to finish the boat and sail it to Nome, and left to go north himself. In Seattle he found that the news of the discoveries at Nome had drawn thousands of people from all over the world. The city was prospering from the influx of strangers, and hotels and private homes , even skyscrapers, were being built. There were rumors of a railroad coming too.

Along the streets posters had been put up by the steam boat companies, shouting: "Travel to Nome! There you will find gold on the beach. Travel to Cape York! New findings have been reported."

Cape York caught the Count's eye. He hadn't heard of a gold field there. He decided it would be his destination as soon as the ships set off.

In the meantime he met a tall, slender girl named Lillian Durant who was fascinated by his gold ring and his stories of the gold diggers' days in San Francisco. Since there was still ice in the northern harbors, he had plenty of time to spend with Lillian and soon met her family. Her father was an engineer of French-Canadian descent, but Lillian had been born in the States and spoke only English. After his time in a tough, male-only, frontier society, the Count felt clumsy in the cozy home setting.

Still, he grew more attached to the 21-year-old girl, and he was torn between two poles. He didn't want to settle in Seattle; he wanted to go back to

Nome and start something new. But he didn't want to lose her either. In this situation he was at a loss for words to explain his feelings.

Finally, as they sat in a park, he told her that he was thinking of buying some property and building a house. "It would be for us two if you want to be in on it."

"Aren't you going to Nome?" she said.

"Of course, but first I'll get a cheap lot in the outskirts and start on the house. Then, well, you understand...We could get married, and you could move into the house and wait for me. I'll send you something so you don't starve."

"Do we have to get married now?" she said slowly.

"Well, I'd like to have all the papers in order before I leave."

Lillian looked at her toes and finally said, "You are in such a hurry." But she liked the idea of the house. She let the Count kiss her, and soon he had the house under way. He bought a lot and plans, organized the lumber, hired workers, and started to dig for the foundation.

Lillian followed the progress with interest. And she asked questions about the Count's plans for Nome too. One day, she asked, "If you should die up there, who would get the house?"

"You, of course," he replied.

"Then," she said innocently, "it would be better to sign the house over to me now."

The Count felt that he had been plunged in a cold shower...How had she learned about all these things? After he left her that evening he tried to put things into perspective. It was clear Lillian didn't want to get married right away. Possibly she wanted to see how much money he would get together in Alaska. But she would love to have the house. She only wanted what the Count brought with him. And so he had one less illusion.

The Count was proud; he'd have to end their relationship, but not the way most skirt-chasers did. He asked the builder how much the house would cost to finish, and then he wrote Lillian a letter enclosing the deed.

Down he went to the harbor where he met up with Clark and Robinson, who had hired a whaling boat to go to Cape York with passengers and provisions. He went aboard, and as Seattle disappeared on the horizon, he reflected on the period in his life that had just come to an end. He felt he had left his lucky days behind him along with Lillian and the house. He had no more capital now than the first time he sailed north. He would have to start from the beginning again.

Chapter Six

Back to the Gold Fields

"In the midst of the sea on the edge of the world."

The barge, Northern Light, left Seattle in May, destined for Cape York. As they approached the Bering Sea, they saw no other traffic. It was still icy cold, and the drift ice was still around. Sometimes they were stuck in the ice for as long as four days before they got an opening.

When they got to Cape York, they were in for an unpleasant surprise. There was no camp, no gold diggers, nothing. The only inhabitant was Charlie McDaniel, who lived by fishing and killing seals. The Count had met him in Nome before Charlie left after some trouble over a woman.

They went up to Charlie's cabin while the other passengers disembarked and started to stake out lots in what they assumed would be the town site for the new gold field. To the Count the rock formations didn't look very promising. He doubted whether there was any gold, and he asked Charlie about it.

"Where did you get that idea?" he said. "There's nothing here. I ended up here by chance. You ought to know how these rumors are started. The steamers want to have passengers and cargo."

Then the Count understood. It was a false stampede, and the Northern Light was the first victim. More would follow. He and Charlie looked back towards the coast and suddenly noticed that everyone aboard a whaling boat that was riding at anchor had begun to move fast. What was going on? They were trying to fire up the engines, and the anchor was hauled aboard.

"What's wrong with the whaler?" the Count asked. "Is it going to leave?"

"Look over there," Charlie shouted. "The drift ice is coming."

The wind was up from the west, and a white belt of ice appeared on the horizon. The whaler was fleeing south to avoid it.

The Count rushed to the beach to get hold of the barge's captain.

"Damn," he said, looking out to sea. "This means catastrophe!"

The whaler had made it out in time, but not the Northern Light. Captain Charleston went out to the barge, dropped another anchor, and brought the shipping papers and instruments ashore. The barge was left to its bitter enemy.

There was a huge crash as the ice came in. Blue-green blocks as big as cliffs swirled around, glittered in the bay, and then were buried as new masses of ice arrived. The whole bay was full and the ice sang as it hit the beach.

Clark and Robertson ran around cursing whoever had lured them up to this hole. But Captain Charleston was philosophical; if you had bad luck, you had to live with it.

The crew and passengers waited with their breaths bated. Would the barge be torn to pieces and sink? Would it be thrown up on land? They imagined that they heard the anchor chains break. But they held. The barge shook as the ice came round its sides and soon it was held fast.

Those who had been in the north before knew it was safe for the moment. But when the ice went back to sea, it would take the barge with it. If it was ever seen again, it would be as a wreck down the coast. Now that the ice was well packed, they decided to rescue what they could.

A donkey engine was fired up, and the winches started to move. They stretched a wire between the barge and the beach to pull things ashore. The 10 flat boats from the Northern Light that usually served to transport passengers and cargo ashore became sleds to be pulled ashore by the winches.

First they took off the passengers, clothes, tents, and other equipment, then some of the provisions. The ice could go out any time , maybe in a few hours. The work went on faster and faster, well into the night.

The passengers and crew spent the night in tents on the beach, while the Count waited with Charlie in his cabin. In the morning there was no change; the ice was still there. Load after load was pulled ashore, but lots of provisions remained on board.

Towards evening a new storm blew up from the south. The barge jumped and canted under the pressure of the restless ice. The hull creaked, and Captain Charleston ordered an end to the unloading. The deserted Northern Light waited for the attack to come.

Back in Charlie's cabin the Count spent the evening with Joe Wallert and Billy Toburn trying to decide what they would do. They thought they would like to look around the surrounding area, but they didn't have any provisions.

"I have provisions aboard," said Toburn. "A whole load, but we can't count on them."

"Why didn't you say something before," Wallert said with a reproachful look.

Then the Count announced: "It's not too late, but it is the last minute...If Charlie would lend us his dog team, we could get there."

"Take it," Charlie said laconically.

No one said another word. The men put their parkas on, and Charlie harnessed his team. Down on the beach, the wind lashed their faces. The camp was quiet, full of sleeping men. They fumbled out to the barge in the dark, holding onto the wire to keep on their feet as the ice cracked under them.

When they reached the barge, they tied up the dogs and went aboard. Down in the captain's cabin in the middle of broken glass and piles of books, they found a whale-oil lamp to provide light. In the cargo room Toburn's carefully wrapped sacks of flour and sides of pork in canvas were not difficult to find. They gradually carried everything up and loaded it in the sled.

Though they could hear the ice cracking, they thought they had plenty of time and decided to relax in the captain's cabin with a five-gallon whiskey jug they had found. Suddenly, they heard the command, "Hands up!" and saw a revolver pointing at them. It was the cook, a huge black man, who had found some whiskey and then fallen asleep before the others went ashore.

"Forbidden to be aboard," he said. "Go ashore!"

Toburn and Wallert were red in the face with anger, but they got ready to jump off, certain that the cook would shoot. Just as Toburn was about to step through the doorway, he turned and knocked the cook to the ground. Wallert got the gun, and Toburn and the Count tied the cook up. Then they sat down to catch their breath.

Now they heard enormous cracks and bangs. Toburn knew what was going on; the chains had broken. The Count rushed up on deck and groped along in the pitch dark. The dog team was gone, disappeared into the ice. The Northern Light was on its way out to sea.

The Count made his way back to the captain's cabin where Toburn and Wallert were making themselves comfortable with a glass of whiskey.

"We should have some fun as long as it lasts, shouldn't we, Joe?" said Toburn.

Wallert nodded, "We can't sing dirges just because the boat didn't want to wait until we were ashore."

The Count pushed his glass aside and said: "First we'll have to see if we're in serious danger. If the boat's leaking, we'll have to start pumping." He took a plank from the cargo of lumber that had been intended for gold sluices and cabins, and went under the deck. There was almost six inches of water on the bottom, but the boat wasn't leaking.

He went back and joined the others. There was nothing they could do as the ice carried them north. The weather was gray and gloomy, and the barge creaked and groaned. Sometimes it shook so badly that they feared it would split up. But it was built for the North, and it was tough.

Suddenly, they were roused by squealing on deck. They had forgotten about the pigs who were aboard to provide fresh meat. They had escaped from their pens and were scrambling about on deck. The noise was awful, but no one wanted to go out in the storm, so they dozed off again.

Eventually, the squealing got on their nerves.

"There's going to be mass murder here," Toburn shouted as he got up. "I can't stand it; it's driving me insane."

They found a pair of axes in a cupboard and went up on deck to start their pig hunt. The driving snow made them blind, and the pigs ran over the lumber and masts as they tried to escape. But finally the hunt was over. They dried the sweat and snow off their faces and looked at the deck full of dead pigs.

Back in the cabin, the Count and Toburn found Wallert lying on the floor covered in blood. He had tripped over a pig and fallen in a pile of broken glass. They bandaged him as best they could, and wakened from their torpor by the pig hunt, they evaluated their situation.

They got wood, rags, hammers, and nails ready in case there was a leak. They checked the hand pumps and found they were operating perfectly. Since Wallert couldn't do any heavy work, he was set to guard Tom, the cook, and to prepare the meals.

As the days passed, they were sure they were still going north, through the Bering Strait and into the Arctic Ocean. They got used to the bumps and the shaking, and when times got tough, they had a glass of whiskey to cheer themselves up. Eventually, they untied the cook's feet so he could move more freely, but they were afraid to untie his hands. Wallert still refused to cook for him and continued to pour raw eggs down his throat.

On the fifth day, it calmed down; the ice continued to move, but it didn't push so hard on the boat. They knew that the maps and compass had been taken ashore, but eventually they found a small pocket compass in one of the cabins. At least it was something to follow. By now there was no doubt. The ice was dispersing and they were in the Arctic Ocean.

Fortunately, the Count knew something about sailing, and he took command. First, the rudder had to be repaired with the replacement part. Sailors who traveled in these waters knew the dangers of the ice. Then they looked at the boiler. Their wood was damp, but it could be split, and they soon started a good fire with paraffin oil so that they could get the coal burning. Now the winch was running.

They put up one of the sails and hoped to spot land. But what would they see? The Count was all for landing on the Siberian coast since it was bound to be the closest. But Wallert and Toburn were terrified of hostile Indians and wouldn't believe him when he said there were only Russians and Eskimos. So it was two votes to one, and they set their course east for Alaska.

It was risky to try to sail that far. It was foggy and they continued to hit blocks of ice, but with three sails up, they made good speed and didn't develop any leaks.

On the fourth day, the fog started to diminish and the sun came out. Straight ahead they could see the coast of Alaska. They had intended to put ashore as soon as they could, but with the good weather and a strong westward wind, they changed their course to south-southeast and raised the rest of the sails. The drift ice had disappeared, and they could proceed at full speed.

When they saw Cape Prince of Wales, they changed the course straight to the east. The wind was still good, and after sailing for 16 days, they were nearly at their goal. On the shore stood Captain Charleston, watching for ships from the south through his binoculars. He was amazed when he saw the Northern Light. He was sure the barge had been lost forever and the men with it.

The Count's seamanship was not expert, but they turned the ship to the wind, set the sails, and cut the tackles. The anchor went to the bottom like a rock, the chain rattled out of the hawser-hole, the sails came down in a rush.

Captain Charleston, Clark, and Robertson rowed out to the boat and greeted them like heroes. How had they managed to survive, and when had they gotten the idea to try to save the barge? It was then they learned that Charlie McDaniel had tried to put a better light on their departure.

"Well," said the Count. "We could see the boat was going to get away, so we went out and took a chance. The pigs are dead, and some of the whiskey is gone, but everything else is in tiptop shape."

At this point the cook ran out and began to tell how he had found the three men in the captain's cabin. But Wallert jumped in, telling Charleston that the cook had been drunk and had tried to stop them doing their job.

Clark asked what they would like as a reward for their trouble. The three men naturally hadn't thought about this possibility since they had actually left against orders. They exchanged glances.

"Charlie should get paid for his dog team," the Count said.

"The rest we can discuss when we are ashore."

In the end Charlie was given a thousand dollars and two tons of provisions for his team, and the other three got $600 and a ton of provisions each as well as a free trip to Nome. Saving the Northern Light was worthwhile!

They spent a quiet week in Cape York while the barge was made ready to sail. They surveyed the area and found alluvial gold and pewter in the valleys, but the first was not to be found in large quantities, and they were not interested in the other.

They were glad to set off for Nome, but they were far from prepared for the commotion they found there.

Chapter Seven

The Nome Scandal-1900

"Here was neither peace nor rest. All was confusion and action."

When the Northern Light arrived in Nome, the Count's party found the biggest fleet of ships they had ever seen. There were passenger and cargo steamers, whaling boats, barges, brigs, schooners, ships from all over the world. And the beach was crowded with thousands of people, all part of the rush to Nome. From the town came the sound of hundreds of hammers; rows of houses were going up to house the invaders.

About 20,000 men and a few women landed that summer of 1900. Not all of them intended to pan for gold; there were naturally those who preferred to acquire riches indirectly by living off the gold diggers. There were promoters, sea captains, brothel owners, pickpockets, card sharks, and above all bar owners as the number of saloons rose to 100.

One of the people who opened a saloon at Nome that year was the legendary Wyatt Earp, sheriff of Tombstone, Arizona. Now in his 50s, he had set off for the North with his wife Josephine in 1897. At first he had taken a job as vice-marshal at Wrangell in the Panhandle. There he went out to arrest a troublemaker who was waving his pistol about in a saloon. The man stopped dead when he saw Earp. "By damn!" he said. "Here I go to the end of the earth, and the first man I run into when I let off a little steam is Wyatt Earp. You threw me and a bunch of the boys in the pokey in Dodge City for the same thing 20 years ago!"

By the spring of 1899, Wyatt was running a saloon at St. Michael. He was earning good money, but he was attracted to Nome when friends wrote him about the great opportunities there. Together with a companion, Charlie Hoxie, he built the Dexter Saloon, one of the biggest in the new town.

When his brother Warren was murdered in Arizona that summer, Wyatt was described by a Seattle newspaper. He is still "grim, game and deadly. He never took water. But he doesn't kill as he used to. Age has cooled his blood. Many wounds have brought him caution."

Wyatt and his wife were seeking a quiet, ordered life, but he found it hard to keep out of fights. One night during a brawl outside the saloon, Earp got into a fight with the vice-marshal Albert Lowe and spent the night in a cell, charged with impeding an officer of the law. Later in the summer he attacked a military policeman who had arrested two troublemakers in the saloon, and in a third fight, he apparently got a bullet in his arm.

Earp continued to run his saloon for another year, but then he left Alaska. Unlike his brothers, all of whom were murdered, he died peacefully in 1921.

The Count had never seen anything like Nome in his gold-digging days before. All along the 30 miles of shore men were packed like sardines, washing for gold with sweat pouring off them. The motor-driven sand pumps coughed and spit, and kerosene fumes hung like a cloud over the beach. The noise was terrible as men shouted at one another and frequent fights broke out.

The Count stored his provisions and took a walk down the beach to survey this strange assembly. In his memoirs he recounted those days:

"You couldn't claim the beach below high water mark. But the ninth paragraph of the laws of Nome said that you owned the ground you were standing on. That meant that all these people owned the piece they were standing on that day. They elbowed each other to get as much room as possible, and the cursing that went on in every language under the sun can be imagined.

"You owned the land you were standing on, but you lost your right to it the minute you left. So you had to get to the beach at dawn to get a good position before the others arrived. This panning was a chancy business. The traces of the previous day's work had been washed away by the tide, and there was no way of knowing if someone had been standing on that very spot the day before taking all the gold out of it."

Some people used rockers, but there were a lot of other inventions in use on the beach, taking out millions of dollars. One old digger had come all the way from Australia dragging a big wash-groove. It had to be pulled along the beach by a steamer, and its owner thought the gold would collect in it. However, he and his strange equipment soon disappeared.

Another gadget supposed to give good results was called the surf washer. It had a groove that went down into the water. Sand was shovelled on top as with the rocker, run through a sieve down into the groove, and was washed by the waves beating on the groove. The sand was washed away, but the gold would stay on the silver plates.

Another fellow had a variation on this device; it was a drum six feet tall, with mercury-covered silver plates inside. He thought sand would be sucked into the drum when the water was high and that the gold would stay on the plates when the sand and water ran out. Some even tried to get gold from the bottom of the ocean outside the beach. They bought boats and sent divers down to investigate, but without any success.

The Count wasn't tempted by the gold on the beach, and he didn't want to stay in Nome either. He intended to go back up to the Snake River. The area had been devastated by typhus during the winter while he was away. Some claimed it had started among Eskimos unaccustomed to the food and the life-style the white men introduced. They traded their furs for sacks of flour and began to make pancakes and bread. Then they got sick, and the typhus spread to the gold diggers in Nome.

Also, because things were still so expensive in Nome and there was such a shortage of household goods, when someone died they would take off his clothes as soon as he went stiff and give them to those who were suffering in the cold, and so the typhus spread. It was a terrible plague.

There wasn't any churchyard or any law about burials. The dead were buried without ceremony up on the Snake River. Moss was shovelled away, and the bodies were stowed in the frozen sand bank; a prayer was said for their poor souls, and then the living had done their duty.

But the newcomers were not concerned about the dead or typhus. They cared only about gold! Soon they heard that there was gold even in the banks of the Snake, and men poured in, digging along the shore. As their picks went into the sand and they began to wash the banks, the dead rose. A white leg would show through the sand, and with the next blow with the pick, the body would appear. These were tough men, and they cursed the corpses before they tried to push them away. The smell of the blackened bodies was nauseating, and neighbors threatened each other with guns if one tried to push the body towards the other.

The spectacle sickened the Count, and he returned to Nome to visit his old friends. By this time worries and uncertainties had increased in the town.

The claim-jumper Carpenter had returned from the south, this time with a judge and a shipful of soldiers in tow. Judge Noyes was installed in his court, and they began to take action, staking out a place for their living quarters.

They chose what is now Barrack Square in Nome for their site. Then there were blockhouses standing there. Without warning they began to tear them down. They made no allowances for previous ownership, and told the mob they were there to stay.

The Laplanders' claims were the first to come to court. When they lost, the claims went to Carpenter, for he had already registered them. A third man who came with Carpenter and Judge Noyes, Alexander McKenzie, was appointed receiver, and all the gold had to be brought to him while the proceedings were going on.

As the *Nome Daily Chronicle* of August 16, 1900, showed, the locals were well aware that the lawsuits were fixed: ''Hardly a day passes but some new suit is filed, and in nine cases out of ten some unfortunate Swede, whose only crime is that he has worked for a fortune that others wish to obtain through an easier process, is made the defendant...The only reason that the war was first opened on the Swedes was that they were foreigners, and, as a rule, any movement against foreigners meets with popular approval. The mass of our people are prone to regard all born outside the limits of the United States, even those who either have already become or have declared their intention of becoming citizens, as interlopers.''

Jafet Lindeberg was also selected as a victim. But he and Brynteson and Lindblom had already formed the Pioneer Mining Company, so the whole company was dragged in. They were ordered to leave their claims within twenty-four hours, and even Lindeberg's good friend Charles D. Lane, by now prosperous and well-respected in Nome, wasn't able to help his claim.

Lindeberg was arrested and held until he paid bail. Now he tried to get McKenzie on his side by offering him a million dollars. McKenzie smiled and shook his head. The law would follow its course. Soldiers were stationed around the claims, and the mining continued under McKenzie's supervision. Every night fully loaded pack horses brought gold down from Anvil Creek to pass through McKenzie's hands.

Charles D. Lane
(Photo-Consortium Library-UAA/APU)

Lindeberg and his friends were not innocents themselves when it came to thieving and villainy. The Swedes rented a room across the street from the bank where McKenzie deposited the gold he had acquired during the course of these lawsuits. There they kept watch twenty-four hours a day. When McKenzie started to leave the bank with a leather bag full of gold, he suddenly found himself surrounded by armed men. Swiftly he retreated with the gold back into the bank. On another occasion Lindeberg and his men hired a gang of thugs to ambush McKenzie's men and drive them away from the claims.

Then it was the turn of C.D. Lane himself. He had bought most of the Laplanders claims, and he was ordered to turn them over to McKenzie.

"I'll close them until the proceedings are over," he said. "They can lie still for a while."

"Never," he was told. The mining would continue.

The soldiers were commanded out again, and they had to follow orders. As a result all the gold coming out of the claims had to be deposited with McKenzie until the judgment was rendered. If it went in the former owner's favor, he would get his gold back. But there were no records kept of the quantities of gold taken out, and there was no control over it, so most of it ended up in the pockets of the receiver and his assistant.

Lindeberg lost his case, and Carpenter got his claims. The situation was critical, and Lane was under strict observation. He consulted his lawyer, who told him he was powerless in law. The only solution was to outwit his enemies.

In the harbor lay the steamer Ohio, about to leave for Seattle. Goods were brought aboard, and boxes and barrels were loaded into the cargo holds. Once the Ohio raised its anchors and was out in the Bering Sea, Lane crawled from one of the oil barrels. He had been smuggled aboard and was headed south to seek redress.

He had to choose his methods carefully, for the people in Nome had powerful friends. Lane went to Washington and looked up a Norwegian-born senator, Knute Nelson of Minnesota. Nothing could keep Nelson quiet after he heard what had been done to Lindeberg and the Laplanders. The Nome Scandal burst into the open.

Noyes, McKenzie, and Carpenter were arrested and brought to Washington for prosecution. They were found guilty but received a sentence of only a year in prison. Not good enough in the eyes of those in Nome. McKenzie had left some $600,000 of gold in Nome.

But the investigation also brought the plight of the Laplanders to the attention of the lawmakers. An investigation showed that they had come to Alaska in the service of the American government, and they certainly had to be regarded as citizens. In fact, on their way North, the missionary Kallman had taken them to the registration bureau in Seattle to get their papers. The clerk in charge had paid little attention since they were apparently off to the North Pole. He issued their papers, but he didn't register them, pocketing the fees for himself.

All this quarreling on the beach and the legal problems made the Count even more eager to get out of Nome. He still had the two claims Lane had not bought from him the year before. He supposed they weren't worth much, but they were worth a try.

He set out for Balto Creek with his spade and pan early one morning. The first pan yielded little, and after a few more he still only had about fifteen cents worth of gold. He wrapped it in paper, put it in his pocket, and headed back to Nome. He knew he would have to have more money to start serious work in the creek.

He went to see Jafet Lindeberg in his office, but he was so occupied with his legal problems and business meetings that the Count couldn't get in to see him. He knew Frank McWellen was back in Nome too, but all he had left was the title he had given himself in San Francisco, the Duke of Lumberland.

Like many of the gold diggers, the Count did a lot of his thinking in the saloons, so he went off to the Alaska Bar to see if he could come up with an idea. The man next to him struck up a conversation, and after they had had a couple of drinks, he asked if the Count had any claims left. The Count recorded how a typical Alaska deal was struck:

"Sure," I said, "I've got two claims at Balto Creek, but I can't do much with them. I need a couple of thousand to get equipment."

The man twisted his blond moustache. I could tell what he was thinking. Why not take a chance? That's the motto up here. And $2,000 is nothing.

He told me his name was Jorgenson. He was a Dane and captained a small schooner. He had a salary, but everybody talked of gold and it had passed him by.

"Is there any gold in those claims?" he asked.

I took the paper from my pocket, opened it and showed him the gold dust. His eyes widened. "Did you get that in one panning?"

"The Irish Duke, McWellen, was on the other side of me." He dropped his glass, and noise of its shattering drowned out my answer. Jorgenson thought I said yes, and that was good. If he had known it was the result of eight pannings, he wouldn't have put up the $2,000 and Balto Creek would have remained untouched, at least for a while.

Jorgenson had gold fever, but he drove a hard bargain. He not only wanted his $2,000 back, he also wanted half the gold taken from the claim. That was a lot for a lousy $2,000. But I had no choice. It was Jorgenson or nobody. So we went to the Alaska Grocery Store, drew up an agreement, and he gave me the money. Now I could begin.

The Count figured he could throw a thousand spadefuls a day into the panning chute. At one cent per spade, that would be ten dollars a day " nothing compared to what he got with rockers the previous year, but it was the best he could do.

Times had changed for the good as well as the bad. Now it was easy to get labor in Nome. Thousands of newcomers had no place to pan, and they had to feed themselves somehow. Georg could get all the men he wanted at $5 a day plus food.

The story was the same with supplies. Cargo steamers arrived in Nome with provisions every day. Whiskey used to cost a pinch of gold; now it was twenty-five cents a glass. It would have been cheaper except that there were no smaller coins.

Georg figured he could feed a man for $2.50 a day, so along with the wages that would leave another $2.50 to be split between Jorgenson and him, if everything went right.

Jorgenson lent him a lifeboat from the steamer to get the supplies up the river. He hired two men, loaded the boat with the equipment, food, tents, and an oven, and the men started rowing up the Snake. After 15 miles, they unloaded the cargo and carried it to Georg's claims on Balto Creek. There they dammed the creek to form a pond, made an opening in the dam, and stuck in a 400-foot hose, 14 inches in diameter. The water flowed through it into two chutes with transverse channels.

Everything was ready to start panning, so Georg went back to Nome and chose another two dozen strong men. ''Come to the Discovery Saloon tomorrow morning,'' he told them. He chose the Discovery because it was the quietest and cleanest in town. It was owned by Magnus Kjelsberg, the Norwegian whaler who had invested with Jafet Lindeberg and made his fortune.

Early the next morning, the men started for Balto Creek. Most of them weren't used to hiking, and there was a good deal of grumbling about blisters and the lack of food. It was dark by the time they got to the claim, and they fell asleep in their blanket rolls after a scanty supper.

The next day they hooked up the hose and began panning. No one knew what the take would be; it was still a gamble. At the end of the day, Georg hurried to put the pouch on the small scale in his tent while the men peered in from outside.

Everyone was quiet while he measured , the take was $3.80 per man. Georg knew he couldn't even pay wages with that! He smiled and pretended everything was fine. Maybe tomorrow would be better. But it wasn't. ''Damn it,'' he thought, ''if this keeps up I'll go broke and get hell from Jorgenson.''

On the third night the scale showed $20 per man; that was more like it. And the result was the same for three more days. Now there was enough for the wages. But just as suddenly the gold fell off again, down to $4 per man. Was it over already?

Georg started digging along the sides of the creek. The gold content increased at one spot on both sides of the stream. He ordered the panning chutes moved, and they started digging. At once they were finding more gold. Slowly but steadily the pouches filled. Georg went down to Nome and paid Jorgenson, and there was still enough to buy another $2,000 worth of supplies.

Georg also hired a foreman, a German named Lutzinger. Now the crew could work day and night. The first gang started at eight in the morning after a good breakfast of oatmeal or hot cakes, dried eggs, ham, and coffee. At one o'clock they had dinner, dried potatoes soaked overnight, fresh potatoes were heavy and too expensive to ship from Nome, and canned meat made into a stew. The next day it would be bacon and beans. There was always a dessert, pie or pudding made of dried apricots or apples. They worked again until seven in the evening when they got another meal. It would be peas or beans fried in bacon fat, more bacon, pie and tea. Georg provided as much variety as he could. When the pack horses came up from Nome once or twice a weak, they brought fresh meat and vegetables, and the crew would feast on vegetable soups and steaks.

The night gang went to work at eight and had the same kind of meals as the day crew. There was daylight almost all night, and the work went ahead very well. When they had an especially good day, Georg would order a case of whiskey, put the bottles out on the table, and tell the men: "Have a drink. You deserve it. But if you get drunk, you're fired." They understood and there was never any disorder on his claims.

Jorgenson came up to the camp after three weeks. He had got his $2,000 back, and he couldn't stay away any longer. He came up the Snake by boat with two sailors, but he had had to travel overland in the end as Georg had done, a tiresome trip for an old sea dog. When he arrived, he was tired and hungry and eaten up by the swarms of mosquitoes he had encountered.

The sight of the men throwing sand into the chutes soon cheered him. After all, what was a little discomfort when there was gold to be had?

"You're living well here," he said, looking at the tents.

"Well, it's all right. Come and have a look at the results," Georg replied.

I showed him the filled gold pouches, and his eyes widened. "Count, we're rich, we're rich!"

"Just a minute," Georg told him. "In this pouch are the wages. We can't touch that. This is the money for food. But this pouch is our little profit on the claim. And Tex has $3,000 on deposit."

He slapped Georg on the back. "You're a regular trump! I've never made a better investment. And no risks..."

And so ended the talk about profits.

(Editor's Note: Many interestingly rich findings of gold were made in 1907 in Nome. Even as of today, Nome's enormous stretch of country that surrounds the great city of the Arctic has scarcely been touched, and yet, it is daily yielding wealth in abundance. Back of Nome, 3-1/2 miles to the north and stretching for ten miles each way east and west, lies the famous "third beach line" which has made the fortunes of many prospectors and is still unexhausted. The season of 1905-06 saw the working of the famous deposits on Little Creek, and the discovery of the Bessie Bench, No. 4 Bourbon, the May fraction, the Pure Gold fraction, No. 8 Cooper Gulch and other claims that yielded all the way from $250,000 to $1,000,000.)

Judge James Wickersham
(Photo-Z. J. Loussac Public Library, Anchorage)

Judge Wickersham was one of Alaska's great pioneers. He eliminated Nome's first crime wave, and won most of the miners gold claims back to the original owners. Much of Alaska's development today can be attributed to his fearlessness.

Chapter Eight

The Great Storm at Nome

"The gales blew, threatening destruction."

While the work was continuing at Balto Creek, the Count made regular trips to Nome. He always stopped for a break at about the same spot in the sand-filled Glacier Mountains. He felt that it showed promising signs, and finally he borrowed a shovel and a pan from C.D. Lane's nearby claim and took a sample. Even on the top layer the first test contained gold worth about ten cents. Deeper down there must be more.

He knew that everything in the area must have been claimed, but at first he couldn't find any stakes. Eventually he found one burned off just above ground level and assumed it had been destroyed in the tundra fire during the summer.

As soon as he got into town, the Count checked with the registrar and learned that the claim was owned by Torulf Kjelsberg, Magnus' brother. He had sold most of his claims the year before, so this one must have been considered worthless.

The Count learned from Magnus that a Lapp up at Nekula Gulch held Torulf's power of attorney, and he arranged with him to get a lease on the claim. But by the time he went back to Nome the following week to sign the contract, he discovered someone else had been working the claim, and as he suspected Magnus and the Lapp had reneged on the deal.

But the Count wasn't through yet. He knew that a claim had to be worked for at least 10 days in the second year and that it had to have produced at least a $100 worth of gold. Otherwise, it was a forfeit. Since he had discovered the gold, he thought he had the right to stake the claim.

Magnus Kjelsberg
(Photo-Consortium Library-UAA/APU)

By chance, he ran into a miner named Gould whom he had known in California and offered him $50 in supplies to go up to Glacier Creek and stake the claim that night. In the morning Gould came by reeking of whiskey, and the Count knew where his $50 had gone. He went up to the creek himself, and there was the Lapp sitting in a tent with 6-foot stakes all around the claim.

The Count checked the stakes to see if any mistake had been made and, as it happened, on two sides the stakes were out too far, leaving a rectangle he could claim. He drove in his stakes and went back into Nome to register what he called the California Fraction after the man whose thirst had cost him the big claim.

Back at Balto Creek the mining was going on successfully, and the Count left Lutzinger in charge while he went north to Teller to look at a new gold field and get some options for C.D. Lane. The stories of gold had been exaggerated as was so often the case, and the Count returned south. On his way to Balto Creek, he was congratulated by the foreman on another claim.

"Damn rich fraction you've got!" Joe Jonsson said.

"That's more than I know," said the Count.

"You're doing great," Jonsson went on. "There are 30 or 40 men working down there."

When the Count got to Glacier Creek, the foreman told him they had bought and registered the claim, and he could see that his stakes were gone.

Digging for Gold in Nome (1900)
(Photo-Carrie McLain Museum, McLain Archive of Photographic Materials, Nome, AK

Down in Nome he learned that the Lapp had pulled up his stakes and replaced them with his own. Then, after he had tested and discovered that the fraction contained far more gold than the original claim, he had sold it for a low price and departed on the next boat.

He consulted with Joe Stone, a Nome lawyer, about legal action, and he posted demands that everyone be off the claim in 24 hours and even had the workers arrested. But they were quickly freed on bond and the work went on. Stone told him that there were big men behind the group at the claim, so the Count abandoned his efforts for the time.

In the fall he went back to his old claim at Anvil Creek and started digging. By the end of the third day he had hit plenty of water but little gold, and as far as he was concerned, the claim was worthless.

A few days later in Nome an old man in ragged clothes approached the Count in the Northern Saloon.

"Been to lots of gold fields," he said, "but right now I'm fresh out of diggings. You got any claims?"

"Yeah," the Count replied. "I've got a bench claim up at Anvil Creek, but I don't think there's much gold in it."

"Well, maybe I could find something there. How about leasing it to me? How much would you want?"

"I'll give you the best terms there are. Ninety percent for two years." As far as the Count was concerned, 10 percent of whatever the old man took out wouldn't be much, but it was better than nothing.

The old man thought and finally he said, "Maybe you'd even be willing to sell?"

The Count proposed a price of $5,000 and accepted a counter offer of four since he felt sorry for the old timer. The old man was in a hurry, and within a half an hour, the contract was signed and the Count had his $4,000.

The next morning he was surprised to get a message that Jafet Lindeberg wanted to see him urgently. What could it be? The year before he couldn't even get in to see him to try to borrow $2,000.

In his private office, Lindeberg came quickly to the point.

"Georg, I'll give you $100,000 cash for your bench claim at Anvil Creek. If you want to sell, that is."

The Count couldn't believe his ears. "I sold it last night for $4,000," he finally got out. And then he told Lindeberg about the old prospector.

Lindeberg laughed. "You've been taken, Georg," he said. Then he told him what had happened. The Northland Mining Company had hit a rich vein that passed through the Count's claim. They knew he'd be suspicious if they approached him directly and that his price would have been a lot higher.

"You know who that was?" said Lindeberg. "King, the Northland superintendent, dressed in rags."

The Count was philosophical. Such tricks happened all the time in Alaska, and at least gold was still coming out of Balto Creek. But even there he was running into trouble. He had staked it his first winter in Alaska, but because it was so cold, he had paced off only 800 feet, not the 1,300 allowed.

Now it was washed out. But it hadn't been a bad season; he and Captain Jorgenson had made $18,000 each. He agreed to sell it to a mining company that was buying the claims through the whole length of the valley, though they offered only $1,500. He said he would take it after he had burned the washers and taken whatever gold remained in them.

But Jorgenson balked at getting so little for the only mine in which he had ever been a partner, and thanks to his stubbornness the price was raised to $7,000. It was a good deal for them since the mine truly was finished, and the company only wanted the claim in order to stretch their hoses over it.

The Count went back to Nome and took a room at the Discovery Saloon, planning to have a little vacation. He bought a quartz claim at Hooker Creek and hired two men to work it. While he was looking for a place to stay for the winter, he ran into the Cooper brothers who had just sold out to C.D. Lane for $300,000.

They were planning to return south to buy a good farm, and they told the Count he could have their cabin. Instead of the usual rough one-room log affair, it was a frame house with two rooms and a kitchen, rugs on the floor, beds, and real windows. This was the way a count should live!

It was there that the Count was living when the great storm hit Nome. He recalled it 30 years later:

"It started in the morning of the twelfth of September with a wind that took hold of the cabins, making the joints creak. The cargo steamers in the harbor quickly raised anchor and sought shelter on the lee side of Sledge Island. The little sailing boats were not so lucky. Their captains knew that they would be driven ashore as soon as they hoisted their sails. So they cast double anchors, and the crews rowed into Nome.

"We had often wondered what would become of all the log cabins that had been built right down to the water's edge when the autumn winds began to blow. There were about 35,000 people in Nome, and there had been a lively speculation in building lots. Lots had been staked out all the way to the beach. The ocean was quiet in the summer, and the waterfront was attractive to farmers and others from inland who had never seen a sea coast before."

The raging storm showed what these beach plots were really worth. The breakers grew higher and higher, pounding far beyond the normal high tide line. The people who lived there fled for their lives. A wave crushed the first house like a hammer hitting a tin can. The two cabins next to it were turned right over. The waves came higher and higher up the beach, washing away the sand. Frame houses fell down like houses of cards and floated away in the foam. The sea took away everything up to the first street.

Oaths and curses echoed on the other side of the road where Georg and his friends stood watching the storm devastate everything in front of them. Men cursed the sea and those who had sold them the lots. They came to Nome with their heads full of golden dreams, and the wind and water stole everything they owned.

By the afternoon the storm became even fiercer. So far the boats in the harbor had resisted, but now their anchor chains broke. One after another the schooners were blown towards the shore.

"Here comes the Seagull," somebody shouted. "And Mayflower!"

Enormous towering waves lifted them up and dashed them against the beach. Their hulls splintered, and cans of food, boxes of potatoes, sides of bacon, kegs of whiskey and barrels of oil were rolling about with all the other debris. Men risked their lives splashing through the water to pick up whatever they could.

A German rolled a cask of whiskey up to the Count. "Do you want to buy this?" he asked. It sloshed inside and seemed to be full, but George shook his head. He was completely occupied with which ship was going to be wrecked next. A miner standing next to him bought the keg, and the German melted into the crowd. The buyer opened the cask, it was filled with sea water. The general chaos had given someone a unique opportunity to trade in false whiskey!

Soon only the schooner General Skookum was left. She was a sturdy, full-rigged ship, loaded with lumber. The men all knew she had very heavy chains and anchors. But could she ride out a storm like this? The betting was frantic and the stakes were high.

"Fifty dollars says she'll stay!" Georg shouted.

"I'll cover it; she can't last another five minutes," Kid Larsen shouted back.

"If you've got money to throw away, I'll take a hundred," Tex Rickard chimed in.

All round the group other men were making wagers on the ship's chances. There hadn't been such a good opportunity to bet for a long time.

It really did begin to look as if the chains would hold. Evening came, and as darkness fell, she was still out there riding the waves.

"Come on up to the Northern, boys," Tex called out. "Looks like she'll be there all night. Let's have a few drinks and relax."

The men took his advice, and soon they were all sitting in the saloon talking about the storm. Then, about nine o'clock they heard a tremendous crash from the beach. It was the Skookum. She had said farewell to her chains and been smashed to pieces on the beach.

When they went down to the beach in the morning, what was left of the proud vessel looked like a lumberyard. The storm had stopped, and the waves had gone down. Wreckage from other ships lay everywhere. There was cargo from the ships, household goods from the houses that had been swept away, and whiskey kegs and boxes of provisions had been thrown about everywhere. One building had remained miraculously intact, and now it was afloat on the calm sea. A sign along the edge of the roof could be seen easily, "Riverside Saloon," it proclaimed in big black letters. It had been a victim of the Snake River, which had burst its banks and carried away all the buildings on the beaches. The Riverside Saloon had served its last drinks.

People collected up provisions and household articles, but nobody cared about the piles of lumber that were all around. What was the use of putting up a house when there was no work and not enough food? Nome was full of

Front Street in Nome after the Great Storm
(Photo-Anchorage Historical and Fine Arts Museum)

dissatisfied grumblers. Hundreds were homeless, and thousands of drifters had no work. They were destitute, and winter would soon arrive. How would they get through it? Starvation was a real possibility.

Violent storms like this were common in both the spring and the fall. The reason this one caused such havoc was that people were totally unprepared. There were many fatalities, the exact number will never be known, but a number of vessels disappeared with their entire crews. Another serious disaster was that most of the coal supply for the coming winter, ten thousand tons, was swept out to sea, and it was too late to get any more fuel.

Crime was rampant, with robberies, break-ins, and murders the order of the day. What was left of Soapy Smith's gang got together again, and a new bunch, Allen's gang, made the whole district unsafe. As men became desperate, more and more of them became outlaws.

Every day corpses were brought into Nome wrapped in tents, usually with their skulls smashed. Sometimes they were half-naked and peppered with shots. One day Georg counted seventeen victims. Your life was in danger if you slept with your head against the canvas of the tent. A passerby could easily smash your skull with a stone, then come in and steal whatever he could find.

One friend of the Count's had a gold mine at a nearby site called Cleary Creek. Pete Larson had washed up many thousands of dollars from his mine, when he decided to go to Fairbanks. One fall day, Pete loaded his pack horse with long, heavy gold bags and started off. The day was cold and dark, and the skies were cloudy, but Pete didn't care about his surroundings.

Pete had worked hard and had a tough life in the cold and dark country of Alaska, but his heart was light at the thought of leaving with money in his pocket. He was rich and intended to go to a much more mild and serene climate. His thoughts ran ahead while his body tramped along the narrow, rocky road that twisted through the heavy woods on the way to Fairbanks. He dreamed about California, beautiful orange orchards and luscious blooming cherry trees. He dreamed about grapes and oysters, ripe, cheap peaches and well-cooked chickens. Suddenly, his reverie was interrupted.

"Hands up!" came a voice from the dark between the fir trees.

Bang! A shot sounded from the woods, and Pete fell down in pain. He had not put his hands up fast enough for the bandit.

After a short while, Pete woke up in misery. The heavy gold bags were gone, and with them all his dreams about the beautiful and fertile country waiting for him. All that was left was Pete's pack horse, which looked at him questioningly with big, sad eyes, and the $5 and $20-dollar coins that the bullet had pushed in between Pete's stomach skin and his intestines. Pete had had the gold coins in his vest pocket, and they had saved his life by changing the direction of the bullet.

Pete picked out the bloody gold coins, and sat up with his back against a large stone. An hour later, two golddiggers passed by on their way to Fairbanks. They lifted Pete up on their horse and took him to the city hospital in Fairbanks.

The story of the assault made a big commotion in the whole area of Interior Alaska, and was the beginning of a very sad era. One golddigger after another was assaulted in the woods between Cleary Creek and the city. Miners did not dare to travel alone through the woods, but instead went together in caravans.

But there were always daredevils who wanted to prove their courage by traveling alone. The assaults did not stop. The only description the golddiggers could give of the robber was that he was always wearing a bluish canvas parka, and that he had a hood of the same material over his head with holes for the eyes. The canvas parka was a common item of outerwear in Alaska at that time, so the description did not give the police much to go on.

Because of the canvas parka, they called the robber, "The Man in the Blue Parka," and rumors about the attacks spread all over Alaska. The robber did not take small sums of gold, but rather millions of dollars. The police in Fairbanks wanted badly to track the culprit down.

In charge of the Fairbanks police department at that time was Marshall Doley. Doley was reprimanded several times by his superiors in the Lower 48. A large reward of $20,000 was promised for catching the robber, and several times searches were organized throughout the woods, but they were always unsuccessful. Even groups of suspicious strangers were taken in for questioning, but to no avail.

Pete Larson started once again to work on his gold mine. He had been thinking about selling his mine, but due to the robbery, he had to continue working on it. Larson was one of the most eager participants in the searches for the Blue Parka Man.

One day, as Larson was sitting in a saloon in Fairbanks, he saw Marshall Doley. As usual, Larson asked Doley if he had found out anything that could lead to the capture of the bandit, but Doley sadly shook his head.

"The only thing that I know about the man is that he has a blue, canvas parka," Doley mumbled. "I can't arrest anyone from that description. I would have to put handcuffs on every second man in Fairbanks if it were for that. The bastard is always alone, and no one has ever seen his face."

A tall, thin man came walking up the street, and Larson watched him through the window. The stranger was carrying two filled gold bags.

"Look at that man," laughed Doley. "He has a canvas parka. Do you think I should put him in jail?"

"Well, Marshall, maybe it would pay to find out where he got his gold," Pete said. "Did you see how big those gold bags were?" he continued in an excited voice.

"Sure I did," nodded Marshall Doley. "I'll look a little closer at him. See you later."

The marshall left the saloon and followed the strange man with the heavy gold pouches. The man walked into a gambling hall. When Doley entered, the man was in the process of changing his gold into bills.

"Hello, stranger!" said Doley. "Where did you get all that fine gold?"

"I washed it out of my gold mine at Cleary Creek, of course," mumbled the man. "What business is it of yours, anyway?"

"I happen to be the city marshall, and I thought I knew all the richer gold diggers in this area. But you seem to be an exception. Where is your mine again?"

"I said, at Cleary Creek," came the curt answer. Doley then asked the man to come with him to his office.

"I just want to get control of things," said Doley. "As I hope you can understand, we must be extremely careful nowadays for strangers around these parts."

Doley could see that the man was Danish, and he gave his name as Robert Henderson. He followed Marshall Doley without protesting, and Doley sent a deputy to Cleary Creek to look at the man's mine. Meanwhile, Henderson had to wait in the jail.

Pete Larson stepped in to see Doley, and while they were sitting talking in the office, Henderson began a loud conversation with his guard. Pete hit his fist on the table and rushed up to Doley.

"You've sure as hell got the right man this time, Marshall! I can recognize his voice. Oh, my gosh! Now maybe I can get my gold back!"

"Oh, don't be so damn silly," mumbled Doley. "It's impossible to recognize his voice. He didn''t talk with you, he just screamed at you to scratch your hands up."

"He's Danish, isn't he?" asked Pete.

"Yes, he is."

"That does it, then," said Pete. "I can recognize that tone in his voice. Just listen to him for a moment."

"Damn fool!" Henderson was screaming to the guard in the jailhouse, and Pete nodded triumphantly.

"You can hear that he does not have that certain tone as you Americans," Pete said. "I'm sure as hell sure of it!"

Doley began to laugh. "There are lots of Danes in this area, and I can't put them all in jail because they're Danish! Hell, no, if his story is true, I have to let him go."

The man Doley had sent to Cleary Creek came back and said that Henderson really had a gold mine there. He had met a companion of Henderson's, and there was no doubt about it. Doley got ready to let Henderson go, but Pete stopped him.

"I have an important suggestion to make to you," said Pete. "You know that I don't unnecessarily put my nose into other people's business. I'm sure that Henderson is the robber, and I would like for you to give me a chance to prove it."

"Why, you can have as many chances as you want," replied Doley, "but I don't understand how you'll be able to prove anything as long as Henderson is sitting in jail. Are you going to find his gold cache?"

"All you have to do is put me in jail with Henderson, and then I will get the truth out of him," said Pete.

"Ha, ha, ha." Doley laughed out loud. "Do you really think Henderson will confess his terrible sins and crimes to you? You are a real dumb shit. I never heard of anything like that before. Besides, maybe Henderson will recognize you and your voice!"

"The hell he will, Marshall," said Pete. "It was so dark in those woods that he didn't see my face when he robbed me, nor did he hear my voice, I'm sure of that."

Pete was stubborn, but after a long discussion, Doley gave in. Pete's optimism was contagious.

Doley took a hold on Pete's coat, and cursed and screamed at him. Then he pulled him toward Henderson's jail cell. When he opened the door to the cell, Pete hit him in the face, and Doley answered by bashing Pete's head on the wall a few times. Then the marshall threw Pete roughly into the cell, where he landed with a hard crash against the wall. Pete angrily started to shout out some rough curses in the Danish language.

Doley closed the cell door and went away.

"Are you Danish?" asked Henderson as he looked with interest at Pete. Pete rubbed his head as he answered.

"Hell, yeah, That's right," Pete said. "What about it?"

"I'm from Copenhagen," Henderson said with a smile. He stretched out his hand to Pete. "It's nice to meet someone from the old country. By the way, those were real knockout punches you gave the marshall."

They shook hands and became good friends as is common among people from the same country. Henderson cursed out Marshall Doley, and Pete agreed with him and found new curses when Henderson stopped talking. None of the guards understood Danish, so the men used their mother language to be able to speak freely. Pete was careful and was satisfied with just talking about their homeland, Denmark. He didn't ask Henderson anything else.

Henderson was of course angry about being in jail, and said that Doley would get his for keeping him in jail without any reason. But Doley came up with one excuse after another to keep Henderson in jail, and the days went slowly by. Every day, the two prisoners could take a little walk outside the jail, but never at the same time. When Pete walked alone, Doley could talk to him. After about a week had passed, Doley had bad news.

"You have been mistaken," he said to Pete. "The Man in the Blue Parka has once again robbed another golddigger, and this time it can't possibly be Henderson. We have to let him go right away."

Pete started to wonder. The robber always worked alone, and Henderson could not have done the last assault. But Pete was stubborn.

"Please wait for another three days more," he asked Doley. "Henderson maybe has a helper who has possibly done this robbery, just to take the suspicion away from Henderson."

"All right," said Doley. "It doesn't make a big difference to me. Henderson seems to be a rich bastard, and if he started to fight after I let him go, I'll be kicked out from my job anyhow, for letting him sit in jail all this week."

Abandoned machine for working the beach, Nome
(Photo-Carrie McLain Museum, McLain Archive of Photographic Meterials, Nome, AK)

"You won't have to let him go. In three days I'll get the truth out of him. I'm sure he's the robber," Pete said.

The conversations between Pete and Henderson became more and more serious. One evening, Henderson asked Pete why he was in the jail.

"I shot Hank Jerney to death," mumbled Pete. "He started to fight against me when I was trying to take the money away from him. Jerney was the cashier to one of the biggest gambling saloons in Fairbanks."

At this, Henderson opened up his eyes wide.

"Then you'll be hanged," he said.

"Oh, there's no danger of that," bragged Pete. "Have you heard of the MacIntosh gang in Nome?"

"Yeah, they're a bad one," answered Henderson.

"Well," laughed Pete, "I'm the leader of that gang now. We're 20 men here in Fairbanks, and at this very moment some of my friends are getting ready to come and tear this old jailhouse down and get me free!"

Henderson stared at Pete with new respect in his eyes, and Pete pushed his chest out, closed his eyes, and bent forward to whisper to him. "Do you want to know how I killed those three Englishmen?"

Pete was talking about a well-known murder that had happened one month earlier at Copper Center, and Henderson pulled back with great surprise. Pete gave him a blood-dripping story.

The following evening, he continued to talk about robberies in Dawson, Circle City and Nome. Marshall Doley had given him many stories to tell, and he knew lots of details. All of these gory stories he told to Henderson. Pete bragged and described the crimes in a nonchalant way.

"When it comes to fooling the police, there's nobody smarter than me," said Pete. "In a few years, I'll be a millionaire."

Doley was desperate and angry when he and Pete met the next day.

"The Man in the Blue Parka has once again robbed a golddigger. If you can't get the proof by tomorrow, I'll have to let Henderson go. This has gone far enough, really way too far."

"Tonight, I'll get everything out of Henderson. I'll find out for sure where he stashed all the gold," Pete said confidently. "But I want you to smuggle out a bottle of whiskey through the window. I'll break the glass in the window, and be sure you don't replace the glass until tomorrow, so then you can stick the bottle of booze in through the window right away. Then listen outside the cell door, and you'll hear what you want to hear. You can better believe that you'll hear his complete confession. Henderson is almost bursting from trying to keep quiet so long."

The evening came quickly, and Pete again started to tell his crime stories. He drank some of the jail coffee, and pretended to get angry. He cursed the taste of the coffee, and broke the window with his coffee mug.

A full moon came up and shone through the window. It was a beautiful evening, and Pete let his fantasy run free.

"Pete! Pete!" came a hoarse whisper through the broken window. A hand came through holding a whiskey bottle.

"Here's a little booze for you; we'll come and help you tomorrow night," said the voice. Pete quickly took the bottle.

"There, you can see what nice friends I have," Pete said with a happy smile to Henderson. "It sure will be good to have a drink. I have good friends, and tomorrow you can come with me away from this hellhole if you want to." The men toasted each other and drank.

Outside the cell door lay Doley and another Dane, as Pete and Henderson spoke mostly Danish. Everything was translated to Doley. Pete bragged again about his bravado. Henderson got angry as he didn't get a chance to say anything. Pete talked and talked until Henderson lost his temper.

"You clumsy fool," Henderson said to Pete. "You're always bragging and continually talking about your crimes. Take a look at me now, I'm the one who really has committed crimes!"

"Ha, ha, ha. You haven't been out doing bad things at all, not as much as I've done," laughed Pete. "Anyone can see that, for heaven's sake."

"Well, what do you know about that? I'm angry as hell, just for listening to you! Can you guess who I really am?"

"Ha, ha, ha. Now I know that the whiskey is going to your head."

"I am the Man in the Blue Parka," said Henderson. He looked questioningly at Pete. Henderson had thought that Pete would be very impressed, but Pete just laughed a little.

"You're drunk," he said. "I heard the other day from the guard that the robber robbed another golddigger while you were here in jail."

Henderson laughed happily. "Oh, one must be smart," he said. "I have a companion, and it's him who done the last robberies, so that I won't be suspected. We both have a worthless gold mine together at Cleary Creek, and no one has the vaguest idea that we get all the gold from somewhere else."

Doley opened the cell door. He had his revolver in his hand and thanked Henderson for all of his factual information. Henderson became so angry that he jumped on Pete without being worried about the revolver being fired, but Marshall Doley hit him on the head with the butt of the gun and knocked him out.

In the morning, Doley and Pete hurried out to Henderson's gold mine at Cleary Creek. At the opening of the mine there was a brownish tent. The men edged up to it carefully. They heard snoring inside and opened up the entrance that kept the tent closed. They found out that Henderson's companion was alone in the tent.

"Hands up!" The men spoke in unison, and the sleeping man jumped up with outstretched arms. He obeyed the command immediately. Doley crawled in the tent and put the handcuffs on him.

"Now you have to show us where all your gold is hidden," Doley said. "Henderson has already confessed to everything, and we know that you have the gold close by here somewhere. Somewhere near Cleary Creek!"

"I don't know where Henderson has hidden it," said the man angrily.

"All right, goddamnit," answered Marshall Doley. "Do you refuse to show use where it is? I'll remember that! Your partner Henderson has already promised to show us where it is hidden, but we thought we wouldn't have to take him all the way out here in the boonies to show us. I'll see you have to pay for all the trouble you're making for us. Henderson will probably get away a little better and easier than you, stranger!"

"But it's he who's done most of all the robberies. He's to blame for all the crimes! Come with me and I'll show you," the stranger said.

Marshall Doley and Pete went with the man to a rich gold cache, and to Pete's astonishment he found all of his gold bags stacked with gold. They were at the bottom of the pile of other gold bags, as he was the first golddigger to have been robbed. Pete could see that the robbers had not been able to spend any of the gold yet.

Pete was once again a rich man, and he did not wait long to sell his gold mine. He was soon on his way south.

Henderson and his companion also went south, but the state paid for their trip. They were both put into San Quentin prison.

Chapter Nine

The Blueberry Kid

"The shame and pity of it; that dastard could receive such gentle courtesy and in vile mood make of his own response death's grisly lure."

Another famous criminal during those years was the Blueberry Kid. The Count went with a friend to Wiseman, then a little mining camp, to search for a new gold mine. Crimes seldom happened in Wiseman, as the Koyukuk country was hard to travel through. On the way to Wiseman, the Count heard the story of the Blueberry Kid.

A beautiful roulette wheel was transported to Wiseman one season, and the community soon had a new resource to draw miners to the town. From all the valleys nearby, mining people came running to try out the elegant wheel they thought would make them rich. Gold sand ran in even streams from the golddiggers' bags. The roulette ball chimed and sang its lullaby to all sober-thinking miners, and the gambling devil laughed so hard that its sharp teeth glittered in the people's black hairy faces.

When all the commotion had died down, two enterprising men named Kelly and Smith built a large log cabin, which housed the roulette wheel. It became a well-liked place to meet for all the miners. Kelly practiced his barbering skills on the men, while Smith, previously a tailor, would make and repair clothes for the men. Kelly would often play the guitar in their saloon, and Smith handled the gambling table with the lively roulette wheel singing its song to the miners who would gamble.

In a short time, Kelly was nicknamed, "Flat Foot," and his friend Smith was named Hobo Smith, because he used to be a traveling bum in the States.

After a year, they extended their business and built more log cabins and saloons. Their riches became greater and greater, but soon the mining camp became boring. It was time for a new sensation.

Pale Mary and Silvertoed Helen heard about the lively camp at Wiseman. They moved from Nome, traveling up the Koyukuk River to reach the remote camp. Lifting their skirts high with one hand, the women jumped ashore from the boat, quickly skipping up to Hobo Smith's saloon. The ladies pulled at the men's beard, telling them how handsome they were, and how they intended to stay in Wiseman. They asked if the business for their trade would be good in Wiseman, and the answer was obviously yes!

Hobo Smith said the two women would be wonderful attractions for his and Kelly's saloon.

Loud noises in the forest could be heard around Wiseman. Once again the Koyukuk men came running from the valleys to throw themselves into dances and gambling games. More women came to the mining camp, and soon Pale Mary and Silvertoed Helen were madams, in charge of several log cabin brothels. The tart ladies were not beauties, but they did have pleasant things about them, and the woman-hungry men were easy prey.

Soon Hobo Smith, Flatfoot Kelly, Pale Mary and Silvertoed Helen became rich and they decided to return to civilization. They'd had enough of the hard Koyukuk country, where it was isolated and wild. Before their departure, they came up with an idea. It was a new sensation! The four invited all the Koyukuk men to a double wedding. Anyone else who wanted to get married could do so, and several miners did.

Hobo Smith began to build a big boat for the wedding trip, and Kelly traveled down the river to find a priest. This party would be the biggest ever known in Alaska. Over 100 golddiggers came for the wedding, and the liquor was free.

Among one of the wedding guests was one gold digger who was called the Blueberry Kid. He had $10,000 in gold sand with him when he arrived in Wiseman. After a few days it was all gone. The roulette devil had eaten all up all of his money. It was gold that the young man had saved up for five years from his mine at Nolan Creek. He didn't complain about his losses, though, but disappeared quickly from the mining camp. Nobody cared about his absence because they were all too busy partying.

On the fourth day after the many weddings, Smith and Kelly put all their belongings into the newly-built love boat. All the gold that they had assembled during their many years in Wiseman they took with them. Some of the golddiggers even sent their gold bags with them to get their gold deposited in banks in Seattle.

The remaining miners at Wiseman cheered and shot off the firearms to salute the happy married couples.

Kelly finally pushed the flat-bottomed boat out into the river, and with Smith steering, they disappeared behind a bend in the Koyukuk River.

The Blueberry Kid had traveled before the group over 100 miles from the opening of the Koyukuk River. It was there he was waiting for the couples. He spent his time building a bark canoe for his escape.

It was a sunny morning when the Blueberry Kid sat with his gun in hand, and hid in a thick bush by the river's edge. The sun glittered on the soft waves from a mild headwind, and dressed the birch clumps along the shore in a shimmering suit of light. Ducks, cranes and geese were smattering quietly in the low groundwater, and swans peacefully glided among them.

The Blueberry Kid sat by a bend in the river, where the pine trees stood black next to the river shore. When the boat went quietly by, he put the opening of his gun through the bushes and aimed. "Bang, bang, bang, bang," went four shots from his gun. The Blueberry Kid was a good marksman, and the boat was not far from him. He killed everyone on board.

The murderer carried his bark canoe to the water's edge and went out to the riverboat. Hobo Smith, Flatfoot Kelly, Pale Mary and Silvertoed Helen all had a rope and heavy rock tied around their necks, and were thrown overboard into the river. He later burned the boat. All of the gold he found on board he buried in the woods.

Toward fall, the Koyukuk men wondered why Kelly and Smith hadn't sent any word. It was learned that the boat had never passed the mining villages further down the Koyukuk than Bettles.

The mining men started to wonder over that and remembered the Blueberry Kid. He had always been so quiet and angry, even during the wedding party, and then disappeared so quickly.

Four men floated down the river on a raft and examined the shores. They found the burned pieces of the wedding party's boat, and a glove that belonged to Pale Mary. After a few days of dragging, they found all the bodies.

A big reward was posted for the capture of the Blueberry Kid. It didn't take long for the people of Alaska to find out that he had been living somewhere in the dark woods near the Koyukuk River. Time after time golddiggers who were on their way down the river with their gold were attacked. Searchers found their boats drifting empty of provisions and gold.

People searched the woods for the criminal. It was easy for the Blueberry Kid to hide, though, as the woods were thick. The law and the golddiggers were often on his trail, but only found his smoking campfires. The Kid became more and more daring, and the reward for his capture grew larger. No traveler was safe from his bullet.

In the place where the attack on Hobo Smith and the others had taken place, they raised a monument with an inscription on it. After that the whole episode was forgotten, and the attacks on miners stopped. Somehow the Blueberry Kid had gotten out of the state.

Many years later, the Count heard the end of the story. World War I had started in Europe. America was pulled into the war on the side of the Allies. Steamer after steamer transported American soldiers over to France, where trains and long rows of trucks took them further on to the front lines.

Pitiful as it was, ambulances filled with wounded Americans started to roll from the front to the hospitals. Among the wounded men was a man named Harper, from Nome. He was moved to a hospital outside of Paris, and he came to lie next to a compatriot named Jimmy Ryan, who said he was from New York. Both men had gas poisoning, and thus could not talk to each other because of the damage to their throats and lungs. Instead they used a small blackboard and a piece of chalk to communicate with each other. They became good friends, and Ryan, who got well first, often came to visit Harper after he had been released from the hospital.

Harper was again sent to the front lines. Finally in an attack against the German lines, the allies were beat back. Harper was hurt in one leg, and had to look for protection in a foxhole.

"Hello, Harper," a voice came from a muddy hole. It was Jimmy Ryan who was lying down in the soupy, dirty hole.

The bombshells exploded around them in every direction. Dirt and rocks flew over their heads. The men could not get back to their trenches, but had to stay there hour after hour in the muddy water.

"Well, this is the end for us," said Ryan. "Soon the Germans will begin their final attack and they'll fix their bayonets and push us through. Can you hear how loud they are bombarding out trenches? They're getting ready for their final move!

"Damnit, life is hell," he continued. "It's really a bastard to die here in this shit. Don't think I'm afraid. I'm really not! You don't know who I am, do you? Let me tell you, I've been in worse things than this before. We won't get out of this alive, so it makes no difference if I tell you about it."

Ryan bragged about his adventures, and told Harper that he was the Blueberry Kid. He boasted about his attacks on the poor golddiggers, and Harper listened, petrified at what he heard. In Nome he had often heard about the Blueberry Kid. He didn't dare to show Ryan his disgust, and besides that, there wasn't any hope that they would get away with their lives.

"That's nothing to talk about now," Harper said. "Help me bandage my leg instead."

Ryan put a bandage on, but continued with his bragging.

The roar from the cannons stopped, however, and it started to get dark. They agreed to try to get back to the trenches. Harper was more afraid of Ryan than of the bullets from the Germans. He dared not turn his back on Ryan, fearing that he'd shoot him down if Ryan should start to regret what he had told him.

Ryan seemed, however, not to fear that his friend would turn him over to the police. He didn't even ask him to keep it a secret. The men both managed to make it back to the trenches where it was safe.

A few days later, Harper told everything to an American lieutenant that he knew from Alaska. The Blueberry Kid was arrested immediately, and a telegram was sent to Seattle. Soon the officials received confirmation that it was really the Blueberry Kid that they held. After a few days of intensive questioning in Seattle, the Kid confessed. He even told where the gold was hidden. There were over $300,000 worth of gold in his hideaway. The Blueberry Kid also paid for his crimes in San Quentin Prison.

Panning for Gold on the fields of Nome (1900)
(Photo-Carrie McLain Museum, McLain Archive of Photographic Materials, Nome, AK)

Chapter Ten

Jack Jolly and Scarface Jim

"With shame-covered faces, ye people, in your tears make a sacred vow, to cleanse Nome from the crimes that stain it now."

The extent of lawlessness in Nome at that time was astounding. Most men wore guns, and robbery and violence were commonplace. Some people lost everything they had because they drank themselves senseless in their tents and were cleaned out. A popular trick was to soak a cloth in chloroform, tie it to a stick, cut a hole in the tent where a man was sleeping, and hold it over his nose. One miner had his bed taken this way; and thieves even stole a stove out of another tent with the fire still burning in it.

Eventually, the news about the needy in Nome reached the south, and the government sent ships to take them south. Many of them departed cursing the day they had first seen Alaska.

But other miners replaced them, coming in from the mountains and valleys with pouches filled with gold and a hunger for good times after their long months in the wilderness. For many their happy days were few as they fell victim to Nome's chief of police and his constable, Jack Jolly and Scarface Jim.

These two villains decided to make their fortunes from the returning miners, counting on them to get drunk and cause trouble. They hired burly men to pick fights with anyone who began to stumble a bit or spoke with a thick tongue. That was the signal for Scarface Jim to go into action.

He would arrest the miner, take him off to the police station, remove his possessions, and lock him up. In court the miner would complain that he had been robbed, but Jack and Jim would swear that he had lost all his money carousing before he had been arrested.

This scheme worked for a long time, but it might have gone on for a lot longer except for a cautious old man they arrested one night. In court he too complained that he had been robbed, and the judge, as usual, paid no attention, fining him twenty dollars for being drunk and disorderly.

The old man looked at the police chief and the constable and shrugged. "All right. Twenty dollars isn't the whole world. I'll pay it right now."

He opened his shirt and exposed a belt filled with gold. Immediately Jack Jolly shot a long dark look at Scarface Jim. Was this the way he searched people? Had he been holding out in other cases?

The Count and his friends never knew what harsh words were exchanged between the two lawmen, but they knew that trouble would come.

A few days later, Scarface Jim was trying his luck at roulette when Jack Jolly came into Reilly's Saloon.

"So That's the way you do your job!" he shot at Jim. "Get out in the street where you belong!"

Jim glared at him without a word, cashed in his chips, and left the saloon. Jack followed, and we watched as the two men disappeared around a corner. A few seconds later two shots rang out, and Scarface Jim was dead.

At his trial Jack claimed self-defense and said that Jim had tried to shoot him because he had raked him over the coals for gambling on duty. And, of course, everyone had witnessed that. But when Jim's girlfriend took the stand, she told how the two of them had been robbing the miners and how angry Jack had been with the constable because he hadn't found the money belt on the old miner. Jim had told the girl that Jack had threatened to kill him.

In the end Jack Jolly went free, but he lost his job as police chief and soon left for Nevada.

Jack Jolly's killing spree in Nome was written up in all the newspapers. In one front page headline from the *Council City News*, on January 17, 1903, it read:

"SENSATIONAL GUN FIGHT AT NOME. EX-POLICEMAN SHOT AND KILLED. BITTER FEELING BETWEEN CHIEF OF POLICE JOLLY AND EX-POLICE OFFICER JAMES CAUSES TROUBLE--THE LATTER SHOT THREE TIMES.--DIED 30 MINUTES LATER."

"A fast, fierce and exciting shooting event took place at Nome at 3 o'clock on Friday afternoon last, when Chief of Police Jack Jolly shot and killed Ex-Police Officer James, known as Scarface Jim.

"The shooting took place in front of the Warwick saloon. A howling blizzard prevailed at the time, and few people were on the street. Those who were in the immediate vicinity say that three shots were fired and a young man who was passing by asserts that he heard Jolly say, "You can't do that with me.""

"The trouble which led up to the shooting arose over the fact that Jim had been discharged by Jolly from the police force, and a feeling of bitterness was thereby engendered.

"Just prior to the shooting Jim was gambling in the Eldorado saloon. He had been drinking heavily and was in a highly excited and nervous condition, betting five and ten dollars a throw on the crap game. Jolly came into the saloon, and Jim spoke to him, but Jolly cut the conversation short by walking out of the place. Jim followed him out and a few minutes later three shots were heard.

"Jim was taken to the hospital on a hand sleigh. In describing the wounds the doctor said that one bullet entered the left hand above the wrist, passed downwards and out through the palm; another bullet entered the head above the right cheek and lodged in his brain, and another passed through his neck. Jim died at 3:30, precisely thirty minutes after the shooting occurred. At no time did he regain consciousness.

"Immediately after the shooting Jolly gave himself up at the Federal jail. He was interviewed by the district attorney, after which he was seen by a representative of the *Nome News*, to whom he made the following statement:

"I discharged Jim from the police force on January 4, and he gave over his star to me yesterday. I knew that he felt very bitterly towards me and this afternoon he saw me in the Eldorado saloon, and began to talk threateningly. I left the saloon to try and get away from him, but he followed me out. I met a friend on the street, and we stopped to talk. Noticing that Jim was following me, I took advantage of the opportunity to unbutton my overcoat so that I could reach for my gun in case of an emergency. I then walked on in the direction of my home, and Jim kept following me. I turned around and said to him, 'This thing has got to stop.' I saw him draw a pistol from his pocket, and I fired. I don't know how many times I fired.' Judge Reed said he would hold Jolly in $5,000 bond, and he would have to appear before the next grand jury."

Apart from these events, there was not much excitement for the Count in Nome that winter. His quartz mine didn't pay off, and he dissipated most of his money playing poker, faro, and roulette in the saloons and giving handouts to friends who were hard up.

Soon he was hard up himself, but he fell in with Grandville W. Long, who invited him to live with him and his wife. After a night's drinking at Reilly's, Long wound up as the owner of the steamship Cleveland, which had been stranded in the storm. As it happened, it carried a cargo of coal and while Long recovered from his hangover, the Count negotiated to sell it for twenty-five thousand dollars. Long offered him half the profit, but the Count told him all he wanted was an outfit. ''I need to get going again, up to Kotzebue to look for gold.''

Mining Operations at Anvil Mountain (1900)
(Photo-Carrie McLain Museum, McLain Archive of Photographic Materials, Nome, AK)

Hydraulic Mining on Snow Gulch in Nome by Pioneer Mining Co.
(Photo-Carrie McLain Museum, McLain Archive of Photographic Materials, Nome, AK)

Chapter Eleven

The Trip to Kotzebue Sound

"Of all heartbreaking labors, that of breaking trail is the worst."

As soon as he had his stake, the Count began to get ready for his expedition north across the Seward Peninsula to Kotzebue Sound. First, he needed animals to pull his sleds. Most who headed North relied on dogs, but he decided to use reindeer since they could forage as soon as they got into

Working on the Nome Beach for Gold (1900)

the mountains. He wanted to take a year's supply of food and ammunition and couldn't spare room for dog food.

He went down to the mouth of the Nome River where the Lapps lived and hired two men named Anders Barr and Rana. He sent them off to the Swedish mission at Golovin Bay to buy seven more reindeer to add to the five he had, and then it took several weeks to tame them.

Meanwhile, the Count continued his preparations and signed on a cook named Stewart who had learned his trade in San Francisco before the gold fever drew him north. What little gold he had found on the beach went straight into whiskey at Kelly's saloon.

The Count's plans attracted attention, and both the *Nome Nugget* and the *Golddigger* published stories about him. These accounts attracted a miner named Richard Howey from Chicago, and soon the Count, Stewart, and Howey signed a contract, with half of whatever they staked to go to Long.

While the Count was packing his equipment a few days later, three men came up to him and introduced themselves as the Mackintosh brothers.

They were big and sinister looking, the kind of men you don't like to meet when traveling alone.

"What can I do for you?" said the Count.

"We want to buy your right to the California Fraction."

"My right? I have no right. The California Fraction was stolen...It doesn't exist any more."

"That doesn't matter. We want to buy the right you had. How about two thousand?"

They went to a lawyer and asked if Georg could sell a right that no longer existed. "Certainly," he said, "you can sell anything if someone wants to buy it."

Georg explained how he had become the owner of the fraction and how he had lost it. The lawyer put it into the contract, and hhe got the two thousand.

The Mackintosh brothers knew what they were doing. Most of the men who had taken the fraction had gone for the winter, and the brothers began working the claim one at a time. When one was arrested, the second took over. By the time he was arrested the first would be free on bail. The third brother was always available in case the system broke down. They took out a lot of gold before the gang returned in the spring.

The Count's Kotzebue expedition with its twelve reindeer and seven sleds set out on February 18, 1901. They had a real Alaskan send-off. People lined the streets and cheered as the animals trotted by. A few of the more enthusiastic fired pistols.

The Count and his partners avoided the bare mountain ranges to the North where the reindeer would find nothing to eat. Instead, they traveled east to Golovin Bay toward the Fish River, intending to go up the river valley. The track to Golovin Bay was well traveled, wide and hard, but after that they would have to make their own way.

The Count went in the lead with the compass, with Howey and Rana close behind. Their wide snow boots packed the snow well enough for the reindeer and the nine-foot sleds. Each sled carried about four hundred pounds of supplies, and the reindeer were tied to one another to force them to walk in the same track.

The seventh sled was a flexible basket sled, made without screws or nails. The ribs, framework, and runners were held together with sinews and straps of walrus hide. It was twelve feet long and weighed less than the others. Its purpose was to act as an insurance policy. They were sure it would not be crushed whatever happened and used it to carry the tent, reindeer-skin sleeping bags, and food enough for several days at a time.

It took them two weeks to reach the Fish River, and then they turned up the valley, through the barren western part of the Seward Peninsula towards the belt of conifers. It was March, so the days were still short, and they traveled seven to ten miles between dawn at nine in the morning and dusk at two-thirty in the afternoon.

Day after day they worked their way through the deep snow of the desolate valley, mostly in silence. From time to time they quarreled over where they were or which route they should take, but once they were snug in their tent, their hunger satisfied and their pipes filled, they forgot their irritations and talked of their past adventures and the things to come when they reached Kotzebue.

When the trees ended at North Fork, they faced uncharted country. From a vantage point, the Count could see that the valley in front of them was at least seventy miles wide. The prospect of such a hike in the open was dispiriting, so they decided to stay in their camp for a couple of days, preparing for the trek. They cooked beans, killed and fried ptarmigan for stew, and collected lichen for the reindeer.

Early on the third morning they resumed their journey, and everything went well for a few hours. Then the wind began to rise, and gray clouds filled the skies. By noon the snow was coming down in gusts, and soon it was mixed with ice.

Suddenly a full blizzard hit them, striking so hard it nearly knocked them off their feet. The Count quickly cut the ropes tying the reindeer together, and they disappeared. They threw the tent down on top of the snow, lashed the sleds together, and crawled under the top canvas. For two days and nights they lay in their sleeping bags without food as the wind howled outside.

When the storm finally abated, they crawled outside to a beautiful clear day. But where had the reindeer gone? The Lapps were sure they were off behind a plateau at the edge of the mountains and set off to find them while the Count, Stewart, and Howey stayed behind to repair the sleds and ropes. It was more than twenty-four hours before they returned, the reindeer full of the moss they had found on the lee side of the mountain.

They hitched up the deer and started out under a full moon, marveling at the dark landscape where the drifting snow had created fantastic shapes.

"There's a strange one," Howey said, "It almost looks like a man."

"I went closer," the Count recorded, "and had a good look at it. I ran my hand over what would be the head and felt a nose.

''My God! It really is a man!''

The old man was just sitting there in the snow. There was frost on his bald head and snow shone in his beard and the hair around his ears. A whole snowdrift had collected at his back, fixing him in his place. He had a biscuit in his left hand, half way to his mouth, and there was a can of corned beef between his legs.

The men hurried back to camp to get axes to chop him out of the snow. Then they dragged him back to the tent and went through his pockets to find out who he was. Eventually they found a paper recording a claim that gave his name as Hark Fries from Council.

They decided they would have to take the body to Council and drew lots. The loser, one of the Lapps, was frightened. He didn't want to travel with a dead man. Howey didn't say anything when he lost the next draw. But the Count knew he didn't want to do it either. So he told the others to press on and headed back to Council, using the biggest strongest reindeer, one they called Bacon John because he pulled the sled with the meat.

The Count put in a long day to reach their old campsite where they had left plenty of wood. Exhausted, he lay awake for a while listening to the click-click of Bacon John's hooves as he chewed his moss and looking at the man who sat at his feet.

"My feet were right up against the dead man's, but I felt no fear or discomfort. In that immense wilderness, you saw death as part of nature, part of life. I thought, ''This is the last journey for Hark Fries.''

With that the Count fell asleep. But a short time later, loud snorts from Bacon John wakened him. He looked into the dark woods on the other side of the sleigh and then out past his fire. Suddenly he saw two pairs of eyes. Wolves! Reindeer were terrified of them.

The Count grabbed his Winchester and fired into the darkness, but angry growls were followed by silence, and then he saw a whole line of shining eyes. They'd take Bacon John and then him! Quickly he threw the reindeer to the ground and bound him tightly, and in desperation he began to throw burning wood towards the wolves. Then he cut down a dead spruce at the front of the sleigh and set it on fire too.

The wolves weren't frightened, but they seemed wary of attacking across the open space on the valley side. They stayed, staring, silent as thieves beneath the trees. The Count was surprised that they didn't howl.

At last dawn came, and the gleaming eyes were gone as noiselessly as they had appeared. As the light grew stronger, the Count could hear their howling from higher on the mountain. A long, desolate song, covering the whole scale and ending in a high treble.

The Count still didn't know whether they would return, but he freed Bacon John and sat down on the sleigh to rest. The corpse had warmed in front of the fire; the raised hand had come down, and the right side of the face was scorched. Now as it was stiffening again, the lip on one side seemed to be cast in a smile.

"You look satisfied, Hark Fries," said the Count aloud. "Well, you got a salute on your last trip."

The Count then hitched Bacon John back up to the sleigh and continued on, reaching Council six days later. There Marshall Donovan asked him whether they had found more bodies. Fries had left with two other men in the fall, grubstaked by Judge Jeffries.

Donovan decided to accompany the Count on the return trip, and they found another body near where Fries had been discovered. Then Donovan decided he would return to look for the third man in the summer, and the Count and his partners pressed on through a pass Howey had found leading down to the valley of the Koyukuk River.

It proved to be a route the reindeer could follow, and soon they found themselves at the head of another valley. As they were preparing to camp, the reindeer began to be agitated, and the Count thought of his experience on the way to Council. They got their guns ready, but they saw no sign of wolves. Then they came upon a snowed-up hut. The Count put his shoulder to the door, and it flew open.

"One look and I stepped backward horrified. On the floor in front of me was a living skeleton, a withered old man. His eyes were sunk deep in his head and his dry, cracked skin pulled tightly over his cheekbones.

"I forced myself to overcome the feeling of revulsion, picked up the nearly dead body, and carried it to the bed. There were no blankets, no sleeping bag; instead the bed had a strange cover of reindeer hair. He stirred and groaned as I laid him down, but his eyes remained closed."

The Count called the others in, and soon Stewart warmed some condensed milk, and they began to feed the old man. They lit a fire and looked again for a sleeping bag. No one would be without one in this icy wilderness. Finally, the Count realized he must have eaten the hide, leaving only the hair. He must have eaten his mukluks too, for there was only straw on his feet. Hunger must have driven him nearly mad.

They gradually fed him bouillon and then solid food, and in ten days he was on his feet. He told them that his name was Jimmy McIntyre and that he had come from Council with Hark Fries and Jimmy Malone. They had built the cabin and claimed a valley nearby. But winter had surprised them, and their supplies started to run out. The other two had tried to make their way back to Council, and they had frozen in Death Valley.

The Count's expedition resumed its journey northward over the mountain shoulder to a tributary of the Koyuk River. They avoided the treacherous lava fields south of Lake Imuruk, the largest lake on the Seward Peninsula. Then they followed the Kougarok and went on to the valley of the Inmachuk. In April 1901 they finally reached Kotzebue Sound.

They put up their tents, cached their supplies on a high platform, and began exploring the surrounding valleys. In some places they built fires to melt the snow and made test washings. They didn't find much gold, but they staked the whole distance of Arizona Creek as their most likely prospect. If they did find something worthwhile, it would be easy to exploit because they were close to the ocean.

However, the partnership was about to break up. The Count and Howey ran into another party of three men from Nome, Davis, McCormick, and Missouri Bill, and worried that they were not the first in the area. But the others had come with dogs, and now they were short of supplies. They had staked some claims, and they were on their way back to Nome. The Count traded a sick reindeer, which was slaughtered to feed their dogs, and flour for three packets of their tobacco, and when the men were on their way, he and Howey checked out their claims.

The next day they staked a few claims on a creek they named Gloriana and then returned to their base camp where they found that Stewart had acquired two Eskimo women as companions. He insisted that he was in love with one of them and was going to return with them to their village as soon as he got his share of the supplies.

The Count tried to dissuade him, but Stewart was deaf to his pleas.

"I haven't done a damn thing wrong," he declared. "We've each got a free will."

Howey and the Count agreed to give Stewart his fifth of the supplies and to kill a reindeer for his wedding trip. But all the rifles and ammunition belonged to the expedition. Stewart agreed readily, and he and the Eskimo girls packed and left.

Howey and the Count then decided to explore in different directions to make the best use of the time before the snow melted. The Count headed east.

Chapter Twelve

The Count Discovers Candle

"The land at the Rainbow's End"

When the Count set out, the snow had already begun to thaw and traveling was difficult. He stayed up on the plateau, descending into the valleys to investigate them and locate claims. Soon it was easier to rest during the day and travel at night when there was a crust on the snow.

When he reached the Kiwalik River, he turned inland and went as far as Koyuk where he staked a few claims before turning back. When he came to the Buckland River, he decided the mountain formations looked promising. In the first stream he went into in the side valleys he washed out about fifty cents worth of gold and wrapped it in paper so that he would have something to show Howey. Maybe, he thought, this valley will be as good as Balto Creek.

Howey had found nothing himself and was eager to set out when the Count showed him the sample. But the Count persuaded him that they couldn't move the sleds now that the snow was disappearing and that they should wait until it was all gone.

When full summer arrived, with green life bursting out on every side, the air full of the noises of wildlife, Howey and the Count set out for their claims. They were unaware of the encouraging reports taken back to Nome by the three-man party with dog sleds. They boasted that they had discovered gold in a valley they had named Old Glory and the rush was on.

The schooner Deering was hastily equipped and sailed round Cape Prince of Wales and Cape Espenberg into Kotzebue Sound. Howey and the Count spotted it from a distance of about twenty-five miles as they were resting at Asses Ears on their way back to their camp. They hiked on through the mountains and forgot the speck until the next morning when they were duck hunting.

An Eskimo boy emerged from the bushes and handed the Count a note: "The schooner J.B. Deering has arrived. Pack your things, bring the reindeer and come down. I'm aboard. Long."

They went down to the mouth of the Inmachuk where the Deering was anchored, and soon found they knew many of the twenty-five men aboard, not just Long and Magnus Kjelsberg, who had made a fortune in Nome through his wise investments and the "respectable" Discovery Saloon, but also Commissioner Noyes who had been sent along to register the new claims. One they didn't know so well, a German named Eric Blankenship, was soon to cause plenty of problems for the Count.

Long was in a sour mood. The coal cargo in the Cleveland had been all right, but Long had decided he could make even more money by salvaging the ship, and he traded the last half of the coal to Reilly for sole ownership of it. He had forgotten about the drift ice, however, and when it went out to sea, it took the Cleveland and Long's hoped-for profits with it. Now he wanted to recoup his losses with gold.

Long's high-handed manner angered the Count, and for a couple of days, it seemed they were at the parting of the ways. But the Count cooled off as he reflected on the difficulty he would have without Long's provisions, and Long decided that he shouldn't waste the Count's experience in exploration. He and the Laplanders would look over the claims that were already staked while Howey and the Count took the canoe north along the coast.

The night before they set off, they spent time in a tent restaurant run by a German girl. The whiskey was plentiful thanks to Magnus Kjelsberg, and after supper they drank and talked with three of the passengers from the schooner, Blankenship, Snyder, and Thomas. In the friendly atmosphere they talked freely about their plans.

By the afternoon of the next day, the two men had paddled past the Kougarok River and reached the Kiwalik. It had started raining, and the wind was gaining strength, driving waves against the canoe.

"We've got to land or we'll be swamped," shouted the Count

They beached the canoe and erected their tent. The Count recorded what happened then:

"It seemed to me that this was not the valley I was looking for, but I was so frozen and wet through that I was ready to dry out and bed down. But I had to try a sample first. I filled a pan with sand and washed it out. There was at least a teaspoonful on the bottom. I showed it to Howey, trying to keep my face expressionless.

"'Hell, Count,' he said. 'You've salted this. You think I'm a greenhorn.'

"'Try it yourself!' I replied.

"Howey scooped up a panful of gold and washed it out. He stood for a moment staring at the gold shining in it. Then he turned to me with a look of wonder on his face.

"'My God! We're rich! Rich!' He poured the gold out on a flat rock. 'Look at that! Gold! Piles of it! We're rich!'

"All the weariness from battling the storm and hiking through rain disappeared in our excitement at the strike. We'd never been in at the beginning before; we'd always come along late, trying to pick up scraps at the edges. But this one was ours. Other men would be the latecomers.

"Gradually fatigue set in and we fell quiet. Too tired to cook, we opened a tin of corned beef and ate it cold. Then we went to bed. Tired as I was, I couldn't help asking Howey what he would do with his money.

"'I'm going back to Chicago to put my father back on his feet. He was a meat-packer, but he lost everything he had betting on the horses. How about you?'

"'I'm going to buy a yacht and sail around the world,' I said as we fell into our golden dreams."

The Count awoke in the early morning and crawled out of the tent to survey the claim that would make him a millionaire. "What the hell was that? A tall stake stood right in front of the tent, a white paper fluttering from near its top. Something was wrong! I ran to look. Rocky Creek, it said. Claimed by Eric Blankenship, Nome! Hell! Those bastards had sneaked after us! They'd pay for it!"

It was as the Count imagined. Blankenship and his two companions had drawn their own conclusions from the conversation in the restaurant and took the land route when they saw where the Count and Howey were headed. The Count grabbed his Winchester and rushed into Blankenship's camp, accusing the three men of claim-jumping and threatening to blow their heads off.

Blankenship at first asserted that they had the same rights as the Count and Howey, but then he said, "We're just trying to get a fair share. We want to talk about it."

First, the Count disputed their new name. He wouldn't hear of Rocky Creek. He wanted to call it Candle because all the little birches in the area looked like candles to him. That was fine with Blankenship: "Let's get to the important part, staking claims."

They finally decided to stake claims in rotation, the Count first, followed by Blankenship, then Howey, Snyder, and Thomas. Soon they were friendly enough to help one another measure and stake the claims, and after nine days, they each had fifteen claims along Candle Creek and the valleys leading into it.

No one else had come into the area, and they hoped it would stay that way. It would soon be winter again, and they could do without gold diggers poking around their claims. They all agreed to keep the find quiet, but they soon discovered that Blankenship was not to be trusted. That night he sneaked out in the dark.

Howey and the Count decided they had better see what he was up to, so they packed their things and paddled south. Within a few hours they saw boats approaching them, many of them strange looking craft consisting of tent canvas stretched over crude frames, sure to be swamped in rough water. As they came alongside, they all asked the same question: ''How far to Candle?''

Blankenship had showed his gold to everyone at Deering, and by the time the Count and his partner reached it, there was hardly a man in the place apart from Thomas Noyes, who had set up his tent and started registering claims in the newly formed Fairhaven Mining District.

Candle City and Kiwalik River after flood of 1903.
(Photo-Anchorage Museum of History and Art)

Now they had new problems with Long. He had decided he wanted a bigger share and refused to pay for the registration of any claim unless he was half owner. They had no cash, and nothing they said could sway him. He gave them a couple of hours to think his proposition over and went off to the tent saloon.

Suddenly, the Count had an idea, and he dragged Howey off to Noyes' tent.

Noyes sat at a table writing on some papers. Georg walked across to the rough plank counter and leaned over it: ''If you register all of our claims, Howey's and mine, and you pay the fees, you'll get two claims for your trouble,'' he said in a low voice. ''But you''ll have to send a man up right away to change the slips.''

''Noyes stared at me for a moment. I knew he was measuring the gold against Long's anger, and I knew that the gold would win. A smile spread across his face. 'Right! I'll do it.'''

Long, of course, found out in no time, and promised he would get even. But for the moment, the Count had other interests. A whaler had arrived from Point Hope that same day. The owner, a Danish fisherman named George Madsen, had an Eskimo woman with him. She had beauty marks tattooed on her face, a large blue star on each cheek and blue stripes from her lower lip across her chin. But it was the boat, not the woman that the Count was interested in. He wanted to use it to get supplies up to Candle.

Madsen agreed to take them, and in the morning they took their supplies and set sail. Then the Count offered Madsen a claim in exchange for the boat. That didn't interest the whaler, but he was interested in the Count's next offer of "supplies", and they struck a deal.

In Candle they found a swarm of men, all of them washing gold from the claims they had staked. With their numbers and no lawmen to appeal to there was nothing they could do. But the Count was eternally optimistic. Over the campfire, he pointed out to Howey that they had come to this valley by mistake; it was not the one the Count had originally discovered. That one was further up.

Howey was eager to set off at once, but the Count reminded him that they did not have enough supplies for the winter. He suggested that he should go down to Nome while Howey remained behind to stake more claims.

When he returned to Deering, there were three steamers and two sailboats lying off-shore. Their passengers were already on their way to Candle Creek. Deering itself now had a number of frame buildings, one of them a store run by a Russian merchant from Riga, Bob Froberger. His business was poor since the miners had departed, and he jumped at the chance when the Count offered him a claim in exchange for slips, pencils, and candles.

On their way back to the creek, Froberger told the Count what Long was planning: "He's going to get revenge on you and Howey by taking over Candle Creek. That's why he's going to Nome, to buy all the supplies he can get his hands on. He'll ship them up to Candle and open a saloon. He'll let the miners buy all they want on credit, and in the spring, when they can't pay up, he'll seize their claims.''

At Candle, Froberger got his claim, and the Count prepared for his trip to Nome. He agreed to take Jerry Hunter and Big Ben, who had made small fortunes washing the beach at Nome, back with him. And he listened to the troubles of Kiddy Braine: "I don't know much about gold mining, Count," he said. "I was a prize fighter down in the States. Baker, he owns a saloon at Nome, sent me up here to stake claims. But, hell, he only gave me four sides of bacon and some flour. Tell him I've got to have more. I'm not going to starve up here."

The Count agreed to do what he could. Then he took Howey and the Lapps up to the valley they had explored and returned to Deering where he picked up Noyes and his wife. The weather was so rough that all his passengers were seasick, and no one could spell the Count at the helm. He was exhausted by the time they reached Cape York and decided to proceed the rest of the way on the mail steamer Sadie with the whaler in tow.

News of the Count's discovery at Candle was soon broadcast in the *Nome Nugget*, which reported his statement that "Candle is the richest creek yet discovered in Alaska and as much as $5 to the pan has been found on the beaches."

He was hauled off for a night of celebration after he attended the first order of business, new clothes from a Stetson hat and a corduroy suit to high laced boots and new guns from the Alaska Commercial Company. He also got a loan of five thousand dollars from Jerry Hunter and sought out Baker's Saloon to deliver Kiddy Braine's message. Baker was shocked that the outfit was insufficient and readily agreed to buy another long list of supplies to send to Candle.

The Count's mind got mistier as the evening wore on. He and his companions toasted one another and assured the eager faces that crowded round that there was plenty of gold.

"When I awoke, I had a dim recollection of going into the Golden Gate, the best hotel in town. Now, though it was still bright, I was cold and grumbled to myself at the lack of heat in the hotel. Soon the cold draft blowing on me forced my eyes open. I was lying on the beach somewhere outside of Nome with the sea rippling close by.

"So this is what it's like to be the discoverer of a new gold field, I thought. Then suddenly I became alarmed. My money? I fished in my pockets. It was still there; at least I could return to the hotel with my dignity intact and clean up.

"As I got to my feet, I saw Big Ben trying to sneak past me. How had he gotten in the condition he was in?

"'Where have you been to smell like that?' I asked.

"'Well, I'm damned if I know,' he replied. 'When I woke up, I looked up and saw a whole lot of round holes. But how did I get there?'

"Now I understood the smell. In certain highly necessary small houses everything was left lying on the floor 'til it froze in winter and could be shoveled out through a big door. Somehow Ben had staggered in there in his elegant suit and laid himself down to rest.

"We had to leave Ben's clothes at the bottom of the sea, and I went off to Cheap John's secondhand clothing store to get some overalls and an old pair of shoes. After a preliminary clean-up, Ben continued his grooming at Elias' bath-house equipped with a bottle of cologne. By evening he appeared in a new outfit."

That evening, the Count went off to a banquet the Pioneer Mining Company gave in the honor of the discoverers of Candle.

All the prominent people of Nome were there to toast the findings at Candle, and after a few hours, bids for the Count's claims started to come in. Lindeberg offered him fifty thousand, sight unseen, for all of them. "That would be insane," the Count told him. Then Kjelsberg said he'd give Georg twenty thousand for the best one, but he didn't like the price.

When Jerry Hunter upped the offer to twenty-five thousand, the Count gave in. He knew his provisions were going to cost plenty, and he already owed Hunter, anyway.

The Count also learned what had happened to his California Fraction while he was away. The old band had returned, and they and the Mackintosh brothers continued to work at opposite ends of the claim, using the old law of Nome that you owned the ground you were standing on. As the banquet was continuing, however, one of Nome's notorious holdups was underway.

A gang of about seventy men dressed with masks over their faces went out to the Mackintoshes' camp, fired some shots, and warned them that they had better get out if they valued their lives. One of the brothers was wounded in the knee, and the others left in their underwear. The other gang stayed on the land, which made the difference when the judgment was finally handed down.

The investigations never revealed who had organized the holdup. The workers who replaced the Macintoshes didn't know anything. They had been paid double in advance by someone unknown, and the masked men had disappeared as soon as they started to work.

After this celebration and excitement, the Count got down to practical matters and ordered twenty tons of provisions from the Alaska Commercial Company, which had everything from pork and beans to Christmas tree candles and glitter. Long was there too, and he told Georg that the expenditures were unnecessary since he was going to bring a schooner full of supplies up to Candle. But Georg was not about to use his friendly services.

He left Nome on the Sadie, which was trailing his whaler as well as a barge with cargo and twenty dogs aboard. Luckily Georg insisted at Teller that the whaler be winched aboard, for just after they left a storm snapped the cable and the barge disappeared in the waves.

When they got to Candle, more surprises were in store for the Count. First of all, he ran into an angry Vogel, who had finished the barge he had ordered in Seattle, sailed it north to Nome with a man from Gotland named Wallin, and then pursued the Count to Candle when he read about him in the paper. In truth, the Count had no answer for him; he hadn't thought of the barge for months.

Winter scene, Nome, 1900
(Photo-Carrie McLain Museum, McLain Archive of Photographic Materials, Nome)

Vogel stood there without a penny, and now the Count had two boats. He gave Vogel and Wallin each a claim and supplies for the winter. Then he hired men to build him a cabin on the other side of the Kiwalik River where the forest belt started, and he arranged for some Eskimos to haul his provisions to the site with their dog sleds

By this time he was wondering where Howey had got to, but he discovered the explanation a few days later. Howey had been staking claims all right, but only one was in the Count's name.

"You were supposed to stake eight for me!" the Count shouted.

"Don't make any trouble, Count. It won't do you any good." Howey replied. "I've got an old school friend visiting, and he's a lawyer."

"Like most old timers, we had no written agreement between us, but the guns didn't come out. It was cowardly to kill anyone fast. We fought with our fists until blood was pouring out of our mouths, noses, and ears. Finally I knocked him down with a right hook, and that finished it. Howey told me in San Francisco years later that his nose still hurt."

The fight didn't stop the men from seeing each other during the winter. They were never resentful and always reconciled. But Georg still wound up with no claim on Bear Creek since he had promised Jerry Hunter one. As it turned out, the creek was not as profitable as it had promised to be. Only about a million dollars in gold was taken out of it.

The Count's hut was finished. It looked like an old wooden church, for he had had a tower built for his provisions rather than a cellar. He put a lantern up in it and it became a good lode star for travelers.

The trail outside became the best used between Nome and Candle, and when it began to freeze, Georg met many of the miners who had been washing for gold on his claims. They advised the young Swede to sell, saying that the gold was gone, but he thought he would investigate for himself in the new year. And so he settled down for a peaceful winter.

Snake River, Nome, Alaska, 1900
(Photo-Carrie McLain Museum, McLain Archive of Photographic Materials, Nome, AK)

(Editor's Note: The *Nome Goldigger*, on March 19, 1902, printed "Count Georg af Forselles came down from his castle last night.")

Chapter Thirteen

Winter at Candle

"Their bristly fur was coated with frost. Their breath froze in the air."

The Count's cabin was called the Count's Castle by everyone in the area, and soon it was known for its hospitality to travelers. The Count built an extra shack outdoors for cooking dog food and built doghouses and erected stakes to tie the dogs to so that they wouldn't fight.

Most of the time the Count and his visitors passed the time playing cards, talking about their adventures, and demonstrating their prowess at bread-baking. But variety presented itself from time to time. One day a pair of Norwegian brothers named Lee came in to tell the Count they had discovered a bear's winter den up in the mountains, and they wanted him to come with his dog team so that they could try to get some fresh bear steaks.

They took their Winchesters and set off. When they reached the den, they could hear the bear snoring deeply inside. So they stacked dry wood in front of the opening and set it alight. When the smoke started to filter into the den, the snoring stopped and a fierce snorting began. Soon the bear began to roar, and suddenly he rushed out through the fire.

Then they could see it was a black bear, not a grizzly. Still the meat would be full of fat and tasty in the early winter. Three shots brought him down, and they went back to the castle with the carcass. They ate the first steaks there in the cabin, and then the Lees took the rest into Candle City.

One of the Count's visitors was a strange serious boy who lived with him for three months but never joined in outdoor activities. He listened to their accounts of their adventures avidly, and then he would withdraw to his corner with paper and pencils. That was all right, for everyone did as he wished, but sometimes their curiosity overcame them and they asked him what he was up to.

"I'm writing a book," he explained.

"A book," the rest of the men snorted. But he was. The visitor was Rex Beach, and the book he wrote in the Count's cabin that winter was *The Spoilers*, stories of the "wild" life in Nome.

Both Rex Beach and the Count tell stories of the Danish whaler, George Madsen. One concerns one of the wildest fights that was ever seen in Candle, when a free-for-all broke out after a boxing match between Kiddy Braine and Charlie Case that had been promoted by Tex Rickard's brother, called Little Tex by the men of Candle. (But that's the next chapter).

Rex Beach
(Photo-Consortium Library, UAA/APU)

2222222

2222222

Chapter Fourteen

The Big Fight at Candle

"With kindly eyes and outstretched hand he stood among the goldminers, giving friendly greetings. Then one came there whose bandaged hand betokened some bitter pain."

One day in the beginning of February, Little Tex came to see the Count and asked him to help put up a saloon in Candle City. The Count wasn't enthusiastic about the idea, but since Tex Rickard and he were very good friends, Georg decided to do Tex's little brother a favor. Little Tex wasn't worth much. He was much too weak for the hard pioneer life in Alaska. Georg put the reins on his dogs and followed Tex to Candle City. There people lived the high life, as there was no police. All disagreements were settled with the fists. There was no lack of whiskey in Candle, as an American by the name of Baker had carried up a whole cargo-load. There were already many saloons, and their owners were doing good business.

The miners had built an office for the mayor-to-be in Candle. It was a large log house that Little Tex thought would be good for a saloon. After arguing with the builder, the Count bought the log house for Little Tex. Then they went to Baker and he gave Tex gin and whiskey on the Count's credit.

The men put the bar together from some large timber stock, and they made two long tables and some benches from planks. On the walls they nailed up papers that they painted red. Behind the bar they put up a large mirror. They changed an empty gasoline barrel into a stove with a lot of hammering and filing. Drinking glasses were hard to find, but the entrepreneurs made their supply bigger with mugs and coffee cups. Finally everything was ready.

Tex strutted around the bar half-drunk and wanted to open the saloon right away. He was very proud of it, and thought the red color was fantastic-looking. No other saloon in Candle had painted walls.

"You should have some kind of attraction to get people here," the Count said. "Show us that you're a businessman now, and take the customers from the other saloons."

Tex tried to think, but he couldn't come up with anything. The men went over to Baker's saloon, where commerce was going at full speed. In that saloon there was always plenty of action. At the bar was the Irishman Charlie Case, and the American Kiddy Braine. They were in a hearty quarrel. They were both boxers, and were arguing about who was the best boxer.

"No one in Candle could beat me," said Case.

"I can make corned beef out of you," said Braine.

"Do you really want to fight each other?" The Count smiled at the men. "The winner will get $500 and the title, "Champion of Candle."

They both looked at Georg with surprise, but then they thought for a few minutes. They had been eyeing each other for a long time and very much wanted to measure the other one's power.

The group decided that the match should be in a few days. There was much to discuss. Baker had a big tent that had earlier been used for a saloon, and the Count bought that for $200. He arranged for the boxing march to be held in the tent. Georg cut a hole in the saloon's wall so that the tent could be put up right next to it and customers could walk directly from the saloon to the tent.

On the following day, Tex and the Count made some more benches and a boxing ring of wood that they covered with an oilcloth. In three days they were ready. During that time, Rex Beach had done the advertising. He had made big posters and put them up on the trees at all the dog roads in the area. The text was as follows:

"Little Tex Saloon in Candle opens the 14th of February at 2:00 in the afternoon. The famous boxers, Kiddy Braine, an American, and Charlie Case, an Irishman, will meet in a ten round match. Bet on who will be the Champion of Candle. The saloon will offer free egg rag. Take your gold bags with you and come!"

In the morning, the golddiggers came to Candle, and the betting started right away. The entrance to the match was free, but everyone who wanted to see the fight had to bet on one of the boxers.

Tex had hired a Negro waiter, and they were kept pouring drinks into the mugs. The atmosphere of the place was rowdy, and there were fights here and there between friends, but they all ended well. The bets became higher and higher.

Most of the bets were on Case, who was bigger and stronger than Braine. At three o'clock, the match began.

The tent and the saloon were fully packed with excited golddiggers. The air was filled with the smell of whiskey and tobacco smoke. Golddiggers screamed out advice for their favorite in the ring, and sent mugs with whiskey to those that Tex and his waiter couldn't reach.

Braine was a technical boxer, while Case was more of a raw strength fighter, and would often beat big holes in the air. He put all his power into each hit. When Braine bent to the side, Case couldn't keep his balance, and often ended up on his back. He then started to use a new tactic, and rushed with his head bent down against Braine. Braine managed to get away several times, but in the sixth round, the Irishman managed to get his head into Braine's face, and Braine was thrown backward through the ropes and down on the golddiggers sitting nearest the ring.

Blood flowed from his nose as he climbed back into the ring. Braine was half-groggy from the hard hit, and the Irishman rushed up with a smile, putting in a few more bobby hits. He put his arms around Braine's neck, holding him with his left arm, and gave his opponent some terrible hits in the face with his right fist.

Braine tried fruitlessly to get away. He wove around the ring in desperation to retreat from the Irishman, and finally sank down to the floor with a swollen and bloody face.

The Americans in the crowd screamed with anger, demanding that the match should be called off, but the referee, an old bald cowboy, waved calmly and started to count.

For a bell, the Count had a tin pail and a hammer. When the referee had counted to six, Georg hit the hammer on the tin pail. The Count wrote in his memoirs that the round wasn't really quite over, but he wanted to give Braine a fair chance as he didn't like the Irishman's methods.

Braine went over to his corner and swallowed a little whiskey. When the next round started, he was again steady on his feet.

The Irishman rushed in the following round, sure of himself, and then aimed one of his sweeping swings toward Braine's head. The American ducked, and his right fist shot out against the Irishman's chin. The hit was hard, and Case straightened up. Fear came over his face, and he fell to the floor. Braine had hit the Irishman on his larynx, and he was groping with his boxing gloves toward his neck, twisting in pain. His breathing was hard and he seemed to be suffocating.

The referee began to count: one, two, three...He didn't get any further.

An angry Danishman stopped him. It was the whaler George Madsen, screaming and pushing into the tent. Madsen pushed away the golddiggers who were in his way, and jumped up on a bench. Madsen weighed close to 200 kilos. He was enormously strong and agile. Sweat ran down his weather-beaten face. His parka was white from hoarfrost, and his light blue eyes were rimmed with red. He stared angrily and shook his enormous fists at the crowd.

"Thieves and bandits!" he screamed with his face twisting in anger. "Goddamn bastards! Come forward, whoever you are, who stole the Eskimos' winter provisions in the caches at the Kiwalik River! I'm going to twist their necks if I find them!"

For a moment the crowd in the tent became quiet. The golddiggers stretched their necks and looked with wide-open whiskey-smelling mouths at the enormous angry Dane.

"Oh, hell," piped up one gold miner. "It's only that squaw man Madsen. He's married to an Eskimo woman, who lives among the Eskimos."

Angrily, the golddiggers waved their fists and began to rush in to crush Madsen. The benches fell over, and the men fell all around, screaming at each other. Madsen was pushed down from his bench, but he fought wildly around himself and made his way up the tent wall. The golddiggers pushed on the tent wall and it broke. Madsen tumbled backward out into the snow, with the stream of screaming men behind him. He shook his fists, threw off the most advanced men, and tried to make peace.

"I don't want to disturb any good people," he screamed. "I just want to catch the provision thieves!"

The golddiggers calmed down a bit, but an American named Jack Brown, who got a real hit from Madsen, opened his mouth.

"Should we let that bummer do whatever he wants to do?" he screamed. "Let's all beat him up, so he'll learn how to behave!"

"Stretch up your arms, gang, for the ones who want to fight the giant," someone hollered.

Almost all of the arms went up, and Madsen couldn't make himself heard. The golddiggers jumped on him again, and the fight was in full force.

"The squaw man should learn his lesson," came a voice from the crowd.

It had begun to get dark, but the sky was covered with stars and the moon threw its light over the snow. The sound of the fight prompted all the inhabitants of Candle to come outside. From a safe distance, they looked on while about 50 golddiggers beat on Madsen.

Madsen became an unpleasant surprise for the fighters. He was agile, strong as a bear, and seemed impossible to pull down to the ground. He hit so hard that the men were rolling in the snow all around him. He took on a couple of golddiggers at the same time, and threw them away, but from every corner, new ones came running at him.

Madsen's enormous arms were moving like a Holland windmill, and his hits were heavy. The men in front of him ran to the side, but others came at him from behind, and hit his head for all they were worth. He jumped all over the place to protect his back. Many of the golddiggers got more than they could handle. Some were sitting and crying in the snow with their hands in front of their stomachs. Some were wetting their mistreated bloody faces with water and snow. But there were just too many golddiggers.

Madsen began to breathe heavily. He slowly fell, and sank down on his knees. He fell forward after a heavy hit on his back. His hands and feet were tied, and the men carried him triumphantly into Tex's saloon.

There was a very loud miner's meeting. The men were excited, but the ones who had not taken part in the fight tried to defend Madsen. They had almost started a new uproar over the tied body of Madsen when Kiddy Braine began to talk.

"Listen boys," he said. "Madsen was fighting cleanly with only his fists, you can see that his knife is still in its sheath, and you can't hang him for beating you up. It's best that you swallow your pride and don't give him any more punishment than he deserves. If you hang him, all of Alaska will put a black spot on you as a bunch of bad sports and murderers."

His words calmed the men down. They decided, even so, that anyone would have the right to shoot Madsen as a dog if he showed his face in Candle again, but that was never made into law. Madsen visited Candle many times without anyone trying to shoot him. On the other hand, another verdict was carried out.

Jack Brown ran out after a young tender dwarf birch limb, and he took the branches off to make a switch. The golddiggers lined up to get their revenge. Madsen's pants were pulled down, and everybody had the right to give him one hard lash.

Madsen and the Count were good friends. Georg had bought a whaling boat from the huge Dane once, and thought Madsen was truly a tough man, yet fair. So the Count helped his friend as much as he could by standing by his side during the beating. The Count made sure that no one hit him more than once with the switch.

As soon as the verdict was carried out, the men freed Madsen from the ropes and then they were ready to talk about the stolen provisions. But Madsen had lost his will to talk, and with his back and behind all beaten and bloody, he walked away. The men who stole the provisions did not get away. They were found a week later, and the Eskimos received their provisions back.

Not until morning did Tex get rid of all of his customers, and by that time his saloon was pretty much destroyed. The red painted paper hung in bits off the walls, and the mirror had a large crack in the middle of the glass. One wall of the tent hung down in rags, and blood spots were everywhere. The site of Tex's saloon would have made a civilized cleaning woman go crazy. Tex wasn't sorry, however. All of the furniture had held up, and behind the bar were many full gold bags.

"You're a dear with that goddamn boxing match," Little Tex said to the Count admiringly.

The Count didn't feel like agreeing. "It's the first and the last time I set up a saloon in a newborn mining town," he retorted.

Georg put the reins on his dog team to return to his castle. Candle was quiet and still, and the Count turned his eyes from the houses. The cold air made him feel good. "Mush on, dogs," he shouted. His huskies put their feet deep into the snow, and started the sled moving. They ran so fast that the Count wondered if even they were happy to leave Candle City.

The Count's dog team at Candle on the Seward Peninsula. The team was named "Spawn of Red MacKenzie". The Count often said, "For the best results from your dogs, feed them bacon and rice of good quality, well cooked, and served warm."

Chapter   Fifteen

All-Alaska Sweepstakes with Scotty Allan

"We would that he could speak the lauds that to the golddigger belong--the bravest and the tenderest soul that men can know."

Soon it was Christmas, and the Count planned a big party. Among the crowd were the Eskimo girls Georg's old friend Stewart had gone off with. They had abandoned Stewart after they had eaten enough of his food and come to Candle.

A big Christmas tree stood in the middle of the floor, decorated with flags, candles, and glitter. Charlie Melbourne played the accordion, and the Count spelled him off with music from the gramophone he had bought in Nome.

"When we got tired of dancing," wrote the Count later, "we ate, drank, and played cards. We had plenty of canned turkey, fresh ptarmigan and reindeer meat, and streams of whiskey and champagne. The party went on for a week."

But the Count had serious concerns too, and after the New Year, he and his neighbor Leo Ivano went out to investigate his claims.

"We burned down to the ground or made holes in the ice to drive our drills into the ground. The layers of earth were as I had been told they were in the fall. Under the yellow clay, there was blue clay, and after that we only touched rock. In some places we found gold; but in other places, it was already washed out. Nowhere was there as much gold as I thought there would be."

After a month, the Count returned to his cabin depressed. He didn't know what to do about the claims; they had lost their luster.

In this mood, the Count was ready to make a deal when a lawyer from Nome offered him $150,000 to transfer all his claims to a new company. The Count accepted the offer and went into Nome too. There he looked at his prospects.

He hadn't heard from Grandville Long during the winter, for he preferred to go outside to San Francisco, and he had left his saloon in the hands of a friend named Barter. The saloon did a roaring business, but all on credit. The provisions disappeared as men ate, drank, gambled, and lived it up in Long's saloon, entering their names on Barker's books after they proved they had a claim.

When Long returned in the spring, he found his saloon open but empty. He took legal action against the miners whose names were in his books and took their claims as payment. The miners parted from them without sorrow, for they knew what Long didn't. The claims were worthless. Only part of Candle Creek had gold; the claims farther up the valley and on the slopes had no gold in them. This was how Long's dream ended; he was never to be the lord of Candle Creek.

The Count, meanwhile, met up with Tex Rickard again. Tex had begun to arrange boxing matches in Nome years before he was to become world famous as a promoter, and now he had a business proposition for the Count.

"I hear you sold out at Candle."

"Lock, stock, and barrel."

"Well, then, you ought to have some money put by. Would you like to be a partner in the Monte Carlo?"

Tex's price for a one-third share was $125,000, and he wanted the money to run a sweepstake. The Count knew that the Monte Carlo was Nome's foremost saloon, two stories high, with a bar and gambling hall on the first floor, and a theater for shows upstairs. When he looked it over, he could see that even in winter there were plenty of people in town with money. It was a deal!

The race that Tex was organizing was the first running of the All-Alaska Sweepstakes, the first dog mushing race in the state of Alaska. The trail went from Nome to Candle and then back to Nome. The road was good at this time of year, and the driver could give the dogs their head. The race was to be the founder of a long tradition of dog racing in Alaska, which has culminated in great odysseys like the Iditarod and the Yukon Quest.

The rules in this first race said that you could have as many dogs as you wanted in the team, but that no dogs could be exchanged during the race. To avoid cheating, any dog that died would have to be brought back in on the sled. Dead or alive, every dog that went out with the team had to be there at the end.

It was the craziest race one could think of; the dogs had to be in harnesses day and night. But the prizes were good. The first three prizes were $25,000, $15,000, and $10,000. A telephone line was even put out to Candle to carry news of the race.

The whole town of Nome was out when it started. Among the drivers of the eight teams were Scotty Allan, a Swede named Jansson, and a Norwegian named Kegstad, who drove the team the Count had bought in Candle. The dogs were the most beautiful that had ever run in the snow of Alaska. Most of them were wolf dogs, but the Count's team consisted of Mackenzie dogs. They were reddish in color rather than the usual gray.

The whips cracked and the starting gun went off. There were shouts from the crowd as the dogs moved off, the snow squeaking under the sleds as they picked up speed and disappeared down the trail.

Tex took care of the betting, and he was up to his ears. The bets went higher and higher as the days passed. Finally it reached such proportions that bickering broke out among those who ran the gambling tables. Their places were deserted. Not a soul was thinking of roulette or faro as long as the race was going on.

The Count did the same as everyone else, betting as much as he could. Scotty Allan was leading in Candle, with Kegstad two hours behind. There was a chance the tough Norwegian would pass Allan soon, and that was how the Count placed his bets. Just to be safe he put some on Allan, too.

The atmosphere in Nome was tense. The bettors paced back and forth in the snow trying to keep warm, cursing the cold and looking down the trail as the hours ticked by.

Finally a black dot appeared far away. It was a gambler named Tom Higgins who had gone out on the trail to make a report. The crowd was silent as he came in with his team.

"Scotty Allan is first," he screamed as he drove by. "Scotty Allan!"

People were cheering and spitting. The cigar stumps went up and down at the corners of their mouths, and calloused hands squeezed the dollar bills.

Another dot appeared on the horizon. The binoculars came out. The dogs were gray. It was Allan. The team was approaching the finish with the breath of the dogs hanging like a white cloud over them.

Shots were fired. Scotty Allan raised his whip, and the tired dogs went faster. Then they crossed the finish line and the crowd went wild, cheering, and screaming, and shooting. People poured over Allan, passing him drinks and helping him untie the dogs. Their fur was full of ice; their eyes were bloodshot and wild; and they limped on their sore paws. The race had taken him only 72 hours. He had let the dogs rest only one hour at night. No wonder the man and his dogs were dead tired at the end.

Three more hours passed, and then Kegstad came in, a solid second. Then the party began, and when everything was settled up, the Count had won $3,000.

With the first All-Alaska Sweepstakes over, business picked up again in the gambling halls. The cash intake at the Monte Carlo was good, but the Count soon knew this was not the life for him.

"As I stood there I watched good-looking young men gamble away their last cent," the Count wrote later. "I knew how they felt. I had done it myself. Now I was one of those taking home the profit from the green tables. The more they lost, the better for me. I couldn't stand it. My attitude was naive in business, I suppose, but that was the way it was. Gamble! Oh, yes! Take a chance, sure! But in the back of my mind I always thought I would earn my own money, not live on the losses of others."

The Count knew a young man named Jack Heart who seemed like he would never fall prey to the roulette wheel. One of the Count's best friends in Georg's first year in Nome, Jack often sat alone in a small log cabin. The Count would often go and visit Jack.

When the Count came calling, Jack would put away his writing things, as he wrote a lot of letters, and sit and talk with Georg until his roommate came home.

Jack was in love with a housemaid down in San Francisco. He showed the Count a picture of her, and the Count could see that she was a beautiful girl. Jack told the Count about his love story very openly.

Jack came from San Francisco where he had been working as a grocery store helper. He was unusually tall, and so thin that the men often joked with him about rattling bones. His hair and eyelashes were almost pure white in color, and his upper teeth shot out between his lips, which gave his face a sheep-like appearance. He was attractive in an ugly way that made people laugh when they saw him for the first time.

Jack was poor, ugly and thin. His parents were dead, and he had no brothers or sisters; they too were dead. His family was at least used to his homely looks, and they were gone.

People smiled scornfully at Jack as he walked down the street in his suit. The sleeves ended halfway down his arms at the elbow, and his legs went beyond his bottom trouser cuffs. His salary was only five dollars a week, and paydays were the high points of his life. On those days he would buy an ice-cream cone and put away twenty-five cents.

One day a young girl named Madge Hopkins came into the grocery store where he worked. She had golden curly hair, beautiful blue eyes and smiled nicely at him as she asked Jack for a can of tomatoes. The first visit was followed by another, and Jack eventually found out that she was working for a local family and that she had recently arrived to San Francisco from the country and that she had no friends in the city. His heart jumped every time she walked into the store. Finally, one day, he got his courage up and stammered out a confused question to her about going to the circus together.

Madge accepted the invitation. Jack walked around all day with a happy smile. He sold salt instead of sugar, dropped dozens of eggs on the floor, and gave ten-cent candies to kids who were buying five-centers.

That evening finally arrived. Jack hurried to the meeting place where he walked around sweating in anticipation and pulling on his sleeves until Madge showed up. That evening became a turning point in his life.

Jack and Madge saw each other often after that night. Jack took out his savings and went to a tailor. For the first time, Jack had a suit that fit him. One day, Madge asked Jack when they were going to get married. She buried her face in his breast and cried out that he was going to be a father. Jack patted her golden hair and tried to think for all three of them.

It would be five or six years before Jack had a salary that would support a wife and children. Jack became very sad, and a longing to get rich quick came over him.

Jack married Madge, but his forehead was wrinkled in thought as the priest made their love official. After the ceremony, Madge went home to her mother and father who had a small ranch a few miles from the city. The newspapers were full of articles about the gold findings in the Klondike and Jack decided to go there. He wouldn't need more than about half a year to be rich up there, he thought. The newspapers said that the river valley in the Klondike were glimmering with gold, like the golden rooms in fairy tales.

Jack wrote to an aunt in Chicago, and asked if he could borrow $1,000 for the trip and supplies. After a while the money came. Madge traveled to the city to say goodbye to her husband. She stood with tears in her eyes, waving when the steamer with Jack on board left the San Francisco pier and started on the long journey north. Madge had promised to wait for Jack forever, and he had told her that he would dig up a pile of gold and that their child would have a beautiful rattle with gold nuggets in it.

Things didn't go exactly as Jack had thought. He was used to the sunny climate in California. He started to sneeze and cough on his trip north, and when the steamer passed Unalaska, with the fog in the Bering Sea, it almost ended life for him. In St. Michael at Norton Sound, Jack became ill with pneumonia for almost a whole month. When he was finally up and around again, he found it was too late to go to the Klondike that year.

Jack had to stay in St. Michael over the entire winter. He wrote a calming letter to Madge, and took a job as a woodcutter for the Alaska Commercial Company.

It was hard work, and Jack had a tough time of it, but after a while his body got used to the heavy work. He became stronger, and he could soon swing the axe with the same speed and strength as his new friends. He also became a good fighter, and answered with his fists when people made jokes about his white hair. Most of his salary he sent to Madge, and he did not spend one penny unnecessarily.

One day Jafet Lindeberg came to St. Michael with a heavy bag of gold. The gold had been found at Snake River on the Seward Peninsula, north of Norton Sound. The place was later called Nome.

Jack quickly left his work and went with a Canadian named Jim Pelter, who had a dog team, and they managed to be among the first to Nome.

Pelter and Jack made gold claims in a valley that was later given the name Bourbon Creek. They built a snug log cabin down at the beach. Around their cabin grew eventually the city of Nome.

The lucky pair had great gold claims. During the early summer, they took up close to $100,000 from them. The gold they deposited in different saloons and gambling houses, as the city was dangerous. Jack sent several thousand dollars to his wife Madge and told her about his good fortune. He planned to make $50,000 more and then go home. Pelter and Jack had 50 men working on their claim, so Jack was optimistic about making that much more money.

One day as Jack was carrying a bag of gold from the claim, the bag broke and the gold ran out on the ground. He then took off his mukluks and poured the gold into them. After that, he walked barefooted to the Northern Saloon, where he deposited the gold.

"You must be a real rich bastard who has so much gold that you have to carry it in your mukluks," giggled Diamond Hady. "Let me buy you a drink, Mukluk Jack, and then your feet will get hot!"

Jack's toes were cold. He had been walking in the mud on the tundra. In the summer the ground melts a couple of feet down, but beyond that it is frozen permanently. Jack took the drink that Hady gave him, and quickly swept it down his throat. Hady filled his glass again and he emptied it one more time. Then she helped him wash the mud off of his legs.

"I hope you'll buy me a bottle of champagne for all this trouble," she giggled as she waved to one of the waiters.

"You're sitting home in your little log cabin all the time alone, and you get sour. It can't be good for you, boy!"

Jack wasn't used to strong drinks, and he had never before tasted whiskey. He liked lemonade better, and always carried a little bag with candies with him. The two drinks made him rather intoxicated, and Hady enticed him to drink several glasses of apple wine after that. He became drunk for the first time.

"Oh, boy, how lucky I feel," he said. "Whiskey isn't bad at all once you get it down. Hello, there, bring over more drinks!"

Diamond Hady arranged so that the waiter left the whiskey bottle on the table, and with an experienced hand, she filled up Jack's glass every time he emptied it.

The whiskey in Alaska wasn't of the best kind, and contained manyother ingredients besides alcohol or water. Booze or hutch, they usually called the fluid, and it worked in many different ways, but every way got one drunk. From some of it, you got nervous and angry. Sometimes you would feel tired and lazy, and some of it you just died from.

Once in Iditarod, the Count saw a man die after three drinks. He fell down to the ground, foaming from the mouth, then he kicked for a short time, then died suddenly. The Count had heard that they made spirits from old rubber boots, galoshes, and old clothes.

Of course, Jack was drinking a much better concoction. For a couple of hours, he sat with Diamond Hady, lolling about. Later Hady suggested that they play roulette.

"Sure, and why not," hiccupped Jack. "Come on, sweetie! Boy, oh, boy, I am so happy!"

They both went up to the roulette table, after having fetched one gold bag each from Tex Rickard's safe. Jack bet and lost, and won and lost. He became excited, putting down bigger and bigger bets. Finally, he didn't have any more gold to pick up from the safe.

Diamond Hady started to take care of other customers. Angry over his bad luck, Jack left to go home. He passed the Barrel House, where he also had gold deposited. Impulsively, he turned and went in. He was sure that he would win his money back. His bad luck couldn't continue forever.

"Hello, Jack," said Gus Seifers, the owner of the saloon. "It's nice to see you here. Do you want a drink?"

Jack swept down a glass and asked for one of his gold bags. Seifers himself was the dealer of a card game, and Jack did not want to appear stingy. He lost all of his deposits of gold at Seifers' saloon. He was broke!

Jack left the Barrel House and went straight to the Eldorado Saloon. He gambled away all the gold he had there, and then went to the Second Class Saloon. Before the morning came, Jack had lost close to $70,000. All he had left from that night was the nickname Mukluk. He was broke!

In those days in Nome, there were many who gambled big, and nobody noticed a person's big losses in the different saloons. Jack slept a couple of hours on a bench in the Nevada Saloon, then went to work as if nothing had happened. Pelter thought that his friend was unusually angry and sour, but he did not ask why.

Tex Rickard at the Northern Saloon, Swede Sam at the Eldorado Saloon, Dick Dawson at the Second Class, Gus Siefers at the Barrel House and Klondike John at the Nevada all knew that Jack had finished all his gold that they had been saving for him, but they did not tell each other about it.

Jack was still considered a rich man. He went back to his little bag of candy and the lemonade, and worked hard to get together a new fortune.

Maja Kry, born in Sweden, arrived in Nome in the early 1920s and became the richest woman in Nome. She owned mining claims, fur stores, and built the Polaris Hotel, the largest in Nome. She died at the age of 89.

Chapter   Sixteen

Mukluk Jack

"Where sultry sun beats down --where shining icefields gleam --where pathless forests reign--where languid islands dream; mankind stands at salute wherever thought has birth."

Some time after Mukluk Jack's gambling, his and Pelter's gold mine at Bourbon Creek began to dry up. There was lots of gold on the top of the claim, but further down in the ground, there was only rocks and mud, like many claims. The men made some very exact measurements, and came to the conclusion that it was best to sell the mine while they could still get a couple of thousand dollars for them. An inexperienced golddigger bought the whole thing for $10,000. The workers' salaries came to about the same amount, and when Mukluk Jack counted up his money, he had only about $5,000 left.

Sadly, he sat in his log cabin, wondering what he was going to do. Madge knew that he had dug up around $50,000 from his mines, and she had written in a letter that that money was plenty for them and he should come home right away. Their boy was now big and clever, but he wondered how his daddy looked, she said.

Jack wrote letter after letter and explained tearfully how he had gambled all his money away. But he never dared to mail any of the letters. Fall came, and Jack bought a new dog team and set out away from Nome.

''I'm going down to Kuskokwim to prospect,'' he told the Count and his other friends. "I won't give up until I become a millionaire."

The men wished Jack luck on his trip. He gave out candies from his supply, joking and happy. For two months he was gone, and the men had almost forgotten about him when he returned around Christmastime. He drove fast through the main street of Nome with his dog team, stopped outside the Northern Saloon, hurried in and screamed for whiskey.

The golddiggers looked at him curiously, as Jack was not known for drinking. They started to gather around him, wondering if he had found any new gold fields. But Mukluk Jack did not answer their questions.

"Bottoms up, you guys! Drink, and I'll pay," he said, and threw a bag of gold on the counter. "Where's Tex? I want to talk to him."

Jack took Tex Rickard under the arm and led him into one of the side rooms.

"I've found lots of gold in a valley toward Kuskokwim," Jack whispered. "Do you want to be in on it? Look here."

He pulled out a couple of handfuls of gold and threw them on the table. Tex examined the rough clean corns. That kind of gold he had never seen before. It was darker than the Nome gold.

"Where have you found that?"

Mukluk shook his shoulders. "For $5,000 I'll make you a gold claim down there," he said. "I'm going to call the valley Flat Creek, but I don't want any gold rush there. Not yet. In the spring I'll let you know where the valley is. Is that all right with you?"

"Well," said Tex Rickard, a little surprised. "do you have to be so secretive? You know I won't say anything."

"Sure, but I want to keep this to myself for a while longer. If it gets out, several thousand golddiggers will rush down there, and there'll only be a bunch of trouble. I'm going to take care of all the gold claims in the valley, and I only intend to let some of my friends in. There's always someone who gossips and tells. If you don't want to be in on it you don't have to."

Tex did not think any longer. Mukluk Jack was a good, careful and well-liked man. Tex had no reason to mistrust him. Tex went with Mukluk Jack to a lawyer and wrote out a notary that Jack owned the right to make a gold claim at Flat Creek and Kuskokwim in his name, and then Jack got $5,000 from him.

Dick Dawson, Klondike Johnson, Swede Sam, Gus Siefers, Louis Hunter, George Hub, Huey Madden and Charlie Peters, all saloon owners and gambling house hosts, had a visit the same day from Mukluk Jack, and he gave them the same offer as he had given Tex Rickard. None of the men said no; they all gave him their authority and $5,000 each.

The Count happened to be there when Jack went to Huey Madden's saloon. The Count could see how Jack pulled at the owner's sleeve and whispered something in his ear. When Mukluk Jack had talked to Madden in a side room, and was going to leave the saloon, the Count stopped him.

"What is going on?" Georg asked. "Are you in such a hurry that you can't even shake hands?"

Madden came up to the men and turned toward Mukluk Jack. "Let the Count in, too," he said. "You know he's a good friend."

"Oh, sure," answered Jack. But he looked a little discomforted.

They went into Madden's office. The Count looked carefully at the new gold and saw that it was a new kind. As he trusted Jack completely, he immediately gave him his authority and $5,000. The Count kept a few of the gold coins as proof.

With the $50,000, Jack left the following day. Tex Rickard sent two men to follow Jack's tracks to see where he was going, but a storm came up and wiped out the tracks.

The story was out, and the *Nome Nugget* newspaper had an article in it talking about a new big gold find in the Kuskokwim area. Several well-know people were already in on it, the paper said, and had claims in the new rich find.

One day a thick letter came from Jack, addressed to Tex Rickard, but written to all of the investors. It contained maps and descriptions of all the claims. Everything was very neat.

The group sent a man down to the area to investigate the claims, but he returned with bad news.

"There is no gold in the valley," he said. "Mukluk Jack has fooled you. He has made gold claims, all right, but there is no gold."

"That's a weird thing," muttered Tex Rickard. "I can't understand why he would want to fool us. He has gold deposited in the saloons here, so we can easily get our money back. How much is it he has with you, Madden?"

"Well, he deposited $15,000 with me, but that he gambled away one night, when he strangely enough was drunk," answered Madden, "so in my place he has no more gold. But I think Klondike Jack has a couple of thousand."

"The hell I have!" said Klondike. "He gambled that away, too!"

The men soon found out that Jack had gambled away every gold corn he had deposited with them.

"Well," said Tex. "he lost more than he stole, so we're not losing too much on him," and with those words it was all forgotten.

The gold was running in floods to the saloon owners' pockets in those days, and a few thousand dollars they felt was nothing to make trouble about. Things changed quickly, but in those days gamblings were high.

Georg never thought he would see Mukluk Jack again, but about ten years later he did. It was in San Francisco.

"Hello, Count," a man said.

The Count looked at the man, but could not remember him. He had dark hair and was very elegantly dressed.

"Have you forgotten me?" he laughed. "Don't you remember Mukluk Jack?"

It was really him. His hair was colored, but otherwise Jack looked the same. Jack wrote the Count a check for the $5,000, and explained the scam.

"It was never my idea to fool you too, but I was afraid that the others would be suspicious if I had said no to you. We were such good friends that it would have looked strange. I hope you understand that."

The two went out to Jack's beautiful home in Oakland. He asked the Count not to say anything to his wife about the story, because she thought that the money he had when he returned was from his mines.

Mukluk Jack had a nice home, indeed. His wife made a good dinner, preceded by some elegant cocktails, but Jack did not take anything. It was instead Madge who said, "Skoal," to the Count.

"Jack never takes spirits," she smiled. "You wouldn't believe how good and careful he is. He sticks to ice cream, candies and cakes, and drinks lemonade when he has a party."

Jack and the Count looked at each other.

"Sure," the Count said. "He was the neatest golddigger in the whole area of Nome when he was up there. You never saw him sitting in the saloons drinking. He was sitting at home alone in his little log cabin all the time, writing to you instead."

Jack's face became red, but Madge beamed with love and happiness.

Nome in 1900. (Photo-Carrie McLain Museum, McLain Archive of Photographic Materials, Nome, AK

Chapter Seventeen

Looking for New Gold Fields

"Reward is his, exceeding great, well won."

Finally Georg became more and more restless. He decided to let Tex and the others take care of his interest in the saloon and got his dog team ready. Spring was now at an end, and the Count was ready to travel north again.

When the Count got back to Candle he checked on his old friends. Two of them, Wallin and Vogel, were living in his castle, and he gave them its contents, including the gramophone. Then he made plans with his neighbor Leo Ivano, an Italian sea captain who had been living outside Candle City with a young man they called Rip Jack that winter. The Count always maintained that Rip Jack was in fact the novelist Jack London, but he wasn't writing that winter.

Before he left for Nome, the Count had often talked with Ivano about sailing the barge that was frozen into the lake at Candle City around the north coast of Alaska to look for new gold fields. He was convinced from his experiences at Nome and Candle that there were certain rock formations that meant that gold would be found on nearby gravel beaches. Moreover, the captain of a whaler had told him the nuggets could be found on the beaches of the high Arctic.

But the Count was restless for another reason too. People were teasing him about the bad deal he had made on his claims. The company that took them over had hit a vein and were taking out millions.

So he and Ivano got the barge ready, put up their tents at Deering, and relaxed in the company of the Eskimo girls while they waited for the ice to go out. It was the last relaxation the Count was to have for quite a while.

Chapter Eighteen

Shipwreck and Return

"The silence of gloom is merciful . . . but the bright White Silence, clear and cold, under the steely skies is pitiless."

When the drift ice finally began to move out, the Count and Ivano got over the Kiwalik River with the help of Eskimos, raised their sails, and went down to Deering to take on a load of provisions. They bought enough for a year and set sail for the north without giving anyone any indication of their plans. The ice was moving slowly and they had to maneuver carefully along the barren coast to stay clear of ice floes.

They passed some small groups of Eskimo hunters as they traveled north, but they did not put in to shore very often. One landing they made was south of Cape Krusenstern on Chamisso Island.

The author on Chamisso Island in 1990

"When we reached the island, I went up to the highest point with my binoculars to find out how far the ice had gone. To my surprise I found an old Swedish copper pot with a broken handle. I thought it would come in handy, and when I picked it up, I noticed a piece of paper underneath it. The paper had been stuck in the ground with a wooden fork and on the back of it was written, 'North East Passage Passed on August 16, 1879. Nordensköld. Palander. The Frigate Vega.'"

The Count carefully put the evidence of these earlier Swedish voyagers back as he had found it and returned to tell his partner about his discovery. Later, his son, Charles af Forselles, returned to the island and brought the copper pot to a museum.

The Count and his friend continued on their way to Point Hope, shooting polar bears which they found to be easy game, but avoiding the walrus.

The walrus were lying on the ice floes basking in the sun. The females looked like giant women, sitting with their babies in their arms. If they are aggravated, they can attack and try to get their tusks through the boat. That's why the Eskimos sneak up on them from land or from ice floes with their harpoons.

The missionary at Point Hope invited the Count and Ivano to stay, but they were eager to press on in their hunt for gold. Now they left behind the slate belts that reveal gold and passed mountains of sandstone and blue granite on their way to Cape Lisburne. Then they went up the Pitmeaga River. There the tundra was difficult to get over, but they could see oil on the surface of water puddles and knew that there was oil under the tundra. On the beach where they had left the barge, coal lay about, and they used it for fuel.

Eventually they reached the location where the whaler had said gold nuggets were to be found, the Kukpowruk River. They went up the river in the two skin boats they had taken along.

Soon the Count understood that the sea people had made up the whole story for the naive captain. There was no trace of gold formations, and the diggings at the beach revealed no gold.

The mountain peaks a couple of miles inland were remarkably steep, but one looked as if its top had been cut off. As the men walked down to the valley below us, Georg could see what had happened. A meteor "perhaps a hundred yards across" had hit it before drilling itself into the valley. Georg found a few fragments, but the metal was so hard that it scratched his axe hammer. He took samples of it and of the rock formations, so they could be analyzed later.

On the way up, the men saw a strange colossus leaning on a sand bank, and on their return they took a closer look. It was the skeleton of a mammoth about twenty feet long and fifteen feet high. One of its tusks had broken off. It was at least twelve feet long and thick as a log. Georg had seen relics of large animals at Kotzebue Sound before, but he had never seen a complete skeleton. It was a remarkable find, but there was no way the men could take it with them, not even the head, so they had to be satisfied with a couple of vertebrae.

By this time the men were discouraged about their chances for finding gold, but they decided to press on around Point Barrow and east to the Mackenzie River. If the fall storms hit before they got there, they would aim for the whaling station at Herschel Island and winter there with plenty of companions.

At Icy Cape they passed some time with an Eskimo group that had made camp there. The Count passed out the religious postcards that Missionary Foster had pressed on him in Candle when he said he was going north, and his attempts to preach about Jesus' journey to heaven amused his friend Ivano greatly.

''I had a ruby ring on my finger that the chief had his eyes on,'' the Count records. "I had bought it in Seattle, and I wasn't interested in trading, but he was stubborn and kept trying to lure me with one thing and another. Finally he dragged out a magnificent parka, made from thirteen black foxes, with all the tails dangling around the hood. I couldn't resist any longer. The ring and the parka changed owners.''

The chief also tried to convince Georg to stay in the village. The explanation was simple. The Count owned a 17-ton barge, and the chief thought if Georg stayed, they wouldn't have to trade their tusks and furs in Point Barrow any more. They would be able to go directly down to the States and make a better deal. His plan showed good judgment, but Georg didn't want to settle on the coast.

The Count was interested, however, in the Eskimo way of life and learned a good deal about their methods of hunting and fishing and preserving meat, birds' eggs, and berries for the winter and the potlatch parties they had with other tribes in the fall, gatherings where the people sang and danced and ate delicacies for weeks.

He found that a good meal could be made out of the berry and egg mixture that had been preserved in a pit in seal or walrus oil. "You dipped sun-dried salmon in the oil and ate the berries with it. The taste of the berries was not less good for having been in the oil. On the contrary, I thought it was a delicacy compared to the way we sweeten them.''

He also noted the devastation tuberculosis had caused among them. "You didn't see it so much in the young, but the older ones were lying everywhere coughing and spitting. When someone was very ill, they called the medicine man, and he went into the hut beating on his drum, waving his knife in the air, and yelling to chase out the bad ghost who had made the person sick.''

After they left the Eskimos at Icy Cape, they went on to Point Barrow, the most northern point in Alaska. By this time the sky and the water were gray, and it was getting cooler. There didn't seem to be anything living on the flat deserted plateau that stretched as far as they could see, and they didn't land again until they reached the trading station.

The missionary who headed the station told them right away that there was no gold to be found, but by that time they were prepared for that. He also warned them about the shallow waters to the east and told them to keep as far away from the coast as they could without losing sight of it.

Four days further into their journey, the wind turned against them, and they had to go further out to sea. They also had to ration their drinking water as ten more days passed. Then it ran out and they had to drink their condensed milk. Finally they were closing in on Herschel Island when the winds got stronger and blew more northerly.

''It made the sea absolutely wild, and waves were slapping over our heads.,'' the Count wrote later. ''It was now unthinkable to try to seek shelter on the coast. We had left the plateau behind, and now there was only a steep, dark, rocky coastline before us. We turned the barge around and tried to sail against the wind to reach Herschel Island.

''But waves as tall as houses came over us, and we could see that we were drifting towards the coast. We tried to hold the wind, but the waves forced us closer and closer to the shore. I was sure we would perish.

''Then for a moment I thought we were saved. Out to sea I saw a whaler that had noticed our dangerous situation and was trying to come in closer. It fought the waves for a while and then signalled that they were unable to help.''

The barge continued to drift, and eventually the Count saw a small sandy beach along the coast. If they could beach there, they had some hope.

In a flash the Count made some preparations for landing. His Winchester was tied to the tiller. He took his raincoat off and put his gunbelt on. They would need a weapon and ammunition if they did make it to the unknown beach.

Then the barge turned, the big sail flew out, and they headed for the beach. A huge wave suddenly lifted the barge higher, then they were down in its valley. A new white wave rose in front of the men and sucked them out again.

"In my ears music roared, and it felt like one big hand was pulling my hair while another tore at my legs. Then everything went black," he wrote.

When the Count woke up, the storm had died down somewhat and the sun was trying to shine. At first he felt paralyzed despite the pain he could feel, and he wondered if he was going to freeze to death on the Arctic shore.

Eventually, however, he found he could move his right arm, and he slowly turned over on his stomach. After a few shaky attempts, he managed to get to his feet.

"The inside of the pants we Northland travelers always wore had a pocket where we kept a knife and a package of Chinese sulfur matches in case we got stranded in the wilderness. I even had the matches inside cartridge cases to be sure they were kept dry. But this time they were damp anyway, and I had to forget about making a fire from the grass that grew close by."

It was a long, chilly night as the Count ran up and down the shore to keep warm, wondering what had happened to Leo. It was too dark to search for him, and there were no Eskimo fires anywhere in sight.

In the morning Georg found some dried apples and a side of pork, all that was left of the provisions among the debris. He ate some raw bacon and then walked on.

He found Leo between some sharp rocks. The Count's throat began to swell when he saw his partner, stone dead and terribly cut and swollen. Georg rolled him further up the beach, but he had no strength to dig.

He threw sand over Leo's body and buried him in this fashion. Then the Count said a prayer that his soul had it better than his poor body and left sadly.

Aching from his injuries, the Count nevertheless decided he had no choice but to follow the river running out on the lonely beach. If it was the Firth, as he assumed, then it would lead him to the Porcupine and eventually to the Yukon, and he would be able to make his way back across Alaska to the coast. He packed up the food he had salvaged, dried out his matches, and set out with his gun and the remaining fourteen cartridges.

He soon encountered an attacking grizzly, and the meat was a welcome addition to his meager supplies. Roasting it over a bush fire gave him hope that he would survive the trip. But fall was approaching, and he knew he had to be far away by the time it came.

"It was the longest march I ever made. I was still sore and in bad shape, so I could never walk more than twenty miles a day, more often only ten or fifteen. I was now close to the Brooks Range, a mountain chain that stretches across Alaska. It was full of bears, and you had to be on the alert. The bears were more interested in me than I was in them; I tried to keep out of their way. It seemed the 'hunt' was mainly for their amusement.''

The Count slept under the open sky, often close to the river. Sometimes he gathered dry grass to sleep on, but most of the time, he was too tired and just slept on the damp ground rolled up in a ball to keep warm.

As Georg hiked through the rugged, treeless land, he also saw mountain goats up on the ledges. But they were shy, and he never got close to them. Nor did he hunt the muskrats in the water; there were plenty of them, but their meat tasted stale.

The Count's plan was to follow the low mountains beside the river in a southerly direction. When he got to the Porcupine River, he would build a raft of some sort and float down it as far as possible. But after three weeks he was lost. Fortunately, he met a group of Kutchin Indians who told him he was on the Chandalar River.

The Indians knew without any explanation that Georg had had a hard time. His face was still covered with scratches, scars, and open sores. He had no coat and his shirt and pants were in rags. Georg's boots were in shreds, the bottoms completely gone. The Indians gave him some moose hide straps to tie around the top leather, so that he had something to walk on.

The Count rested with them for two days while they deliberated on how they could help him. Then they gave him a canoe and a supply of dry fish. With the remainder of his bear meat, he felt well equipped as he set off. Now there were trees and the weather was better, but the Count had no time to appreciate the scenery.

The trip went more slowly than he hoped since he had to portage over many rapids in the river. It took him a full two weeks to reach the broad Yukon River, and it was with great relief that he paddled up it to Fort Yukon.

Tommy Forrest, whom the Count knew from Nome, was the first person he met when he stepped ashore at Fort Yukon. He couldn't believe his eyes as he stared at a man in rags saying hello to him. After a closer look, he recognized Georg. Then he took the destitute Swede to the closest saloon, ordered up a large glass of whiskey, and demanded to know about the Count's adventures.

As the story unfolded, Forrest became more and more amazed, interrupting again and again to say, "Are you serious? You must be crazy, gold mines in Candle, the Monte Carlo in Nome. What the hell were you doing in the Arctic Ocean?" The men had a good evening together, and best of all, Tommy owed the Count some money, which he paid on the spot. The

Count then had enough for new clothes and a ticket down the river to St. Michael.

By this time the golden days of the Klondike were over, and the steamer Margrethe was one of the few boats still navigating the Yukon River. It was the Count's first ride down the river, and he enjoyed the leisurely ten-day trip, especially since the Swedish captain, who knew his old companion from Balto Creek, Captain Jorgenson, made sure he had a good time.

At St. Michael, he boarded the steamer Ohio headed for Nome. There Georg was hit with bad news.

The green tables had not prospered during the summer. The Northern Saloon was closed, and the bar was now managed by John Murphy. The other partners in the Monte Carlo had disappeared. Tex Rickard had left for South Africa to dig for diamonds. The Monte Carlo, the most famous saloon in Nome, had gone broke and was now closed and deserted. The Count was again in Nome with two empty pockets.

Chapter Nineteen

Fairbanks

"The men of the camps and trails unbent, and jest and song and tales of past adventure went round the board."

Not only was the Count broke, everyone in Nome had thought he was dead. His obituary had been printed in the local papers after the whaler who had tried to save the pair on the barge had reported the shipwreck. He had learned in Point Barrow that the Swedish Count was one of the two aboard.

In the circumstances, the Count wasn't surprised that his partners in the Monte Carlo had split everything that was left when the saloon closed and forgot completely about Georg. He had no relatives in the country. He did get a couple of thousand from John Murphy, the only one left, and Georg lived in the following days by cashing in on debts. He had plenty of these. The big debtors tried to ignore him. The Count saw no sign of. Little Tex, for instance, who owed him $7,000 for food, whiskey, and buildings from their joint venture in the saloon business. The small debtors understood, however, and tried to pay back as much as they could.

The Cooper brothers' cabin had disappeared in the storm, and Frank McWellen had sold the one the Count had built. But Georg found a home for the winter in Joe Kennedy's cabin and bought a supply of food. There wasn't much mining going on around Nome except up in the mountains. The Count's old bench claim, Anvil Creek 2, had been turned into a huge tunnel after a large gold-bearing vein had been discovered and almost two million dollars worth of gold had been taken out of it. Other gold strikes like this in the North were made at Circle City in 1893, and at Dawson and Rampart in 1896.

In the new year, rumors came down from Yukon that a new gold field had been discovered at Fairbanks. Some people in Nome were excited and got their dog teams ready, but many others were skeptical. There had been so many rushes in the last few years to places where no gold was to be found, that they thought this one might be a false claim too.

In fact, however, a strike had been made on July 22, 1902, by an Italian named Felix Pedro, who had spent four years feverishly searching for "Lost Creek," a gold-bearing little creek he and a partner had located and marked with an upside down boat in 1898. . . . and then lost! The thought of the lost treasure burned in his mind and he dug and washed every day that he could until he hit a vein that he named Pedro Creek, north of the Chena River.

But the Count was tired of inactivity, so he bought a team of huskies and a sled. An old friend, Billy Taylor, asked if he could come along, and they outfitted themselves with a tent, sleeping bags, and food before they left Nome at the beginning of March 1903.

At first, all went well. The trail was in good condition because it was regularly used for the postal service. They planned to drive over Norton Sound to Unalakleet and then to Kaltag after they left the postal trail.

But soon Billy was sick. The Count knew he couldn't take him with him up the Yukon or leave him either. So he drove him down to the garrison hospital at St. Michael and left money for him to leave with the first boat. Then he proceeded back to the trail they had planned to take.

When he reached the Indians' winter camp at Nulato, he rested his dogs for a day and bought more food. Though it was March, it was very cold and the dogs were suffering. They had plenty to eat, rice and dried salmon mixed with bear and moose fat. One died, and the Count rested the others for another two days before he continued up to Fort Gibbon and then east along the Tanana River. Miners who had preceded him had made the trail easy to follow, and he reached the new town of Fairbanks at the end of April.

"A tent city had mushroomed," the Count said. "I put up my tent, chained the dogs, and started to look around. There were a lot of people from the interior of the country " Circle, Fortymile, and Dawson. There were saloons everywhere, and many more were being built. Gambling was now illegal in Nome, but there was plenty of it here."

During his stroll, the Count ran into Tommy Forrest again. He had started a saloon, and charged high prices as everyone did in all the new gold areas. A small glass of whiskey was a dollar, and a bottle of beer cost five.

He also ran into Dave Petre from Lummelunda, a big, fat friendly Swede who had married an equally big Indian woman and started a tent saloon. He had a great business trick that he practiced with success. He always had only one bottle of whiskey on the counter, and the customers raced to empty it. Then he would produce another one. It became a sport to finish his supply, and it was a standing expression to say, "Shall we go down to Dave's and drink his last bottle of whiskey?"

One night at Dave's the Count met a miner named Ford who didn't know much about claims but had $25,000 he was willing to bet if the Count could find a claim. They struck a deal and set out for the gold fields twenty-five miles out of town early in May. Now that the snow was melting, the dogs were of no use, and the Count left them at Dave's.

Soon after they reached Fairbanks Creek, they were offered work by the foreman of Number 7 mine, but they were determined to find their own claim. The Count located a possibility, but Ford didn't think much of it and then he questioned the legality of a contract written in pencil. While he went back to Fairbanks to consult a lawyer, the Count struck up a friendship with a shaky alcoholic named Jack Welsh who sent him off to buy two bottles of whiskey.

The gold pouch he gave Georg must have had $3,000 in it. They treated gold the same way here as had the men at Nome, giving a full pouch to a stranger and telling him to take what he wanted.

When he returned and started to drink with his new friend, the foreman soon showed up and told him it was illegal to buy whiskey for a "siwash," an expression of contempt for the Indians. Jack took offense, and he and the foreman were soon in a fight.

As it turned out, Jack Welsh had tenant's rights on the claim, so he fired the foreman and hired the Count as his replacement at a hundred dollars a day plus food. The Count had his own ideas for improvements to the methods used for washing the gold, and things worked well except for his problems with men who didn't want to work for a Swede and with the cook.

The Count knew their aversion to Swedes. Jack London had tried to give him an explanation when they were all in Candle. He said he knew the Irish mentality and that they learned to hate Swedes in school for religious reasons. They were told that it was Swedes who had put the first bombs under a Catholic church during the Thirty Years' War.

Welsh replaced the Irishmen, and that caused the problem with the cook, Mrs. Gillroy. She thought an injustice had been done, but she didn't want to leave her own job because she had a young son. She was a Londoner who had come to Alaska in desperation trying to find a way to look after a sick husband. Now she was saving every cent to return to him. The Count used the boy to get around her.

"He looked at me as if I were the devil, but he was interested in the gold too. I found him washing for gold on the beach, and occasionally he found a small nugget left behind when they had been using grooves that were too short," the Count wrote.

"I gave him a real gold pan and took him to the potato crates that were filled with black sand and magnetic iron from the old grooves. The previous foreman had not bothered to worry about the gold in the bottom layer. The boy's eyes shone when he saw how much was in the first pan he washed. I told him he could keep what he found, and from that day on the food was much better."

Soon enough the summer was over, and the order came to put the fires out under the boilers. The men all went down to Fairbanks, where they were paid off at Dave's saloon. Now it was no longer in a tent.

Dave from Lummelunda had become a fine man and built a two-story saloon with a dancing palace and girls, a room for card players too, he didn't want to hear of roulette, a first class bar, and a bank for gold deposits. There was no more talk of the last bottle of whiskey at Dave's.

The Count had to find a place to spend the winter in Fairbanks. His friend Billy Taylor had shown up as well as Laddy Goldspring, and they built a cabin with a basement at the edge of the woods. The other two were broke, so the Count had to buy the kitchen utensils and the eight tons of food they would need for the winter. Then he nailed up the house rules.

They assumed guests would arrive, and they were welcome, but they had to follow their laws. In the first paragraph the Count let them know that he would be going out on discoveries during the winter and would not be doing any household work. He didn't think it was too much to ask when he was feeding the whole gang.

No one could stay in bed after eight o'clock in the morning. The daily work was split up. One cooked and brought water, one chopped wood, one hunted for small game, and so forth. Every chore lasted for a week at a time. It was very effective. It wasn't very long before there were seven men in the cabin, and by spring there were eleven.

The men talked about mining and told stories. They visited the saloon and played cards. Often there were disputes about the chores, but not about the cooking. The law said that anyone who complained had to take over. So compliments were plentiful. Even burnt porridge was said to taste like honey. The men had good food too, though, especially stews made of rabbits and ptarmigan.

Serious crime was rare, but that winter Fairbanks had a murder. The Count had never met the victim, a Dalmatian named Slescovitch who dried fish for a living and lived like a hermit. He went by his place one day while he was rabbit hunting because he knew the rabbits liked the salt and he had found plenty in the nearby woods.

"When I came to the drying place, I found to my surprise that the cabin and the tent used for drying were gone. I was sure Slescovitch wouldn't have burnt his own cabin up. I started to kick around in the rubble, and a skull flew up in the snow. I thought there must have been an accident, but when I examined the skull I found a small hole in the back of the head and a large part of the bone on the forehead blown away.

"I put the skull back down beside the body and headed for Marshall Toburn in Fairbanks. He came back to Tanana with me, and we agreed that it looked like Slescovitch had been shot by a 30/30 Winchester, but a lot of us had guns like that. In fact, I had two myself."

Then the Count remembered that Laddy Goldspring had vouched for another Dalmatian named Perovitch when he came one evening asking to borrow a gun to hunt mountain goats with. He had taken one of Georg's rifles. Georg told Toburn that he hadn't gotten the gun back, and he said he would check it out, but how could anything be proved? No one knew anything about when Slescovitch had been shot or what possessions he had had.

The Count was very surprised when Perovitch showed up at his cabin that very night to return the rifle. Georg told the man about the murder, and it was like he had had a cold shower.

His face turned bright red, but all he said was that he had known Slescovitch and had visited him in the summer.

Perovitch disappeared that night, but he showed up at the cabin of two wood choppers 75 miles away a few days later asking for a night's lodging. No one ever turned down that kind of request, and they took him in.

One of the men was an inquisitive Scotsman named Keynes, and he noticed that Perovitch was wearing a watch chain made of nuggets and a ring like one he had himself. It was a very popular ring at the time, gold with the words Klondike and Nome engraved on it. Naturally, Keynes wanted to know how much Perovitch had paid and where he got it. He was furious when Perovitch told him that he had bought it from the same jeweler as Keynes had but had paid ten dollars less. That was something he wouldn't forget.

In the morning when Perovitch was about to leave, the marshall showed up looking for him. He arrested him and took him off to Fairbanks. But he returned a couple of days later to ask if the wood choppers had learned anything suspicious when Perovitch was there.

Keynes told him about the ring, and Toburn said that Perovitch was nothing but a rogue and must have gotten rid of it before he came. They remembered that he had gone out before the marshal showed up, so they went and began to dig around the outhouse. Eventually they found both the watch chain and the ring.

In the ring, the name George Slescovitch was engraved. That solved the case. Perovitch confessed. He had shot his fellow countryman while they were eating, taken the jewelry, and set fire to the cabin with kerosene.

He was sentenced to 99 years in prison, the harshest sentence. But he was later hanged on a bridge over the Tanana. His body was left hanging for a long time as an example to anyone else who thought of breaking the law in this northern place.

Life returned to normal after this excitement, and the Count and his friends returned to talking about their summer plans. Soon the Count was to be off on another adventure with an old friend.

Chapter Twenty

A Winter Trip

"And then arose the long wolf howl, swelling to a great heart-breaking burst of sound, and dying away in sadly cadenced woe."

While the Count was working at the Number 7 mine, all the claims around Fairbanks were taken up. During the winter, he and his pals talked about their chances. Some were going to go to the Klondike or to Fortymile or even further east. But the Count thought that gold could still be found farther down the Tanana River and up the Nenana.

He planned to go alone, but one day an old friend from Candle, Jack London, walked into the castle, shaking the snow off his clothes. He had just come up the Yukon River, and they had lots to talk about for much had happened during the year since they had last seen each other.

Jack had never done any mining or owned any claims. He went from camp to camp and enjoyed the hospitality, for the law of the north is that any one without food is welcomed wherever there is any. He had listened to the woodcutters talk and hung around in the saloons to listen to the gold diggers' stories. Now he had a head full of ideas, but he seldom talked about them.

Jack London (Photo-Oakland Public Library)

Jack was eager to go with the Count, as was a third man named Falkenberg, so they made their preparations.

The Count retrieved his dogs from Dave Petre, but they were in poor shape. They had spent the winter lying around his stove and eating anything they could find. Now they had lost weight and their fur was full of bald spots. Petre said they were useless and should be shot. But the Count said he would fix them up and took them back to the castle along with Dave's own dogs, which he had given him for free.

He built doghouses with beds of moss and gave them strengthening food. At first they howled all the time, but soon they got used to being outdoors again. After a week, he thought they would be strong enough to pull his twelve-foot sled and they set out.

On the way the Count continued to doctor his dogs, feeding them whole rabbits he shot. He was convinced that the dogs had worms and that the worms would be absorbed by the rabbits and pass out with the waste. Soon the dogs were fatter, and their bald spots began to fill out.

They followed the Tanana down to the Yukon, stopping for a day at the woodcutters' hut where Keynes stubborn curiosity had led to Perovitch's arrest. Then they continued up the Nenana valley with its magnificent view of mighty Mount McKinley far to the south.

About 30 miles up river, they met an Indian whose gun attracted the Count's attention. He had two rifles himself, a 30/30 and a 30/40, but they both had short barrels, and so they weren't suitable for hunting the shy mountain goat from a distance. In the end, he made a trade. He soon had a chance to try it out on a bull moose up on a ridge five hundred yards away.

Though they didn't need the meat yet and couldn't carry it all with them, they seized the opportunity. They camped and feasted for three days. The dogs too had hearty appetites. They were now fully recovered and their fur shone.

While they were camped, the Count explored the area and found some gold in a valley they named First Chance. But they found no more on this side of the mountains, so they marched twenty miles over the crest and located some more promising rock formations.

They followed a number of valleys that came out in a small river that flowed into the Tanana. The sand banks were of alluvial gravel, and the Count estimated he could pan out gold worth at least ten dollars a day.

They stayed in the area for several weeks, making claims and naming the creeks: Elsie Creek, Rex Creek, after Rex Beach, California Creek, and Grace Creek. But they had no name for the river itself. They met some Indians and asked them what they called it.

"Totatlanika," they replied. "Further up, it's called Tatlanika."

The Count didn't really understand what they said, but he tried to put it down on paper anyway. When he went to register the claims it was just as much a mystery to the registrar.

"Can you show me on the map where it is supposed to be?" he asked.

The Count climbed a ladder and drew the river on the big wall map. The area had been blank until that time, and later on the name Wood River was given to it.

There was plenty of wildlife in the area' mountain goats, rabbits, ptarmigan. But the staples they had brought with them, including flour, salt, sugar and beans, were running low after six weeks in the wilderness. So they decided to head towards the mouth of the river to find a place to trade.

The weather was still beautiful, cold with short days and long nights. There was plenty of dry wood for fires, and they camped early.

One night as they sat talking in the tent, the Count got the feeling that nature had wakened up around them:

"It must be my imagination," he thought, "You can't hear an animal sneaking around in soft snow." But then he heard a scratch on the canvas. The dogs wanted in. Alaska dogs don't sleep in tents; they dig a hole in the snow at night. It didn't look good when they wanted in.

He got up and went out. The night was ice cold, and the stars were shining like diamonds. The spruces sank under the heavy snow. There was no breeze, and it was totally silent.

The dogs, however, were standing with their backs arched and their noses trembling. They sensed something and were waiting for them. It seemed like everything was holding its breath.

"Ahooo!" came the howls from far away. "Ahooo!" it rolled down the valley. And "Ahooo!" came the echo.

The Count hurried into the tent, and Jack and Falkenberg demanded to know what was wrong. "Wolves," Georg said. "They aren't far away. We have to tear down the tent and make a fire outside."

The tent came down in a flash, and the men tied it over the meat-filled sled. The men lined up their weapons and ammunition on top of it, three Winchesters, one shotgun, and two Colts.

On the side where the riverbank was they tied up the dogs so close they could hardly move. On the side facing the valley, they cut down more spruce and made the fire bigger.

It was lively in the woods. The trio could hear the horned owls warning each other, "Hooo! Hooo! Hooo!" The moose were coming closer; foxes were barking in their high-pitched voices.

Falkenberg tended the fire, and Jack and Georg were ready with the guns. They waited: no sounds; the woods were quiet again.

Suddenly the dogs let out low growls, and another growl answered from the woods. The men threw more logs on the fire so they could see when the danger came.

Then they saw them. The wolves had surrounded the group without a sound. Their eyes shone and glistened, reflecting the light of the fire.

"Watch out," the Count said to Jack. "We can't let them get too close."

Alaskan Timber Wolf, Canis lupus   (Photo-Wolfsong of Alaska)

The men both fired. The shots echoed between the valleys, and a wild howl came from in front of them. They fired again, and what seemed like a chorus from hell resounded.

The men could hear the snapping, driveling jaws and the crunching of bones as the wolves threw themselves over their fallen friends.

The fire was burning too fast; the men had to have more wood. Falkenberg dragged in more spruce, while Jack and Georg continued to shoot. One, two, three; Georg shot nine, one after the other. Their death howls, the savage tearing, pulling, bones being crushed; the sounds echoed in his mind for days.

As one wolf fell, another one beside him put his teeth into him before he hit the ground, tore fur from his side and began to swallow it. He chewed for all he was worth, but it stuck in his throat, and now he, in turn, was defenseless. The rest of the pack soon perceived his state, threw themselves on him, and tore him to pieces. It was a terrible, unforgettable scene of savagery as man's mortal enemies turned on each other.

Then, in the light from the fire, the men could tell from the others' behavior that all the lead wolves had died. The survivors didn't dare to attack and stayed back in the dark.

In the morning the wolves had disappeared. The men had counted approximately one hundred wolves when they first came. It was difficult to say how many had survived. They cleaned up after themselves, and all that was left behind were puddles of frozen blood and chunks of fur.

With bloodshot eyes and burned clothes, the trio sat down to rest. They didn't stay that way for long, however. They didn't want to fight wolves another night, and they wanted to reach the Tanana as fast as possible. They fried up some slices of caribou on the embers of the fire, sitting on the sled. Then Jack became talkative.

"Now I know what I want to do," he said between bites. "I'm going to write a real story about wolves and call it, Cry of the Wild."

The Count was surprised, maybe he had gone crazy too, or else, like Rex Beach he thought he could make a living that way. Certainly it was the first time he had ever mentioned that he could handle a pencil.

Jack noticed Georg's surprise, laughed, and changed the subject, asking what the Count planned to do. Georg told him he was going to continue washing for gold until he got on his feet again.

And that was what the Count did for another couple of years, adding to his store of adventures, but not getting a great deal richer.

Chapter Twenty-One

Travels with Nick

"Nature has many tricks wherewith she convinces man of his finity . . . but the most stupefying of all is the White Silence."

Georg af Forselles spent two more years in the wide open spaces, always awed by the wilderness. Once on his way to the Tanana River he explored a massive glacier in the Wrangell Mountains with a friend, a relative newcomer named Nick Anderson.

Crossing it proved more precarious than they had thought. The surface of the ice cracked open; crevices closed without warning. Finally, they realized they would have to spend the night on top of the glacier. It was far too dangerous to continue across the treacherous surface after sunset.

They had no tent, and they couldn't lie down on the ice. In desperation, they finally spread out their pork and dried potatoes and made a makeshift camp.

"I have never felt so small and meaningless before nature's majesty as I did that night on the glacier," the Count said later. "Above us lay the big sky, and that is where the Northland's cold starts. All around us there was nothing but ice and more ice. And under us the big glacier was working. It sounded like organ music when the ice cracked. Sometimes the sounds became louder and mightier, like trumpet blasts, it was nature's voice resounding through the night."

With the early morning light the two half-frozen prospectors carefully started their descent from the glacier. Exhausted by the time they reached their cache, they camped for the night. Another shock was coming to the inexperienced Nick.

"We didn't have much bedding, so to make it comfortable, we used a piece of pork as a pillow. Nick was dreaming about gold when he was suddenly wakened up in the middle of the night by a big hairy beast that was standing in front of him and making terrible noises."

"What is it, Nick?" I whispered, still half asleep.

"A BEAR, A BEAR!" gasped Nick hoarsely.

"I could hear how frightened he was. I jumped up and started shouting 'HO! HO! HO!' as hard and loud as I could. It didn't take much more than that to make the big dark figure lumber away.

"I thought I was a goner," said Nick. "He was breathing in my face."

"I told him the bear had only wanted the pork. It was only an ordinary black bear, not as dangerous as a grizzly.

"I could hear Nick's teeth chattering as if he had a fever, and he wanted to have a fire. I finally got him calmed down, but there was no more sleep that night."

The next day they continued their trip, following the Nizina River, but the conditions got worse, and they decided to stay for a few days at an Indian village. This was another new experience for Nick.

Instead of putting up their own tent, they accepted an invitation to stay in one of the village's three-room tents.

The men slept on a bench against the wall of the first room of the tent with their food cache underneath it so they could keep an eye on it. Nick was on the outside of the bench, and Georg was inside against the wall."

Suddenly Nick pinched the Count awake and whispered, "Look at that crazy Indian; I think he's going to murder us." Georg had been sound asleep so he hadn't heard anything.

The Count rubbed the sleep from his eyes and looked out through the door to their part of the tent. In the dark he could see a big Indian in the next room with a knife in each hand. He was cutting the air with them. He had red lines painted on his face, and there were feathers in his hair. He seemed to be in an ecstasy. His eyes shone, and he snarled and made other strange noises.

The Count tried to calm Nick by explaining that the Indian was a medicine man and that he was trying to drive the bad spirits away from someone who was sick in the next room. The medicine man continued to jump up and down, slashing the air and chanting, but soon he uttered a whistling sound and retreated.

Georg knew that Nick was still scared and that he had a lot of experiences in a short time. In the morning the Count discovered that there really was a sick child in the next room, but he was able to get the Natives to give them space in another hut anyway.

By this time the Count had acquired a fair amount of knowledge about Native customs, but he was always interested in learning more. On this occasion he got quite well acquainted with a seventeen-year-old boy he called Jim who hung about their cabin.

Jim was wearing tendons of moose hide around his arms and legs and torso, and the Count asked him what they signified. Jim said that the medicine man had told all the boys they must wear them until they had killed six goats, three elks, and a bear. Then they would be men.

Jim also had a sister. He told Georg that she was fourteen and that she had menstruated for the first time, so now she had to spend about three weeks alone in the woods by a fire in order to become a woman. Food was put out for her, and when she returned she would be ready to be married.

He also told Georg that there was a lake near the village that contained strange fish and that the medicine man had forbidden them to catch or eat them.

Naturally, the Count was curious, so he set off for the lake. As he looked through the clear water he soon saw the forbidden fish; they were eels. He always carried a few sticks of dynamite among his supplies. Now he took one out, lit the fuse, and tossed it into the middle of the lake. Boom! After the explosion hundreds of eels floated to the surface. The Count and Nick had a feast of fat and delicious boiled and fried eel. But the Indians wouldn't touch them.

Jim's older brother mentioned to the Count that there were some white men up in the mountains, so he and Nick had a new direction to follow. They left the camp and started walking, looking at formations and taking samples.

However, they only found a few traces, and most of the metal was copper. Since they weren't having any luck in their prospecting, they were glad to sign on for a summer of work at Esterly's mine when they came to it.

Nick had never done any gold mining, so he was to help the cook, and Georg was to handle the dynamite and the blasting. Esterly's mine was worked hydraulically with high pressure hoses washing the banks. When big rocks were in the way, it was the Count's job to move them with the dynamite.

The work was easy and enjoyable. There were plenty of woods; the birds sang; and the sun shone. What more could you ask from the wild?

Nick's work was heavy, however, and he didn't like washing dishes or setting the table. After a month he had had enough. One day he had a fight with the head cook and came to tell Georg he was going to leave.

The Count tried to persuade his friend to stay until the fall, but when he wouldn't, Georg decided he would have to leave too. "I had brought him in, and I would take him out," the Count said.

Esterly was reluctant to see the men go. He said that Georg could be the boss next summer if he would stay and watch the camp during the winter. Esterly suggested that Nick wait until the packhorses came in from the coast with the monthly mail and then go out with them.

Georg wasn't interested in staying for the whole winter, and Nick was determined to leave at once. So the Count bought some lumber from Esterly's sawmill and built a riverboat with two strong oars for the river currents.

When you break up from camp, it seems as if the wanderlust is contagious. Esterly tempted one man to stay with a bottle of Johnny Walker, but an Englishman named Jewitt decided to come out with the Count and his friend. The fourth passenger was a brown dog some others had left behind.

They set out on a fine sunny morning, and the trip down the Nizina River went smoothly at first. They could see the mountains ahead of them and seemed to be closing in on them quickly. Suddenly they were in trouble.

"We floated into a basin I had never seen before. The current went faster and faster, and walls of rock loomed up in front of us. A hole opened up in the mountains, and the river was foaming through it."

The men were forced into a steep gorge, and the boat started to turn sideways. "Row, row!" Georg screamed at Nick and Jewitt. "Don't look around, just row!"

The dog began to panic, and the fear in his eyes shone just as the gorge swallowed the men into its blackness. They continued to go forward and to spin sideways at a terrifying speed. It was as if they were on a floating ice rink.

"Foam splashed into our eyes, and as I wiped it away I could see rocks sticking up in the river. I shouted orders wildly, trying to avoid them. I knew the Nizina Canyon went in the shape of a W, but that was all I knew about its path."

"More to the right! More to the left!" The Count shouted as Nick and Jewitt bent over the oars. He held tightly to the rudder. Who would ever have believed there was such a fierce river?

Then it became lighter in front of the men, and Georg could see the walls of the cliffs. The sun was shining, and it was as if they had come out into a green paradise. Georg steered into the bank, and the exhausted party tied up and rested.

Indians came running from a nearby village. They wondered how the group had managed to get through the four-mile-long canyon, and they pointed out sixteen graves of gold diggers who had died trying to go through it. How many had really died, nobody knew.

"We felt very tame as we floated the rest of the way down the Nizina and the Copper River to the sea. When you have been so close to death, you feel like a school boy for a long time; God has given you a powerful lesson."

When the Count and his companions arrived at Cordova, there were a lot of rumors in the air about what was going to happen at Seward. People were talking about railroads and coal fields.

U.S. Government had discovered and was going to exploit coal fields situated by Cook Inlet, just south of the Aleutians.

But it wasn't only coal. The story was that they would build a navy base at Seward and a railroad to run to the coal field. Then there would have to be a new city there.

"Do you want to buy some property?" I asked Nick. "It's a good opportunity to make some money."

"O.K.," he said. "Why not?"

By the time the men got up to the coal field, they knew they were a little late. Thousands of men from Valdez and Cordova had descended on the area. Many had already staked out their property, sure that the piece they had chosen would be in the center.

The two staked anyway, and after a number of meetings, a plan was laid out, with a First Avenue, Washington Avenue, Miners' Avenue and so on. They rubbed their hands in satisfaction over the good property they had found and wondered how much they would get for it.

But the bubble was soon to burst. One day a big ship steamed into the harbor and anchored. Workers, soldiers, and engineers were put ashore. They were led by a big major with a big moustache.

The major stood looking at his papers and then at the entrepreneurial pair where they were standing happily, ready to make their fortunes. "What does this mean?" he said when he saw their stakes.

"The city is already staked out." the men said. "These are our properties. Maybe we can sell you some."

"Are you crazy?" he screamed. "Don't you know the city plan was prepared in Washington?"

The design didn't sound as good as they had thought.

"Clear out!" said the major.

As it turned out, the city was built up on the plateau and named Anchorage. The navy got new ships that were driven by oil instead of coal, and so the planned navy base fell apart.

There was nothing for Nick and Georg to do, and they decided they had had enough of the property business.

The Count and Nick went back to Cordova and spent some time partying and doing nothing. By the end of November, however, the Count had a new plan. He had never been to the far north, the Koyukuk country; that was where the best gold in Alaska was supposed to be.

Nick was willing enough to go along, and they said goodbye to their hosts, Hans and Charley. They loaded up a new 12-foot sled with gear and provisions and set off. They didn't take dogs because the Count knew there would be no food for them.

They went over to Valdez and took the difficult road over the glacier. But at the end they could follow the road made by the packhorses into

They went over to Valdez and took the difficult road over the glacier. But at the end they could follow the road made by the packhorses into Fairbanks. By that time there were inns along the way, but they avoided them, camping in their silk tent and cooking in their Yukon stove.

They reached Fairbanks just before Christmas, and there Nick began to have second thoughts.

"How far is it?" he said. "Is the road going to get any better?"

The Count laughed, "The walk's been child's play so far. This is where the hard part starts. We'll be going down to the Yukon, and after that across very desolate country."

"Well, I can think of nicer things to do," Nick said, looking as if he were going to turn around right away.

"Come on," the Count said. "We'll go down to Fort Gibbon. We can follow the Tanana. There's always some kind of road there. The walk will do you good."

"Count," Nick said seriously, "I'll compromise on south Alaska where it isn't so goddamned cold. Can't we turn around? You can make some money down there."

"I don't care about the money," Georg roared. "I want to see the Koyukuk country. If you don't want to come, that's fine with me."

"I'll turn around," he said shortly. And that was the end of that. Nick went south to the copper mines, and the Count stayed over Christmas with old friends in Fairbanks.

He left just after New Year's. As he thought, there was a road along the Tanana down to Fort Gibbon, and the Count had no difficulty finding his way to the Yukon. From there, he planned to cut across to Bettles by way of the Koyukuk River.

After resting for a day, the Count put on his snowshoes, took out his compass, and started pulling his sled on what he knew would be a long, arduous trip. And so it was, mile after mile, day after day, through the silent, frozen wilderness.

In some places, the snow was so hard that Georg only had to walk over it once to make a path. But more often it was so deep that he would have to leave the sled and stamp out a path in advance.

When it snowed, he stayed put, and when he walked on, he often felt serious, thinking of how small he was, swallowed up in the isolated valleys. The silence was awesome, and even a breaking branch would sound like a pistol shot. But Georg was grateful when he heard any sound, a woodpecker in the distance would sound like it was encouraging him.

But he was not so glad one day when a wolf turned up in the middle of the afternoon. He could see another two or three in the distance, and he knew they would be the leaders of the pack, checking out the terrain.

He had his Winchester ready in the sled, and he knew the pack wouldn't be very large, twenty at most. Before it got dark, he put up his tent, cut a lot of wood, and made a big fire. The Count was ready to stay awake the whole night, but in a couple of hours he could see a ring of glittering eyes around him.

The Count fired into the darkness. The shots sounded like thunder in the silence. Soon he could hear the wolves fighting over the corpses of their dead mates. He could see their eyes, but with the leaders dead, they were no longer a danger. At dawn they left, and he never saw them again.

Finally, Georg reached Bettles, and there he found a trail along the Koyukuk River. The way was much easier then, and so one day at the end of March he reached Wiseman, his goal. It felt strange to walk into Hobo Smith's saloon, order a whiskey, and sit down in a corner. It was a very simple place, with handmade chairs and tables, but it was warm and the Count felt like he had returned to civilization.

Chapter Twenty-Two

The Best Gold in the World

"North and South, as far as the eye could see, it was unbroken white."

Just as he accepted the failures in his claims and other speculations, so the Count was philosophical about events on the trail and the behavior of the sourdoughs he met.

"Wild and desolate was the Koyukuk River country," he later wrote in his memoirs, "and its citizens were strange. They wrote their own laws and lived their own lives far away from the big cities and towns."

It didn't take the Count long to find out the rules of the town. As he sat reading a two-month old paper that first night, most of the customers simply drove up in their sleds, came in and barked an order for a gallon or two of whiskey, and left again. But eventually one stayed to have a drink with the host, and soon they asked the Count to join them.

"I realized that was the custom in the Koyukuk country. No one empties a glass in a saloon unless everyone is doing the same. I knew I should take a turn, and I wondered about the price of drinks. I had seven silver dollars, and I was sure that must be enough for one round at least."

"I threw them on the counter, and Hobo Smith and his pal began to laugh.

"'That's cheechako money,' they said. 'Uncle Sam's silver dollars, a sound from home.' Then they began to talk about their youth, what they had done in the States."

When Hobo Smith's friend left, he began to tell the Count about the area. Not only was Wiseman the most northerly mining camp in the world, he said, "They take out more per person than anywhere else, and it's the most valuable in the world, nineteen dollars an ounce."

The Count told Hobo Smith that he had got $17 in Nome, and he asked where else he had been. Georg told him about discovering Candle, and the doubt in his eyes was clear.

"No," he said. "It was the Swedish Count who found Candle."

"I am the Swedish Count!", Georg replied.

Hobo Smith's eyes became big and round, and then he said, "You must know the guy over in the corner then, Jimmy Hill."

Hobo Smith called him over and said, "Do you know this one?"

Georg was pretty grimy and heavily bearded after the long trip, but after looking curiously, Jimmy said, "By God, it's the Count!"

The men sat down with another drink and laughed over some of the old stories from Candle, like the time they sent Ben down to the pharmacy in Nome to help him with his seduction of an Eskimo girl named Kitty. The pharmacist was in on it, of course, and Ben was very chagrined when the vial of houseflies he was given didn't work.

The men drank to Ben and then Jimmy said that another old friend was up here too, Lawrence Civily, who had run a saloon in Candle. He had a mine seven miles out of town, an Indian wife, and three children.

The next day Jimmy and the Count went out to see Lawrence, and the Count learned how difficult and expensive mining was in this area. Lawrence had taken out a pile of rock from his mine during the winter, and he estimated that there was $50,000 worth of gold in it. But he had to work the gravel with a steam pan, which took a lot of wood at fifty dollars a cord. He thought he would be lucky if he had $10,000 left when he paid all his debts.

The Count, as usual, was short of "working capital," and he soon got tied up with a greenhorn worse than Nick.

This time it was a man named Nuicebaum who had arrived in Wiseman with the postman on his monthly trip. Nuicebaum had had a restaurant and barber shop in Fort Gibbon, but now he had decided to try gold mining. Since he had no idea how to go about it, he was eager for the Count to become his partner.

Hobo Smith suggested that the team go up to Gold Creek about twelve miles north, and they took his advice. They met two brothers named Brown, and they were willing to lend the pair some of their equipment. When they went into the cabin to see it, Nuicebaum pulled on his long nose as he always did when he was upset.

The Browns said that the pair could help with the washing and keep 85 percent of what they took out. The Count told Nuicebaum it was a good deal, but he wanted to look around for a while longer.

Farther up the valley they came to Cassiar Jim's claim, and because the summer was so short, he didn't have time to wash much of the gravel. He was willing to let the miners have part of the claim if they gave him 10 percent and said he wouldn't take anything for any day when they didn't take out more than a hundred dollars.

Nuicebaum pulled his nose again and asked the Count what they would need. He told him that food, pack horses, and equipment would cost about two thousand dollars.

"No," he said. "I don't want to go in on that. Let's go back to the Browns and look at their claim again."

Nuicebaum asked the Browns what they wanted to let the men wash through their gravel heap and they said 10 percent.

"By gosh, That's 5 percent better than before," Nuicebaum said, making his usual gesture.

The Count was losing his temper by this time. He explained that they would have picked out most of the gold while they were digging and that all that would be left would be fine gold that would hardly pay. Still, he had spent all my money living it up, and his punishment was to follow newcomers who wanted to be part of the action but didn't dare take a chance.

When the men got back to Wiseman, Hobo Smith had another suggestion, Mascot Creek. There the gravel lay on a mountain ridge. The rains had washed some away, and you could see gold shimmering in the sun. Naturally, Nuicebaum was excited. "Dos gegelt mir! (This pleases me)", he exclaimed. (Nuicebaum, a matey person, would often speak the Yiddish language to himself when he got excited. It's spoken by many European Jews, a high-German dialect that's written in the Hebrew alphabet.) Nuicebaum's dirty worn-out hat had a small brim, and crown in the shape of the top of his head. His dark beard and hair were long and thin, but matted.

The Count told him they wouldn't get much, but they had to do something. They dug a small trench and as soon as the water ran into it they started washing. Their happiness lasted about two weeks. Then the snow from the mountains that had provided the water was all melted; they had made about $700 each.

It was full summer when they turned back, and it was not what the Count had hoped it would be. He was very angry by the time we got to Wiseman, but Nuicebaum was cheerful after he had had a few drinks and wondered if they couldn't try somewhere else.

"I still have my $10,000."

"You can go to hell," the Count told him calmly. "You better go back to Fort Gibbon. You and the $10,000 will fit in fine there, but not here!"

Then Georg went off to Hobo Smith's in a fighting spirit, and there he joined his friend Harry Owen in a few beers. He pointed out a tall gold digger as the toughest man in camp, Jimmy Scofield. Jimmy saw the two looking at him and was soon at their table spoiling for a fight. That was all right with the Count. It happened so fast the others didn't even have time to lay their bets.

Jimmy rushed at the Count, and he stepped aside. Then he came again, and Georg dived down to his side. Then Georg managed to get a good blow in and blood was dripping out of Jimmy's mouth. The Count avoided most of his punches, but one hit him in the eye and he flew backwards.

Then the Count was even madder and charged back. He knew his eye was swelling, and he could taste blood from a cut in his lip. But he couldn't feel any pain, and the cheers of the crowd made it seem like a big party.

Finally, the Count landed one on Jimmy's chin, and he fell with a huge crash over the bar and lay still. "Thank God for Kiddy Braine," Georg thought; "I really needed his boxing lessons."

The Count wiped his face and dried his mouth. "A good fight," he heard someone say. "Now, let's all be friends and have another drink." That suited the Swede. He was in a good humor again, and he had almost forgotten about Nuicebaum and his nose.

The miners were also pretty uncouth on the rare occasions when they saw a woman. At least, that's what Gold Poke Annie, a dark-eyed big-bosomed French lady, told the Count when she came into his tent one day.

She and her husband Louis had owned a saloon in Dawson, but it had closed when the rush ended. They journeyed up the Yukon and Koyukuk in 1905 to the small town called Wiseman. There they rented a small house among the crude tent town and began to serve up strong drinks to the rowdy patrons.

"What strange, uncultured people there are in this wild place," Annie said as she came into the Count's tent and collapsed in a heap on his bed. "I haven't slept for a week, and I can't take it any more."

She explained that a party had been going on for days at their establishment, when one group had fallen under the table or disappeared, another would show up. Now Sammy had passed out, and the party goers not only wanted her to sing constantly, but they also wanted her to open her dress so they could touch her.

"Jesus," she said. "It makes you crazy."

"But you must be doing pretty well moneywise," the Count said. "I hear you charge twice as much as Hobo Smith for liquor."

"Yes, That's true. Otherwise, I wouldn't take it. We've been working steady for a week, and we've got ten thousand bucks! But I can't sing twenty-four hours a day. Can I sleep here to get away from those crazies for a while?"

"Okay," the Count said, and she was soon asleep.

Rumors abounded that Annie's was a sinful place, and the prospectors came in droves looking for women and drinks. They didn't care how much it cost as long as there was a party going on.

Gold Poke Annie and Louis disappeared soon after that. They had made enough for a new saloon.

That's how people were up there in those early years. Gold diggers only pleasure in the winter months was going to saloons where there was whiskey and music and other temptations for men who had been without love for a long time. They would stay in a place like Wiseman for a week or a month, until their gold was gone. Then they went back digging, a little quieter and more sour. That was the gold digger's life, more digging, more fun, more trips.

All of these strands of life on the gold frontier came together for the Count in the adventures of Jack Mider that summer he spent in Wiseman, women, whiskey, and the law of the camp.

In Wiseman there were all of three white women, and it was Jack Mider's dream that he would take each of them in his arms and kiss her. And as soon as he came into town, he tried to make his dream come true.

He went into the Golden Gate Hotel and had a few drinks, so he was prepared when the owner, Miss White, came into the smoky room. He swept her into his arms and kissed her hard on the mouth. "Number one," he said.

Now, Jack was a nice-looking fellow, and Miss White probably didn't mind all that much. But Marshal Murphy was also in the saloon, and he decided to go to her aid.

The Count wasn't quite sure why the government had sent a marshal at all, for nothing really bad ever happened up there, and everyone was reasonably well behaved.

Anyway, a fight naturally broke out. Jack wasn't much of a fighter, and he got a good beating before Marshall Murphy dragged him off to the blockhouse. The marshall wasn't sure how he would punish Jack. The crime wasn't bad enough to send him down to Fort Gibbon, so he had to think up something himself.

While the marshall was thinking it over, the news that Jack was in the blockhouse went flying up all the valleys of the Koyukuk.

"What does that newcomer think he's doing?"

"Doesn't Jack belong to our gang?"

Well, the upshot was that they called a miners' meeting. Originally it had consisted of the first seven who had arrived there, but now there were a lot of others because it was a matter of community interest.

Scarlet Jim ran the proceedings, and after a lot of screaming and talking, he wrote down their decisions on a roll of toilet paper he had found somewhere. The Count had borrowed a tired old horse so that he wouldn't miss the occasion, and so he rode off with all the others.

The long row of armed men descended on Marshall Murphy's blockhouse, shooting in the air and demanding that he come outside. The men saw Jack waving from where he was working in the marshall's garden, but they ignored him.

When Murphy came to the door, the crowd fell silent.

"Hands up!" a deep voice said. "You, Jack, beat it over the mountains, and you, Murphy, come with us."

Murphy was tied hand and foot, and slung on the back of a horse. Then they all rode out into the woods where they had built a gallows with a ladder leading up to it.

They carried the protesting marshal up on the platform and put the noose around his neck. Big Solomon beat on his washing pan " bang, bang, bang" like a drum roll. Scarlet Jim then came up and read from his toilet paper.

"Paragraph one," he said, loudly and seriously. "It has to be known by everyone in the Koyukuk country, and especially Marshall Murphy, that we make our own laws, which we try to follow."

Big Solomon banged the pan again.

"Paragraph two. We, the miners at this meeting, agree that anyone who breaks our laws will be hanged the by neck until he is dead."

It was dead quiet. You could hear the wind in the trees. Bang, bang, bang went the pan.

"Paragraph three. We, the miners, say that the one who has taken the law into his own hands and treated Jack Mider badly should be hanged till he is dead, dead, dead."

He spoke so seriously that the Count could feel shivers up and down his spine, and it fell quiet again.

"Fire!" said Scarlet Jim, and all the revolvers and Winchesters went off. The shots echoed through the woods as the whole cavalcade rode off.

The men laughed as they headed off to have a few whiskeys to celebrate Scarlet Jim's wisdom and left the marshall where he was. He tried to get out of the ropes, but they were tied too tight, and he was being eaten alive by mosquitoes as the sun went down. Who knows how long he might have stayed there if Hobo Smith hadn't happened along and cut him down.

Nothing more was ever said about the matter. The marshall decided he didn't want to stay in such a country, so he resigned and headed south.

Jack Mider, whose dream had started all this, was forgiven, and there was no talk of punishing him for his kissing party. But his punishment was to come in another form.

To get to the layers where the gold was, one had to dig through a lot of gravel, and the miners decided that they should buy a keystone drill and a digging machine. They would cost about $25,000, so they had to choose someone to go down to the States and buy them. They knew from what they saw in Dawson that a lot could happen to a man with that much money.

At first, they thought they should send two men, but then they decided that was no good for two would be company, and you never know what they might get up to. They thought and thought, and eventually Jack Mider came into their minds. He didn't drink as much as most of the others, especially not whiskey, and what had happened before he left Wisconsin was nothing, just silliness over a lady.

So they approached Jack and he agreed. They advised him not to go by way of Dawson but to head instead for the Yukon River and then go straight down to St. Michael where the boats between Nome and Seattle always came in.

Everything went fine as far as Seattle, but Jack had $15,000 of his own as well as the miners' money. He thought he might as well have a good time while he was in the city, and besides he had met a cute little dancer at Donovan's Dance Hall. She had everything he wanted in a woman.

Like the women in Nome she needed rings and bracelets and dresses, and Jack wasn't stingy. That word was hardly known in Alaska.

In the spring, a sad letter arrived in Wiseman. Jack had followed all their advice and behaved himself, but he had been mugged! Now he didn't even have enough money to get home.

The news of the letter and the mugging went around. No one said much; the miners' meeting would have to decide what to do.

Strangely, everyone was of the same opinion. They couldn't just leave Jack down there. They all nodded and passed the hat. Travel money was sent down to Jack, and he came up with the Yukon boat. A lot of people came into Wiseman when they heard that Jack was back.

To Jack it seemed like everything was going fine. He had barely arrived and said hello, when they asked him to come down to Hobo Smith's saloon. There everyone who had put up money was waiting for him.

It wasn't long before he found out what was up. Scarlet Jim could talk, but he didn't need a paper this time. A lot of hands suddenly grabbed Jack, and he was laid over a table. Then he got two lashes from everyone who had helped him have such a good time in the south.

They were strange people up there. Not a word was said about embezzlement. They just took things into their own hands. It was said from that day that Jack Mider never looked at a woman again.

By the fall of that year the Count was back in Nome for the winter. He lodged with the Danish whaler George Madsen and his Eskimo wife. Madsen had decided the mining life wasn't for him and he was working in Nome as a stevedore.

Then Nome was peaceful. Salmon fishing had brought prosperity, and the tent city and shacks destroyed by the storm of 1900 had been replaced by wooden buildings. The town stretched about a mile and a half along the beach. But it was still only three blocks wide, and it was still unprotected from the weather.

Late one stormy night the Count was talking with his friend Kurt Evans at the Golden Gate Hotel. Since the weather was so bad, they decided they would spend the night there instead of returning to their homes.

"In the middle of the night," the Count records, "I woke up and felt that something strange was going on. It was very light outside. I blinked my eyes a couple of times, then I jumped out of bed. I ran to the window and saw that a big fire was blazing. At the same time a spark ignited the windowsill of my room.

"'Get up!! FIRE! FIRE!' I screamed, and then hurried to pull on my pants."

The Count could see it was burning on the other side of the street as well. A window cracked and shattered; the flames were licking around the window frame, and then it started to burn in the hotel. The windows smashed and shattered, and people ran by in the hallways, screaming and shouting.

Nome Fire, 1905 (Photo-Carrie McLain Museum, McLain Archive of Photographic Materials, Nome, AK

Just as the Count opened his door and rushed out, he collided with Mrs. Peterson, the hostess in the hotel, who had the room opposite his. She was dragging a heavy sewing machine.

"Save my sewing machine," she wailed.

It seemed ridiculous in the middle of all this turmoil and confusion, but a sewing machine was worth a great deal in the north then.

"To hell with the sewing machine," the Count said. "Where's the exit?"

"My sewing machine," she cried again.

So Georg grabbed it and threw it out of a window. Miraculously it landed undamaged on the sand below.

As soon as they reached the street, they could see how big the fire was. In the east it was a raging inferno. The storm was blowing from the southeast, driving the fire further down into the western part of town. People were running about with their furniture, household utensils, clothes, whatever they had grabbed in their panic.

The fire brigade and the military were working feverishly; they blasted whole houses trying to stop the fire. But it was hopeless. Sparks flew up into the air and smoldered for a moment; then the wind would come, and the fire would flare up. The sounds of collapsing roofs and houses came from every direction.

The fire department arrived with their horse teams and wagons; their water hoses were stretched everywhere. The Count and his housemate rushed down the street, coughing from the smoke.

They saw Sam Pepper at the door of his bar. Whiskey, beer, and brandy barrels had all been rolled out into the street, as sweaty men worked frantically to save what they could of the booze.

"Come on, boys," Sam shouted. "Have a drink, the last one Sam Pepper's bar is serving before it goes to hell. Tonight you can drink for free!"

The Count stepped in. There were 20 men dirty from the smoke inside. It was hot, and the whole inventory was swept down. Glass crunched under Georg's feet. "Skoal, Sam Pepper, for old times sake!"

The Count rushed on. The next saloon was Tex's old place, filled with memories from the time of the pioneers. In ten minutes the fire would get to it and lick along the tables and the roulette wheel where so many fortunes had changed hands.

He ran past Floridora's dance hall where the champagne had flowed every night. There would be no more cancans on these floors; no more weatherbeaten gold diggers would sit on the hard benches clapping their calloused hands to the music.

The frivolous golden years of luxury were gone. All the old memories were disappearing: Floridora's, Hunter's, Alaska Second Class, Hubb's, and the Monte Carlo, they were all in flames. The temple of the gold rush was going.

The Count followed the stream of people down to the beach, and many of the belongings people had saved disappeared in the chaos and disorder as lightfingered men took advantage of the darkness.

He eventually heard how the catastrophic fire had started. The Duncan sisters had been fighting over an old, drunken gold miner's pokes of gold dust on the second floor of the Alaska Saloon. During their scuffle, a kerosene lamp fell on the floor and ignited the curtains. The whole saloon quickly caught on fire, and the gale force winds whipping Nome fanned the blaze that turned the whole town into a pile of smoldering ruins.

Nome was rebuilt, but its day was almost over. By 1910 only a few stubborn sourdoughs continued to try to scrape out a living there. The Census that year declared Nome's population to be 2,600, down from 12,488 in 1900.

The Count continued to pursue his golden dreams, and he spent two more years back in Fairbanks. But within a few years his base was in San Francisco. He tried copper mining in Arizona, and almost wound up engaged there in 1918.

Instead he wound up on the Barbary Coast as part-owner of the Comstock Saloon in the years before Prohibition.

Whoever named the street it was on, Pacific Street, had a sense of humor. This rough area of the city was quiet enough by day, but at night all kinds of rowdy visitors roamed its streets.

"The policemen always walked two by two when they made their rounds," the Count said. "And they certainly needed to do so for their own protection. Music, singing, laughing, screaming, cursing all resounded in the air, and fights and muggings were not unusual."

The Count's new business had no special attraction inside except for the pretty pictures along the walls, naked women, as was the taste in those days.

At first he had business troubles too. He wasn't making the money he thought he should, and he soon found out the reason. His partner Walter was too stingy to hand out eye-openers to customers who had drunk up all their money the night before, and they were taking their business elsewhere.

Fate was soon to provide the Count with a way to solve his problem. Walter was worried that the books weren't balancing, and he began to suspect that their alcoholic janitor was supplementing his wages with free whiskey.

Soon they caught the janitor swigging while he worked, and after that the books were all right. But the Count noticed that his lesson hadn't seemed to sober the janitor up,

He always smelled of liquor when he left the Comstock, but the bottles behind the counter were never touched again. One day after the janitor left, the Count decided to check out the basement.

It was full of dusty old packages, most of them filled with clothes people had bought and left behind in the saloon. Could this be where he was hiding his liquor?

He started to search carefully, and it wasn't long before he saw something that looked like a long snake. It was a red rubber hose, and when the Count followed it he found it was attached to a huge barrel of rum.

The Count knew that his partner had originally purchased the saloon from a widow, and he figured that the former owner had hidden the barrel of rum for his own use. He locked the cellar, and then he asked his partner if he could give the packages to the Salvation Army.

His scheme worked perfectly. Now the rum barrel was all that remained in the basement, and Walter knew nothing about it.

The Count used it for eye-openers for good customers, serving one and two drinks and sometimes even a small bottle free. The word spread, and the bar started to fill up. In fact, he didn't have time for many escapades.

These glorious days ended with the coming of Prohibition, and the bar closed down.

Georg still had a good part of Alaska to explore. He continued on one gold expedition after another. More often than not, he came back pale, tired, hungry and broke, but just as often, he returned with his gold bags filled to the brim! It was an exhilarating life that suited him. Georg never saved any of his gold. When he found it, he spent it quickly grubstaking other prospectors and blowing it in dance halls.

Georg finally created within himself a strong urge to visit his Swedish homeland, to visit old friends and kinfolk. It was there he met a very pretty young lady, who stole his heart. He was indeed very much in love. In fact, it was the catalyst which gave Georg a completely different motive for seeking yet another fortune in the wilds of Alaska! Until Georg met Elisabeth, he never gave marriage a thought. He often frequented saloons and places which provided the pleasures of talking and mingling with friends, and occasionally, ladies of the night. He could often be seen throwing gold dust about from his pouch, to the rhythm of plinking piano keys, as he joined in the wild, frolicking dances which often took place. Dance-hall girls and friends went wild over the glorious sprinkles of flying gold dust which came from the inimitable, incomparable and unforgettable character, Georg af Forselles!

Georg had hardly ever come in contact with many of the more "refined" type of woman during his rip-roaring, carefree adventurous life, until he made a visit to his Swedish homeland in 1920. There he met a very beautiful, gentle, refined lady, whose name was Elisabeth. Love soon blossomed into courtship. It didn't take long to propose marriage. This twist of fate overwhelmed them both with a wonderful happiness and a new kind of contentment.

Erik O. Lindblom standing in front of his hotel, The Claremont, in Berkeley, California.
He bought this hotel with the riches he discovered at Nome. This is how he dressed in Alaska.

Elisabeth and Georg had a huge, typically Swedish wedding. It would be one of the most solemn moments in his life! As the church organ began to play the wedding march, to Georg, it sounded like a gentle wind blowing through the tall trees of an Alaskan forest, as he escorted his light-haired, blue-eyed bride slowly to the altar.

Dressed in a newly-bought tuxedo with a fancy high collar, he suddenly found himself somewhat surprised as he realized he would be assuming new responsibilities. "What am I getting into?" he pondered nervously. As the priest read the marriage vows of fidelity, Georg's muscular body swelled under his beautiful new suit. His arms hung down heavily as if they were a couple of large sledge hammers under those big white cuffs. His starched shirt breast popped out in a bow, as a tuck of wiry hair stood straight up from the middle of his head.

"The worst of it all," exclaimed Georg later, "were the trousers! For a while I thought they had fallen to the floor. I was accustomed to wearing a belt, but had been convinced somehow that suspenders were more appropriate. In the middle of the solemn ceremony, I missed my belt, which normally pushed comfortably against my belly. I broke out in a cold sweat, thinking that I would lose my pants!"

The planned honeymoon was to take place in sunny California. Georg had been gone too long from his native Sweden to want to settle and live there. Elisabeth also agreed that it would be good to settle down in America. It would be a new and exciting adventure for them both. They chose to live in Oakland, near the golden San Francisco Bay. There, they built a nice little home overlooking the bay, to live a blissful life together. The gold-digging days for Georg would be an adventure of the past, with fond memories and adventures to pass on to his children. He took a steady job and became a good reliable worker and a loving devoted husband.

Georg was blessed with an abundant amount of strength and stamina. He never got tired of working for his home, wife and family. He named his first child, who was born during the first year of the marriage, Thomas. Two years later there came another son, whom he named Charles. Then, six years later came his first lovely daughter, Lillian. These were indeed happy, contented times for Georg. It seemed that no one in the entire world could have had a more contented life.

After a hard day's work, Georg enjoyed sitting outside in the California sun with a happy feeling in his heart. He enjoyed bouncing the little ones on his knee, and with a glass of milk in hand, he would tell them of his many exciting adventures in the wilds of Alaska.

A man like Georg always had lots of good friends and acquaintances, always eager to listen to his adventurous experiences and who admired him greatly. His house situated high on a hill commanded a magnificent view of San Francisco Bay, where steamers and sailing vessels would pass for him to see. There were about a dozen small, peaceful communities sprinkled along the coast which could be seen from the vantage point of his verandah, whose spectacular lights glimmered like shining diamonds upon the waters of the Bay at night. He was happy and content with his little family and the life he had created for himself.

As the years passed by, Elisabeth became involved with a women's organization that believed an individual's fate was guided by astrology. Georg began to notice a difference in her attitudes, as she became more and more involved. The members were required to write horoscopes which supposedly predicted future events.

Every week, Elisabeth would receive a package containing horoscope materials to work on. As she became submerged in the complexities of the work, her countenance and attitudes seemed to change. The beautiful blue eyes which had captured Georg's heart looked less frequently toward him, as she sat more and more often slouched over her typewriter day after day, writing horoscopes for people. As she studied the stars in the heavens, she learned to believe she could predict many things about an individual's life.

The horoscope organization seemed to make good money from this work, but none of the funds were passed on to its members. Instead, they would receive various medals of different types and sizes, or an honor certificate. Elisabeth was infatuated with the belief that horoscopes could really foretell and predict future events. Georg simply laughed, and thought the whole thing was a foolish waste of time.

Ten years had passes since his marriage to Elisabeth. Georg was not working, and it was difficult to find a job to his liking. He began to yearn for his beautiful Alaska, and he conjured up visions of the past. He knew that the great land to the north was still largely unexplored. Finally, he got in touch with a mining company, and was hired without delay. His duties would be to examine and explore an area in Alaska. If it proved to be gold-bearing, he would be given a large percentage of the take from the mine.

Georg knew the area well, and he also knew that mining on a large scale would make him wealthy once again. Once again, he would be on his way to becoming a millionaire.

A few days before he began the long journey north, a salesman knocked at the door. He stretched his right hand out, giving Georg's a brisk shaking, as he introduced himself as Tim Brass. He was as pleasant as a Swede at a smörgåsbord table.

"Is the little woman at home?" the salesman inquired with a smile. "I have something special that will surely interest her. It's a new item that no woman should be without!"

Georg hesitated for a moment, as he didn't particularly take a liking to this tall, fast fellow who so familiarly pressed his cold, wet hand into his. Elisabeth came stumbling down the stairs to the front door, inquisitive about the stranger.

"Look here," laughed the man, addressing himself to Elisabeth. "The lady of the house!" His eyes looked lustfully at Elisabeth, as she bashfully lowered her head. "I see that the little lady, like all beautiful women, wears silk stockings!" he exclaimed as he extended his hand to her, holding a small needle. "And how often do they get snagged, leaving unsightly runs in them? Those lovely expensive stockings could be ruined!"

Mr. Brass, the smooth-talking salesman, stopped for an artful second, waiting for a response, as Georg coughed in irritated aggravation. The smiling salesman eagerly continued his pitch.

"Look again carefully at this magic needle. It quickly and inexpensively repairs all kinds of silk stockings! It surely doesn't look like much, but look at this! It's quite simple for such an important job, don't you think?"

The salesman quickly plucked a stocking filled with runs from his case, and very skilfully stitched away his demonstration.

Georg expressed no interest in the confounded contraption, and wished the salesman would disappear. Elisabeth, however, leaned over with great interest, as the salesman skilfully captured her attention.

"It certainly does mend nicely," Elisabeth responded.

"Yes, it's truly a wonderful invention," sighed the salesman.

What came next made the hair on the back of Georg's neck stand on end. Brass took hold of Elisabeth's hand, placing the confounded needle there. "Now, let me show you how it's done." His arms were now around her, and his hot breath caressed her ear, as Georg's face turned a bright angry pink. Elisabeth held the needle in position for the demonstration, as Brass caressingly guided her hand. Georg's face was red hot as he felt anger surge through his veins.

"Why, it's a wonderful invention," Elisabeth sighed, seemingly enjoying it all as the warmth of Mr. Brass' breath heated her neck. "A wonderful discovery, don't you think, Georg?"

"Yeah, wonderful," replied Georg, gritting his teeth, trying desperately to control his temper. Georg diverted the conversation to his new Alaskan adventure. It was nearing departure time, and it was all he could think of to distract the attention of this confounded salesman.

"Alaska!" Brass exclaimed, dropping his smooth-talking sales pitch. "That must be a wonderful country. I hear there are lots of opportunities there in the gold fields." He eagerly forgot about selling his "magic" needles and began to express his secret desire to find his own fortune in the northern wilderness.

Georg grinned with satisfaction, quietly claiming his victory over vamp as his blush quickly faded.

"Well, why don't you come up with me?" said Georg, bumping his elbow against the crafty salesman. Brass eagerly became involved with enthusiasm as Georg's adventurous yarns held him spellbound, filling his greedy soul with visions of wealth. He said he would give a lot of thought to accepting the invitation, saying he was already quite a wealthy man and could well afford the trip. Georg chuckled to himself, knowing how a greenhorn like this would be quickly fleeced out of his stake, heading back to civilization with holes in his pockets.

"I'll come back in a few days, after I've given a little more thought to your offer," said Brass, as he gathered up his demonstration. Elisabeth bought two of his "magic needles" before he departed. It was plain to see that sparks were still flying between them as he gave an eloquent departure pitch, holding her hand as if he were Galahad himself. Georg shrugged as he mumbled to himself, "Sure hope I don't have to look at that fast-talking bastard again!"

Salesman Brass visited Georg's home twice after that before Georg's departure for the Alaskan gold fields, each time complaining that he had a difficult time selling a chicken farm he owned. He said he might have to go with Georg another time. Georg, on the other hand, did all he could to make Brass feel uncomfortable.

As the time neared for Georg's departure, he arranged for his family's comfort and security. He rented a beautiful summer bungalow before he left for his family to enjoy. Marie, a friend of Elisabeth's, would stay with the family in his absence. In addition, he hired a nurse to help attend to the children's needs.

Finally, it was time to say farewells as he departed for his journey north.

Georg's work took him far in to the northern wilderness. For six months, he fought pesky mosquitoes and worked hard under exhausting conditions to accomplish his major objectives. He thought often of his little family and wondered how they were faring.

Elisabeth had written only once in the time he was away. The letter which he received said that she and the children enjoyed Camp Meeker, the location of their summer cottage, very much and had good company. They swam, lounged in the sun and appeared to be healthy and in good spirits. Georg noticed something else in the envelope, however. It was a photograph. As Georg pulled the photo out, the first thing that caught his attention was that pesky salesman, Brass!

"That big skinny bastard," Georg mumbled, as he blushed with the indignity of it all. "Look at him standing there in his damned bathing suit next to my Elisabeth. Why is that son-of-a-bitch hanging around my wife?"

As Georg's anger cooled, he turned to thoughts of his wedding and the precious intimate moments spent with one another, and his heart was heavy.

"What have I done wrong?" he asked himself. "Elisabeth was always a good woman and a good mother. I've always trusted her and have never had a reason to doubt her love for me and our children." Georg pulled out a photo of his little family that he always carried in his pocket. A smile came upon his face as he came to realize that his real treasures were not gold and adventures, but in his posterity. Then he spoke his thoughts aloud to

From left: Charles, Thomas, Lillian, Elisabeth and friends at Camp Meeker, California, 1933.

himself. "Towards fall, I'll be ready to return home!" That would be the time when his mining contract would end, and he would return with a very handsome sum of money!

Georg sent a telegram to Elisabeth the very next morning, announcing that he would soon be home. The time passed swiftly, and he soon found himself homeward bound, filled with great anticipation of being with Elisabeth and the kids. In his mind, Georg envisioned how he would tell her the good news as she sat on his lap, hugging him after the long separation. It would be the culmination of his hard work, sacrifice and effort. His greatest reward would be to hold her in his arms once again, to share his wonderful adventure and experience, not to mention the monetary rewards it had brought to them as a family. Smiling to himself, Georg painted a rose-colored future in his mind, with dreams of a joyous reunion...

The steamer finally edged into its berth in the port of San Francisco. The familiar skyline made his heart beat a little faster as he stepped along the gangplank, eagerly looking for Elisabeth.

"There, there she is," he muttered softly to himself. Elisabeth waved her hand. "I can't wait to hold her in my arms again," thought Georg. He envisioned himself enveloping her in his arms, close to his bosom, lifting her from the ground that her lips might touch his own. Georg's heart picked up a few more beats as he drew closer, sat his sea bag down and held his arms outstretched to receive her. But Elisabeth, uncommonly cool and quiet, simply held out her hand to him as if welcoming a stranger.

Her face wasn't filled with anticipated joy, but held a solemn look of concern. Georg's countenance changed with disappointment as Elisabeth's hand fell coldly into his. There were no smiles, no warmth. It was obvious that something was very, very wrong.

"She appears so quiet and unhappy," Georg thought as he looked deep into her eyes as if to reach her mind. "Has anything happened that I should know about?" Georg asked.

"No...a..no," she said, looking at him in a rather nervous and curious manner, as her eyes glanced downwards. "Why?"

Georg didn't respond. It wasn't the time or the place to talk about it. He could wait, gather his thoughts, then talk to her when he could find out for himself what was really going on.

As they arrived home, the children happily clung to Georg's tall figure like monkeys in a banana tree. Little hands poked into his pockets to see what surprises he might have brought home for them.

With little Lillian on his right arm and his baggage in his left hand, little Charles and Tom clung tightly to his trousers, eager to receive their daddy's affections. Georg's heart pounded with the excitement of seeing his little ones and to receive their genuine unadulterated love. It felt warm inside to be loved, wanted and needed. While he laughed and shared their joy, he quietly wondered why Elisabeth was so cool and quiet.

The welcome home dinner seemed almost dreary. Georg readily detected a look of dispirited gloom upon his children's faces. "Strange," he thought. "They must know something I don't know." The clicking of spoons against china soup bowls broke the solemn silence.

As dessert was being served, the startling ring of a telephone broke the silence. Georg began to lift himself from his chair to answer it, but Elisabeth was quick, even eager to catch it; was it to get to the receiver first? She spoke softly for a while and finally ended her conversation. As she returned to the table with a pleasant smile on her face, she said, "Georg, would you mind if I go over to Marie's this evening for a little while? We have a few important things to put together for clients, which simply must be mailed out immediately."

Georg looked down at his plate, coughing suspiciously into his napkin before he answered. "Of course, you can go, if you want to," he replied.

Five minutes later, after applying fresh makeup and changing clothes, Elisabeth hastily said her goodbye. As the door slammed shut, Georg's face filled with a sense of disappointment and suspicion, as he tried desperately to cast fearful thoughts from his mind.

Georg stared down at his nearly empty plate, and then a smile shone upon his face as he looked up at his lovely children. Their faces were somber, but as he slowly smiled, they did also. He pushed back his chair as his children lovingly gathered around him, each chattering like a chipmunk. "Okay, okay," he exclaimed. "I know what you're looking for, and have I got a lot of exciting adventures to tell you about!"

Georg began to spin his yarns of the beautiful wilderness of Alaska, the Eskimos, the Indians, and the adventurous gold diggers, until the evening sun began to set. Darkness filled the sky, and it was evident that Elisabeth was not coming home. The nurse took care of Georg's precious little ones, and saw that they were comfortably put to bed for the night.

As early dawn pierced the stillness of the night, sounds of chirping sparrows woke Georg. He blinked, finding himself still sitting in his favorite rocker by the bedroom window, wrapped snugly in a woolen blanket. Fresh rays of morning sun shone peacefully upon his face through the window panes. He looked toward the big empty canopied bed. His heart sagged in silent despair as he drank in the beauty of his surroundings, lamenting the loss of Elisabeth's loyalty and love. He rubbed his eyes, threw back the blanket and headed for the washroom. "A good shave and a hot bath," he thought to himself, "and I'll feel a lot better!"

The house was still quiet as Georg walked down the corridor. He opened the door to the children's bedroom slowly. A smile swept across his face as they lay there, sleeping so peacefully, sweet and innocent. "She'll never have my kids, never," he mumbled to himself, fighting hard not to be depressed.

There were stirrings in the kitchen, and the sound of eggs sizzling enticingly in a pan. As Georg approached the door, anticipating that it might be Elisabeth, he found the nurse preparing the morning meal. The radio played a soft music as she hummed in quiet unison. Georg smiled, even whistled softly in tune. It was a pleasant feeling to hear a sound of happiness in the house. His terrible depression began to fade, in acceptance of the fact that the cards would have to lie where they fell.

With his belly full of breakfast, and still feeling a bit of anguish, Georg began to whistle again in order to bolster his own morale and to fight off the terrible loneliness which engulfed him. It still plagued him and his heart hung heavy. "It will take time," he kept saying to himself. "It will take time." Soon the day had passed and he still felt the pangs of hurt and depression. "Damnit! I need a good, stiff drink," he thought to himself. Georg advised the maid that he would be going out for a spell, to visit a friend across the street. The maid, with a look of concern, pulled the curtains back slightly to observe Georg heading for the cafe and bar across the street.

Georg knew Joseph, the Italian owner and the bartender, very well. He and Elisabeth had enjoyed an occasional dinner and drink there. He knew that his friend would be surprised to see him, as indeed he was. Georg bought a bottle of wine and sat quietly at a secluded table to sip and think. His friend Joseph casually walked over with a cup of coffee and a ham sandwich in his hands.

"Here, this is on the house, Georg. What's disturbing you, my friend? I can see by your face that you are concerned about something."

"Thanks, Joseph, I do have a bit of a problem," he sullenly responded.

"You know, Georg, I have a hunch that I know what it might be," Joseph said with a serious look on his face. "Elisabeth has been seen a lot with another gentleman around town while you were away, and he just didn't appear to be a relative." Joseph's eyes penetrated into the soul of Georg's thoughts.

In a burst of intense anger and emotion, Georg screamed, "That's a Goddamned lie!" He buried his head in his hands on the table as his big Italian friend wrapped his arm around him in solace.

"My friend," the bartender said. "I wouldn't lie to you. It's just a fact you must face."

Georg's muffled sob shook as his body trembled, and he knew in his heart that it meant the end of his marriage to Elisabeth.

Joseph explained to his friend that almost every evening while he was away, a lone gentleman stopped his car outside of Georg's house, unlocked the garage and drove the car inside. He would not be seen until early the next morning. "Now, were those the regular habits of a gentleman!" the big Italian exclaimed. "Of course, we thought it might have been a relative."

"It was not a relative," Georg said somberly. "I know who the bastard is!" As Georg described the man Brass, Joseph confirmed that it fit the description of the man perfectly.

The evening passed, and in the silence of the fog-filled evening, Georg slipped into his coat and walked home feeling more able to accept all that had happened. He knew for certain now what he must do to rebuild his life.

The new day began with radiant sunshine beaming through his bedroom window. Georg blinked as its rays cast streams of light across his bed. He felt better about himself now. He had accepted the facts as they were, and was determined to make the best of it.

He wondered if Elisabeth would ever come home for the sake of the children, and prepared himself for the worst. This time, when he came downstairs for breakfast, he would be smiling. The children eagerly greeted him. He saw a bit of himself in them as their innocent smiles shone brightly. "Thank God, in their innocence, they would not be hurt. And why should I hurt?" he asked himself. Georg couldn't help joining the smiles of the most wonderful treasures of all, his beloved children.

When Elisabeth finally came home, she appeared as if there were nothing wrong. "The horoscope studies we had to prepare were so interesting that Marie and I worked until very late into the night. I thought I might as well stay there until morning," Elisabeth explained. Georg did not respond, as he looked away to hide the smirk on his face. The next morning, she told him that she had to go back to complete their work, in order to get in into the mail.

"Sure," said Georg, shrugging his shoulders, as Elisabeth punched a long hatpin through her bonnet. She left quietly, without saying another word.

During the next couple of weeks, Elisabeth continued to claim how well they were doing and how busy they were. Telephone calls, seemingly requiring her assistance became more and more frequent. While Georg suspected that she was seeing Mr. Brass, he went along with her excuses while he determined how to handle the situation.

One evening while little Charlie, who could also sense in his childish way that something was wrong, was busily playing near the telephone when it rang, Elisabeth answered it, saying, "Oh, hello, darling!" Without hesitation, anger whipped through little Charlie. Tears suddenly burst forth from his eyes as he cried out in a loud and heart-rending tone, "Papa! Papa! It ain't Marie! It's Mr. Brass!"

Elisabeth, with a frightened, guilty look upon her face, quickly put the receiver down. Her face turned pale as Georg, who was also suspicious, clenched his fist and gritted his teeth as anger and disappointment enveloped him.

Frightened, stunned, Elisabeth stared into his angry face as tears welled up into her eyes. "I love him," she cried hysterically. "I can't help it, I love him!" She ran into the hall, pulled her hat and coat out of the closet and quickly made an exit through the front door.

During the next fourteen days, Georg lived alone with his small children, bolstering their spirits as well as his own. Their emotions and disappointments calmed as they began to adjust to their lives, knowing that they might never have a wife and mother to comfort them and console them again.

The weeks passed in slow somberness. The children longed for mother's comfort. Georg felt an emptiness in his heart as he wondered why these things should happen. The children had revealed to him many incidents which had taken place while he was gone. Brass and Elisabeth had been living together at Camp Meeker. He had beaten and punished the children when they had observed obscenities taking place between Brass and their mother.

Then one day there was a knock at the door. As Georg opened it, there stood Elisabeth. Tears of sorrow and lament welled up into her eyes, as Georg stood silent, trying to fight the hurt of betrayal. Elisabeth claimed that she would write a letter to Brass, telling him that it was over between them as she pled for forgiveness to return to her family. She claimed that she realized her folly and had fallen in temptation from the smooth words of Mr. Brass, and desired to keep her family together, begging Georg to forgive her.

After hearing all of the facts from Elisabeth, Georg concluded that if there was a real chance to preserve his family relationship, he would give it a little time to see if things really could work out again. Elisabeth agreed to write a letter to Mr. Brass, approved by Georg. She did so, and Georg took it to the post office himself. He envisioned a last opportunity to bring their home and family together once again. Yet, in his mind, he remained skeptical. Things seemed somewhat normal for a while at first, however, as time passed, Elisabeth again began to spend more time away from home.

Little Charlie, in his childish, straightforward manner, related to his father how terrible the man Brass had treated them. The children, even in their innocence, had an inbred distrust of the man. They suspected that their mother might be seeing him again.

Georg, still hoping to preserve his family unit, turned away from any negative thoughts and began to drink more often. They had been married for ten years. It seemed a lot to throw away. He waited patiently, wrestling with his own conscience of times he himself had been unfaithful when visiting Eskimo villages, living their ways of life.

One evening, little Charlie asked if he could go to the neighborhood store to purchase some dinner rolls. Charlie reached into his pocket for some loose change, but found none. "No luck, son, maybe Mama has some change." He reached for her purse. As he looked within, Charlie's eyes suddenly widened. His face turned an angry red. There he beheld a photograph of Elisabeth and Brass, both naked as a jay bird, holding hands on a beautiful sandy beach.

The divorce was drawn-out and bitter. In the final decision of the court, Elisabeth was awarded the custody of the children. Georg was required to pay alimony until the youngest child was eighteen years of age.

Although he rebelled against this judgment, in the end, Georg gave up his children.

Georg wandered sadly around the empty house in a daze, realizing that he was now totally alone. He sat in his chair to dwell in the unbearable silence, concerning all that had happened to him. Tears rolled gently down

Thomas, Lillian and Charles.

his cheeks, dropping discouragingly into the palms of his open hands. He peered into a large mirror which hung upon the wall as suddenly his expression changed to anger and outrage. Clenching his fist, he stood erect, exclaiming in a loud coarse voice, ''Should the Count of Alaska sit and cry like an abandoned child? Hell, no!" Anger boiled within him. "It's a good thing Brass left San Francisco," he said, as his fist shook violently in the air. Georg paced the floor like a bear in deep thought. Something had to be done. But what? Then within a few minutes, he solidified his thoughts into a plan which suited the dictates of his own conscience.

Georg sat at the table and began to compose a list of names and telephone numbers of his friends who had stuck by him during the divorce. Then, sitting at the telephone, he began calling them one at a time. His message was simple and to the point. "Come over to my home now. You'll do me a favor to come right away," he said. "I have many fine gifts for you and my loyal friends."

Georg ordered two large trucks to move furniture. When his friends arrived, Georg sat on a stool on the porch, greeting them with a happy smile. "Come, my friends. Come and take whatever you want of my possessions," he said with his thumb pointing into the house. "But don't fight over anything. Go ahead, I am serious. It costs you nothing."

With amazement and delight, Georg's friends obliged his wishes, taking all of the fine furniture he had acquired, placing the pieces in the waiting trucks to be delivered to various places. Georg smiled, knowing he had made many people happy that day.

"Thank you! Thank you, Georg! God bless you, Georg! Good luck," they said in gratitude, patting him on the back, shaking his hand and wishing him well. Many of them had never had such fine things to beautify and bring comfort to their homes. Georg just smiled, feeling good about himself, as they gradually emptied the last few remaining items.

Georg walked through the emptiness of his home, reminiscing about the better times with his family, whom he would most likely never see again. As he closed the door, an echo reverberated throughout the empty halls and rooms.

Georg smiled in satisfaction as he stood on his porch, thinking about his good Italian friend. He walked calmly across the street to have a beer, and talk to him for perhaps the last time. His friend filled their glass and placed the pitcher on the bar. His sympathy and sorrow for Georg was genuine.

"My friend, you have been good to me. I'm going away and I'd like you to have my beautiful home," said Georg, pointing across the street. "There is no happiness there for me now."

The Italian didn't hesitate to accept this most unusual gift, as Georg smiled in satisfaction and graciously gave his good friend a signed deed to the property.

On the following day, a policeman came to arrest Georg for not paying his ex-wife's alimony. However, Georg had already departed and was well on his way to Sweden. As the policeman talked to Georg's friends and neighbors, he shook his head and with a smile said, ''I hope they never catch him! That man has a lot of guts and a lot of character!''

Georg was free, and he was happy! As a wanted man he could no longer seek new fortunes in gold. Alaska was soon to become a territory of the United States of America. He was never able to fulfill his contract with the mining company.

Georg justified his actions in a letter written at the time. "Should I start supporting both her and her fiance Mr. Brass? Hell, no! I gave everything away, two houses and everything I had! I don't want nor need money! From here on, I'll work myself down financially, instead of working myself up! When I saw to it that everything had been given away, I said farewell to all of my good friends and took the train which traveled eastward. I moved as far as I could away from California, with their 'Women's Rights Laws'!''

"I knew I was getting old," he said. Times were hard in America, and the Great Depression raged across the land. With all his possessions given away, the Count decided to leave San Francisco.

He learned of a new discovery in Sweden from friends in the Eldorado Bar, and he believed there was still gold for him to find. He decided to travel to Sweden and continue with his life's love, searching for gold.

The Count accepted a bet for $1,000 one night; it was to provide his fare.

All he had to do was travel across the country to New York hobo-style, without a penny in his pockets. When and if he made it, the money would be wired to him.

He wanted to leave right away, before he had a chance to think about the challenge he had accepted.

Georg's daughter, Lillian af Forselles, a beautiful Swedish woman in her 20s.

Chapter Twenty-Three

Across America

"Not deck'd in warrior spoils; not who grandly dragg'd a groaning train of conquered wilds behind his chariot; but one who led the hemispheres in triumph at the wheels of peace."

Having accepted the bet, the Count decided he would show everyone he meant business. He took his friend Al back with him to his apartment, changed into old clothes, and gave Al a seaman's sack containing the rest of his belongings to take care of. Then he started walking out towards Oakland.

It was a warm, late summer evening. A mild wind was blowing over the golden fields. Lights were shining from the houses he passed, and he could see men smoking their pipes, children playing, women cooking. The Count realized he was a hobo! It was the whiskey that had made him accept this stupid bet!

He knew he had to keep out of sight of the detectives who watched for people trying to board box cars, so he headed out to a spot where he could still see the brightly lit station and people loading a freight for its trip east.

An hour passed, and then he heard ''singing'' on the rails. The big locomotive began to wail its lonely sound. By the time it reached Georg it seemed enormous, its noise deafening. He tensed as he stood there, and then he jumped in the direction of the train.

As he caught hold of a ladder, he thought his arms would be pulled from their sockets. Georg climbed up the ladder to the top, and stretched out along the board walk. His pulse was beating hard and the cold wind chilled his sweaty forehead.

The Count ate the two sandwiches he had brought with him, and then he dozed off. In the morning, he met others traveling the same way. One of his new friends was called, ''Seven-Day Joe,'' because he bragged that he never worked anywhere for more than a week at a time.

Joe taught the Count how to fill his stomach while riding the rails. When the train slowed down, the two would jump off and disappear into the surrounding area for a short time. They found huge buckets of fruit in the orchards and took whatever they wanted. They ate all that they could and then filled their pockets with apples and pears and peaches.

The fruit train passed over the Sierra Nevadas into Reno, and the travelers slept in a park before hopping a morning freight for Ogden, Utah. Now there were more ''free'' passengers, and they lay out in the sun, admiring the scenery.

When the train arrived in Ogden, the travelers were all very hungry. They had heard that there was a shelter in the town, and three of the men found it. They gave the travelers fruit and coffee and a slice of bread. There weren't any beds, so they had to sleep on newspapers, seven in one room. There were people of all ages and occupations, driven onto the open road by the hard times.

The Count (on right) and friends.

In the morning they were served porridge and milk. They were hardly finished when two broad-shouldered policemen came in. The group thought they were going to be arrested.

The police took the vagrants outside to waiting police cars and only asked a few questions, though.

''Where are you going?''

''East.''

They bunched us up in the cars and took us to a place outside the city. They stopped the cars and escorted us to the railroad tracks.

''Well, boys,'' one of them said. ''In five minutes there's a train going east. If you don't make it, you'll have to work on the road crew.''

The Count knew that old story. If they didn't manage to get on the fast train, they'd have to work on the road gang for three months without pay.

The train rushed towards the group. The Count clenched his teeth and jumped like lightning. Instinctively, he held on as he was tossed about, and then he slowly climbed to the roof. Three cars down, he could see another man. The others hadn't made it.

The Count jumped off before the train pulled into Salt Lake City because it was known to be tough on hoboes. He walked in and found a Salvation Army shelter for another night. The food was poor, beans without pork, hard bread, black coffee, and porridge and raw carrots for breakfast." But no one complained.

The next stage of his journey east was interrupted when armed guards stopped the train and loaded the ten men aboard into a cold box car. Eventually they were released, close to the tracks, and soon they were aboard another train, this time to Grand Junction, Colorado. There the Count hid out in the hobo jungle.

It was located near a stream of water in the woods. People hung their belongings in trees and bushes, empty cans used as pots, primitive cooking utensils, ragged clothes. Sad, scruffy faces could be seen round the camp fires. Poorly dressed people turned ashes in the fire to heat up their food...if they had anything to cook. The Count thought he had come across an outlaws' camp the first time he saw the poor, desperate. starving vagabonds.

Some were running around almost naked while they were boiling their clothes free from the lice they caught off the ground. There were factory workers, farm workers, office workers, and others who had lived the good life, but they seldom talked about it. Only first names were used, and that was all you knew about them. Most of them were drifters, going slowly from one town to another trying to survive.

The hoboes in the jungle lived by begging and stealing and anything else they could find to bring in a little money. If they couldn't find food in the city, they'd kill the first hen they came across. Georg even saw a little pig in one of the pots. They dug up potatoes from gardens and took apples from the orchards.

He met these destitute people when there was sun and the summer heat. How would they make out in the winter?

The Count's luck varied. One night he was soaked in a rainstorm; another time a friendly ''hillbilly'' gave him a train ticket good to La Junta, Colorado. He got a steak dinner from a steward for peeling potatoes and then had to spend another night in the ''jungle'' to avoid train detectives.

By the time he got to Kansas City, he found the streets were full of tramps. Even the Salvation Army had nothing left to give them. An organization called the Helping Hand took the drifters in, disinfected their clothes, and gave them showers and hot soup.

They took down names, occupations, and where you came from. The Count told them he was from La Junta and was out for the melon harvest. He had learned the trick of giving the nearest town as your place of residence. Otherwise, they would have discovered that he was a roving tramp and that would mean trouble.

Soon the Count hopped another train for Chicago, and spent another night with the Salvation Army. The preacher warned him to be careful of the Lake Erie Railroad and said it would be better to try and get aboard a sheep train heading for New York via the Lakawana line. He took the advice and after brief stops in Cleveland and Buffalo, he arrived in Jersey City, almost at his destination.

For the first time the Count had to beg. He needed six cents for the underground train between New Jersey and New York. There were no freights on that line. To his great surprise, the hand-out came from another hobo!

The Count landed in the Bowery in New York on a Sunday. It reminded him of the Barbary Coast. The Swedish consulate was closed, so he set off for the Seaman's Mission. There he sent off a triumphant telegram to his friends in San Francisco.

"The bet is won. Arrived New York. Please send the money. City Bank. Count."

He was shocked at the reply:

"Lady White left with mysterious gentleman. Taken all money. It's being sought after."

The Count sent another telegram:

"Please send Seaman's sack."

The Count of Alaska stood beside New York harbor with empty pockets. He would have to find work. It was 1933 and he longed to return to Sweden. When the sack arrived, he sought out the Swedish ship Kungsholm and was hired aboard as a food service man.

When the ship sailed, Georg af Forselles bid farewell to America.

"For the last time I saw the beautiful Statue of Liberty disappear in the distance. I had spent thirty-five years in her arms; thirty-five years of freedom and democracy, in the United States where the people had ensured the blessings of liberty for themselves and their posterity. It had been a free and wonderful life."

EPILOGUE

The old sourdoughs from Alaska are a special kind of people. It takes several years to become a true one. The oldest ones have left this earth, and some left the big winter country in the north and settled in Seattle. Some Alaska travelers have returned to Sweden with their gold nuggets well kept.

George af Forselles, called and known as the Count of Alaska, has spent several years in Sweden, and many people wonder how he invested his life there. Here in the U.S.A. we do not know. We would like to know more about him! He has a proud, sophisticated title, "Count", which he has always kept, and it is reminding us readers of his many thrilling adventures in Alaska. He is a complete success in his native home in Sweden. In Västerbotten, Sweden, gold deposits were discovered by the Count, and a large company was founded by him there. Several years ago, he also claimed and discovered a rich gold claim close to the city of Krångfors, Sweden, where he worked last summer, as an old professional Alaska gold-digger. So far, there has been no mining company that can compete with the mighty and well known Boliden Mining Company, that is so wealthy and famous in Sweden. But who knows? Maybe one day Count Georg af Forselles will come up with more great gold finds, that will put the Klondike in the shadow of wealth!

(Editor's Note: The above was extracted from a newspaper article of approx. 1943 vintage.)

End of the trail. The burial for Georg Jakob Hjalmar af Forselles was at Lindingö, Sweden, on April 15, 1952. He was born at Borås, Sweden, on April 15, 1878.

After his return to Sweden, Georg met and married Signe Adams, the owner of a chain of movie theaters throughout Europe. She was a millionaire and probably the richest woman in Finland. The Count was known as "King of the Movie Films" when they were married in 1945.

Georg af Forselles and his wife, Signe. (Photo taken in 1946 at Helsinki, Finland. Note that Georg has lost his left leg. Amputation was necessary because of gangrene setting in to ingrown toenails, possibly due to his tramping all over Alaska in inadequate footgear for many years.)

GLOSSARY TERMS OF ALASKA PLACES

ANVIL CREEK: stream, flows N to Cripple River, about 24 mi. NW of Imuruk Lake, in the Seward Penin.

ANVIL MOUNTAIN: mtn., 1,134 ft., 4 mi. N of Nome, in the Seward Penin. Name was reported in 1899 because of anvil-shaped rock formation on mountain's flank.

ANDREAFSKY: village, pop. 220, on N bank of Andreafsky River, 3.5 mi. NE of Pitkas Point, and 37 mi. NW of Marshall, Yukon-Kuskokwim Delta. Was established about 1898 or 1899 as a supply depot and winter quarters for the Northern Commercial's riverboat fleet.

ARIZONA CREEK: stream, flows SW 1.8 mi. to Taylor Creek which flows to Kougarok River, 7 mi. SW of Midnight Mts., and 46 mi. NW of Imuruk Lake, in the Seward Penin.

ASSES EARS: peaks two, extend 200 ft. above a bench, elevation of W peak 1,995 ft., 2 mi. SE of Black Butte and 8 mi. N of Imuruk Lake, in the Seward Penin. (ASSES EARS was so named on August 11, 1816, by Lt. Otto von Kotzebue, because "its summit is in the form of two asses ears.")

BALTO CREEK: stream, flows SW. 1 mi. to Snake River, 9 mi. NW of Nome, in the Seward Penin.

BEAR CREEK: stream, heads on SE side of Anvil Peak, flows SE 3 mi. NE of Nome, in the Seward Penin.

BERING SEA: sea, N part of Pacific Ocean, between Siberia on W and Alaska on E, enclosed by Aleutian Islands on S and Komandorski Islands on SW, and connected by Bering Strait with Chukchi Sea on N.

BERING STRAIT: water passage 55 mi. wide, connecting the Arctic Ocean and the Bering Sea and separating Asia and North America.

BETTLES: village, population 77, on the West bank of Koyukuk River 1 mi. SW of its junction with John River, and Kanuti Flats.

BONANZA CREEK: stream, flows NE 2.3 mi. to Jasper Creek which flows to Salmon Lake, 29 mi. NE of Nome, in the Seward Penin. Name was reported in 1900.

BOURBON CREEK: stream, flows SW, and is 3 mi. to Snake River at Nome, in the Seward Penin. (Prospectors named it in 1899).

BROOKS RANGE: mtn. range, 4,000-9,000 ft., and extends E-W about 600 mi. from Canada on E to Chukchi Sea on W and forms divide between Arctic slope drainage to N and Kobuk and Yukon Rivers.

BRYNTESON, MOUNT: mountain, 1,757 ft., 9 mi. N of Nome, Seward Penin. Reported as "Brunteson Peak" on the 1900 "Map of Nome Peninsula" by J. M. Davidson and B. D. Blakeslee. Named for John Brynteson, one of the "three Swedes" who discovered gold in the Nome area in the summer of 1898. Brynteson, a native of Sweden, was 40 years old in 1898 and an experienced coal and iron miner wo went to Alaska to search for coal.

BUCKLAND RIVER: stream, formed by its north and south forks, flows NW 67 mi. to Eschscholtz Bay, 40 mi. SW of Selawik, Kotzebue-Kobuk.

BUCKLAND VIILLAGE: on the Buckland River, 54 mi. N of Haycock, in Seward Penin. Population was 52 in 1920; 104 in 1930; and 115 in 1940.

CALIFORNIA CREEK: stream, flows NE 1 mi. to Ophir Creek which flows to Niukluk River 38 mi. NE of Solomon, in the Seward Penin.

CANDLE: village, population 103, on the left bank of Kiwalik River, 54 mi. NW of Haycock, in the Seward Penin. A mining camp established in 1901. Post Office was established in 1902.

CANDLE CREEK: stream, flows NE 16 mi. to the Kiwalik River at Candle, 54 mi. NW of Haycock, in Seward Penin. Prospectors name reported in 1903. The name was derived from a bush or shrub that grew along the banks of the stream, which resembles "candlewood" or "greasewood" in that it will light afire easily. Greasewood is a stiff, prickly plant. Candlewood is any resinous wood used for torches or as a substitute for candles. There are various trees or shrubs yielding such wood which burns brightly.

CAPE ESPENBERG: locality, on the Seward Penin., at the mouth of Espenberg River, on the Chukchi Sea, 50 mi. NW of Deering.

CAPE KRUSENSTERN: point of land, on Chukchi Sea coast, N point of entrance to Kotzebue Sound, 35 mi. NW of Kotzebue.

CAPE LISBURNE: promontory, 1,500 ft., on the Chukchi Sea coast, 40 mi. NE of village of Point Hope.

CAPE NOME: point of land, on Norton Sound, 12 mi. SE of Nome and 20 mi. SW of Solomon, in the Seward Penin."C[ape] Nome"appears on the 1853 Brit. Adm. Chart 2172. Its origin is generally attributed to an Admiralty draftsman's misinterpretation of "? name" annotated on a manuscript chart constructed on board the H.M.S. *Herald* about 1850-1852. The "?" mark was taken as a "C" and the "a" was thought to be an "o". This is the explanation given by the Chief Cartographer of the British Admiralty in 1900.

CAPE PRINCE OF WALES: point of land, westem most point of Seward Penin., 55 mi. SW of Teller, in Seward Penin.

CAPE YORK: point of land, about 6 mi. SW of York Mts., on Bering Sea, 35 mi. NW of Teller, in Seward Penin. Name in 1827 by Capt. Beechy, RN (Royal Navy) in 1831, ''in honor of his late Royal Highness,'' the Duke of York of England.

CHAMISSO ISLAND: island, 1 mi. long in Spafarief Bay, 57 mi. SW of Selawik, 3 mi. S of Choris Penin. Named in 1816 by Lt. Otto von Kotzebue, IRN, for Louis Adelbert von Chamisso, a member of his expedition.

CHANDALAR RIVER: stream, heads at its North and West Forks, and flows SE 100 mi. to the Yukon River 20 mi. NW of Fort Yukon.

CHEENIK: at Golovin village, population 160, on point between Golovin Bay and Golovin Lagoon, 42 mi. E of Solomon, in the Seward Penin. This Eskimo village has been reported in 1842-44. About 1890, one of the employees of the nearby Omalik mines married an Eskimo woman and established a trading post here. This man, John Dexter, became the center for prospecting information on the Seward Penin. With the discovery of gold in 1898, Golovin became a supply-relay point of the Council goldfields north of here. In 1899 the Cheenik Post Office was established here. It was discontinued in 1903. In 1899 the Golovin Post Office was established south of here, at Golovin Mission; it was discontinued in 1904. John Dexter was listed as postmaster at both of these post offices. A new Golovin Post Office was established at this site in 1906 and was discontinued in 1958.

CHENA RIVER: stream, heads at junction of North West Forks Chena River, flows SW 100 mi. to Tanana River, 6.5 mi. SW of Fairbanks.

CHILCOOT PASS: pass, 3,739 ft. on Alaska Canada boundary, 4.1 mi. NE of Mount Hoffman, and 17 mi. N of Skagway.

CIRCLE: village, population 41, on left bank of the Yukon River, 130 mi. NE of Fairbanks, at Yukon Flats. So named because the village was thought to be on the Arctic Circle. A mining town established in 1887.

COPPER RIVER: stream, heads on the N side of Wrangell Mts., and flows S 250 mi. through Chugach Mts. to the Gulf of Alaska, 20 mi. NW of Katalla. Meaning of Copper River in 1779 was "river of the lost."

CORDOVA: town, population 1,128 on SE shore of Orca Inlet, opposite Hawkins Island.

COUNCIL: locality, population 41, is on the left bank of Niukluk River, 33 mi. NE of Soloman, in the Seward Penin. Site of village and recording office in the center of the Council gold mining precinct. "Council City * * * was first started by Mr. Libby [Daniel B. Libby, a member of the von Bendeleben expedition of 1866 and who with three others found gold in the area] and party in the fall of 1897. * * * In October, 1898, the city consisted of about fifty log houses, and probably about 300 persons were then there, the majority of whom had come in during the months of August and September, after the news of the first discoveries had reached St. Michaels."

DEATH VALLEY: basin, is 6 mi. across, along the Tubutulik River, on E side of Darby Mts., 37 mi. SE of Imuruk Lake, in the Seward Penin.

DEERING: village, population 95, on the Seward Penin. at the mouth of Inmachuk River on Kotzebue Sound, 57 mi. SW of Kotzebue.

DEXTER CREEK: locality is along Seward Peninsula's Railroad, SW of King Mts., 6 mi. NE of Nome in the Seward Penin.

ELSIE CREEK: stream, flows NE 13 mi. to California Creek, 38 mi. SE of Nenana.

FAIRBANKS: city, with population of 13,311, located on Chena River. Founded in 1901 when a trading post was established here by E.T. Barnette. The town began as the supply center for the mining region to its north after gold was discovered by Felix Pedro in 1902, and has since become the commercial and transportation hub of north and central Alaska.

FAIRBANKS CREEK: stream, flows SW 8 mi. to Fish Creek, 20 mi. NE of Fairbanks, Yukon-Tanana.

FIRST CHANCE CREEK: stream, flows SW 16 mi. to Koyuk River, 26 mi. NW of Haycock, in Seward Penin. Reported in 1903.

FIRTH RIVER: stream, heads at E end of Davidson Mts., and flows NE 125 mi. across Alaska-Canada boundary to Beaufort Sea, SE of Herschel Island, in Yukon and Canada. Named in 1890.

FISH RIVER: stream, heads in Bendeleben Mts., and flows S 47 mi. to Golovin Lagoon 35 mi. E of Solomon, in the Seward Penin.

FORT YUKON: located 140 mi. northeast of Fairbanks, and about 8 mi. north of the Arctic Circle.

FORTY MILE: locality, at junction of Bullion Creek and North Fork of Fortymile River, and 37 mi. SW of Eagle, Yukon-Tanana High..

GLACIER CREEK: stream, heads on E side of Mount Brynteson, flows SW 6 mi. to Snake River, 6 NW of Nome, in the Seward Penin.

GLACIER MOUNTAIN: mtn., 5,915 ft., 10 mi. SE of North Peak, 21 mi. W of Eagle. Prospector's name obtained in 1898.

GOLD CREEK: stream, flows N 2 mi. to Seventy-mile River, 20 mi. NW of Eagle.

GOLOVIN BAY: now Golovnin Bay: bay, once called Golovin Bay. An Eskimo named "Tatchik," meaning "bay," heads at Golovnin Lagoon and extends S 12 mi. to Norton Sound, 45 mi. E of Solomon, in the Seward Penin.

GRACE CREEK: stream, flows SW 2 mi. to join Warner Creek to form Wade Creek, 45 mi. SW of Eagle.

ICY CAPE: point of land, on the Chukchi Sea coast, 48 mi. SW of Wainwright, on the Arctic Plain. It's so named by Captain Cook in 1785, who wrote on August 15, 1778, "The eastern extreme forms a point which was much encumbered with ice; for which reason it obtained the name of Icy Cape." This was the northern limit of Cook discoveries. The Eskimo word "Utoqaq" means "old" or "ancient" place.

INMACHUK: Eskimo name reported in 1901 as "Ipnichuk," meaning "big cliff," however, the present spelling of the name would indicate it may mean "new salt water."

INMACHUK RIVER: stream, on the Seward Penin. that flows NE 30 mi. to Kotzebue Sound, at the village of Deering, 57 mi. SW of Kotzebue.

KALTAG: village, pop. 147, on the N bank of Kuskokwim River, 24 mi. W. Aniak.

KIWALIK: village, pop. 10, on NE coast of the Seward Penin., between Spafarief Bay and Kiwalik Lagoon.

KIWALIK RIVER: stream flows NW 58 mi. to Mud Creek Channel Kiwalik River, 55 mi. NW of Haycock, in the Seward Penin.

KOTLIK: village, pop. 116, on the E bank of Kotlik River, 0.3 mi. S of Apoon Pass and 35 mi. NE of Kwiguk.

KOTZEBUE: town, population is 1,290 on NW shore of Baldwin Penin. Kotzebue was established as a permanent Eskimo village when a reindeer station was located here about 1897. Prior to then, it was a summer fish camp first mentioned by Lt. Zagoskin in 1847. That name was then recorded as "kikikhtagyut."

KOTZEBUE SOUND: bay, that is 35 mi. wide and 80 mi. long, on the W coast of Alaska, N of Seward Penin. Named by Lt. Otto von Kotzebue for himself after discovering the bay in 1816. KOYUK: village, pop. 129, on the right bank at the mouth of Koyuk River, 31 mi. NW of Christmas Mts., in the Seward Penin.

KOUGAROK RIVER: stream, formed by junction of Macklin and Washington Creeks, flows S 45 mi. to Kuzitrin River, 47 mi. SW of Imuruk Lake, Seward Penin.

KOYUKUK: village, W of Koyukuk I, and 16 mi. NE of Nulato.

KOYUKUK RIVER: stream, heads at its Middle and North Forks, flows SW 425 mi., to Yukon River 22 mi. NE of Nulato.

KUKPOWRUK RIVER: stream, the heads in De Long Mts, flows N 160 mi. to Kasegaluk Lagoon, 9 mi. S of Point Lay.

LAKE IMURUK: lake, 8 mi. long and 5 mi. wide, and is 37 mi. NE of Mount Bendeleben, in the Seward Penin. Eskimo name reported in 1901.

LINDBLOM CREEK: stream, flows 1.6 mi. to Snake River, 8 mi. NW of Nome, Seward Penin. Reported as "Lindbloom" on a map by S. E. King, dated 1900. Named for Erik O. Lindblom, one of the "three Swedes"who discovered gold in the Nome area in the summer of 1989. Lindblom, a native of Sweden, was 30 years old in 1898, and for several years had been a tailor in San Francisco. He joined the stampede to Kotzebue Sound, but ended up in Council where he met John Brynteson, a Swede, and Jafet Lindeberg, a Norwegian. These three, often called the "three Swedes," sought new territory and prospected along the coast of Norton Sound where they found gold along the Snake River.

LOST CREEK: stream, flows NE 2 mi. to Nome River, 6 mi. NE of Nome, in the Seward Penin. Prospectors name reported on a map dated 1900.

MELSING CREEK: stream, flows SW 8.5 mi. to Nuikluk River at Council, 33 mi. NE of Solomon, in the Seward Penin. Prospectors' name reported in 1899.

MOUNT MCKINLEY: a mtn. in Central Alaska; highest peak in N. America (20,300 ft.).

NEKULA GULCH: ravine, trends NW 0.6 mi. to Anvil Creek N of Dexter Peak and 6 mi. N of Nome, on the Seward Penin.

NENANA: village, pop. 286, mi. 411.7 on The Alaska RR., on the left bank of Tanana River, E of the mouth of Nenana River, 45 mi. SW of Fairbanks.

NIZINA RIVER: stream, flows 37 mi. S and W from Nizina Glacier to Chitina River, 12 mi. SW of McCarthy, in the Wrangell Mts.

NOME: town, pop. 2,316, on S coast of Seward Penin., on Norton Sound, in the Seward Penin. "Was first called Anvil City, and Nome City, now officially Nome."

NOME RIVER: stream, heads 4.5 mi. W of Salmon Lake, flows S 40 mi. to Norton Sound, 4 mi. SE of Nome in the Seward Penin. Prospectors' derived from Cape Nome and reported in 1899.

NORTON BAY: bay, extends NE 50 mi. from NE end of Norton Sound; it is defined on S by a line between Cape Darby and Cape Denbigh.

NORTON SOUND: gulf, 125 mi. long and 70 mi. wide, extends E off Bering Sea, between Seward Penin. on N and Yukon Delta on S.

NULATO: village, pop. 283, on right bank of Yukon River, 25 mi. W of Galena.

OLD GLORY: stream, flows NE 7.3 mi. to Pinnel River which flows to Inmachuk River, 17 mi. of Inuruk Lake, is in the Seward Penin.

OPHIR CREEK: stream, flow NW of Cripple River about 25 mi. NW of Imuruk Lake, in Seward Penin.

OTTER CREEK: stream, flows SE 3.6 mi. from Nome River, 4 mi. SE of Nome in the Seward Penin.

PEDRO CREEK: locality, on Pedro Creek, 10 mi. NE of Fairbanks.

PITMEGA RIVER: stream, heads in De Long Mts., flows NW 42 mi. to Chukchi Sea at Cape Sabine, 40 mi. NW of Mount Kelly, at the Arctic Slope.

POINT BARROW: point of land, between Beaufort and Chukchi Seas, in the northernmost point in the United States, Arctic Plain.

POINT HOPE: village pop. 324, on foreland terminating at Point Hope on the Chuckchi Sea coast. This Eskimo village locally referred to as "Tikiqaq" or Tikarakh.

PORT CLARENCE: bay, 18 mi. across on S coast of Seward Penin., between Grantley Harbor and the Bering Sea, W of Teller, in the Seward Penin. Named in 1827 by Capt. Beechy, who said, "To the outer harbour I attach the name of Port Clarence, in honour of his most gracious majesty, then Duke of Clarence.'' This feature was known to the Russians as Zalivkavyayak, "Kavyayak Bay." According to Martin Sauer, of the Billings expedition in 1785, the Eskimo name is "Imagru."

PORCUPINE RIVER: stream, right-hand tributary to Skagway River, about 5 mi. NE of Skagway. This river, crossed by a horse bridge on the "Skagway Trial" to White Pass, was well known during the Klondike gold rush.

REX CREEK: stream, on the Seward Penin., flows NE 4.9 mi. to Kotzebue Sound, 16 mi. W of Deering. Prospectors name reported in 1901.

SEWARD: town, pop. 1,891, on the Kenai Penin., at NW end or Resurrection Bay at the Chugach Mts. Named for William Henry Seward. 1801-72, Secretary of State, 1861-69 who negotiated the purchase of Alaska. The town was founded in 1902 by surveyors for The Alaska Railroad.

SEWARD PENINSULA: peninsula, extends W 200 mi. from line between heads of Eschscholtz Bay and Norton Bay; founded on S by Norton Sound, on N by Chukchi Sea, and W by Bering Strait. About 1898 Governor John Green Brady suggested the peninsula be named in compliment to William Henry Seward, 1801-72.

SINUK RIVER: stream, heads N of Tigaraha Mtn., flows SW 48 mi. to Norton Sound, 25 mi. NW of Nome, in the Seward Penin. Eskimo name reported in 1900.

SKAGWAY: town, pop. 659, at the mouth of Skagway River, near head of Taiya Inlet, 90 mi. NW of Juneau Coast Mts. The name derived from Skagway River. "The town is called The Gateway to the Golden Enterior," and was founded in 1897 by Capt. William Moore, who had a cabin here, when gold was first discovered in 1896 near Dawson, on the Yukon River.

SNAKE RIVER: stream, formed by junction of Gold-bottom Creek and North Fork Snake River, flows SW 15 mi., then SE 5 mi. to Norton Sound at Nome, in the Seward Penin. The local name reported in 1899. So named in 1898 because of its serpentine-like course by the three men who found gold in the area; John Brynteson, E.O. Lindblom, and Jafet Lindeberg.

SPECIMEN CREEK: ravine, former tributary of Gold Creek, about 2 mi. W of Juneau Coast Mts. Also there is a Specimen Gulch: a ravine; trends W 1 mi. Anvil Creek, 5 mi. N or Nome, in the Seward Penin.

ST. MICHAEL: pop. 205 on the E coast of St. Michael Island in Norton Sound, 43 mi. SW of Unalakleet. About 1833 the Russians established a stockaded post, which was named after Capt. Michael Dmitrievich Tebenkov, afterward governor of the Russian-American colony. The St. Michael post office and an American military post, called "Fort Saint Michael," were established in 1897, following the Klondike gold strike and the subsequent increased Yukon River traffic, most of which originated at Saint Michael.

SUNRISE CREEK: stream, flows NW 1 mi. to Fox River between Slate and Windy Creeks, 22 mi. NE of Solomon, in the Seward Penin.

TANANA RIVER: stream, formed by confluence of Chisana and Nabesna Rivers at Northway Junction, flows NW 440 mi. to Yukon River, 3.5 mi. E of Tanana. The Tanana village, a pop. of 349, is near the junction of Tanana and Yukon Rivers.

TOPKOK: locality, at mouth of Topkok River, N shore of Norton Sound, 15 mi. E of Solomon, in Seward Penin. Former Eskimo village reported in 1880. This town established in 1898 as a debarkation point, with an excellent ice-free harbor, for men seeking a route to the Klondike gold region. It was originally called "Copper City" but name was changed when the Valdez post office was established in 1899.

TOTATLANIKA RIVER: stream, heads at junction of all Gold and Dexter Creeks flows N 63 mi. to Tanana River, 10 mi. E of Nenana. Tanana is an Indian name meaning "Totatla Creek." Totatlanika is another Indian name.

VALDEZ: town, pop. 555, on E end of Port of Valdez, 45 mi. NW of Cordova and 115 mi. E of Anchorage.

WRANGELL: town, pop. 1,315, on N coast of Wrangell Island. Wrangell began as a stockade built by the Russians occupying the island in 1834 "to prevent encroachment by the Hudson's Bay Company traders."

WRANGELL MOUNTAIN: mtn., 14,163 ft., 15 mi. S of Mount Sanford, Wrangell Mts. named by the Russians for Baron von Wrangell, and reported in 1895.

YUKON RIVER: stream, is about 1,500 mi. long, heads in Marsh Lake in the Yukon, Canada, and flows NW into Alaska Fort Yukon, then SW to Bering Sea at Norton Sound.

The stairwell in the House of Nobles in Stockholm, Sweden, known as one of the most beautiful buildings in Northern Europe. It dates from the first decades of Sweden's era as a great power, the "Age of Greatness." After having earlier held their meetings in an insignificant building, which has now disappeared, the nobility bought the present site close to the Riddarholm Canal in the spring of 1641. (Upper left corner is the af Forselles coat-of arms).

Georg af Forselles, Count of Alaska, with his son Charles, Helsinki, Finland, 1947

Family portrait of the Magnus Georg af Forselles family. Photo taken circa 1885 in the family mansion in Stockholm, Sweden. Adults seated are Magnus Georg and his wife, Emma. Around them are their three sons, Carl, Albert and Georg. Georg is the little fellow leaning on his mother. This is the earliest photograph available of Georg Jakob Hjalmar af Forselles. Here he is about 7 years old. In another ten years he will be off to sea to fulfill his great thrill for adventure.